International Buffer Stocks:
Theory and Practice

European University Studies

Europäische Hochschulschriften
Publications Universitaires Européennes

Serie V
Economics and Management

Reihe V Série V
Sciences économiques
Volks- und Betriebswirtschaft

Vol./Bd. 460

PETER LANG
Berne · Frankfort on the Main · New York

Alis Medzikijan

International Buffer Stocks: Theory and Practice

PETER LANG
Berne · Frankfort on the Main · New York

CIP-Kurztitelaufnahme der Deutschen Bibliothek

Medzikijan, Alis
International Buffer Stocks: Theory and Practice/
Alis Medzikijan. – Berne, Frankfort/M. (Frankfurt am Main),
New York, Lang, 1983.
(European University Studies: serie V)
Economics and Management: volume 460)
ISBN 3-261-03318-5

NE: Europäische Hochschulschriften

To André

To my parents

ACKNOWLEDGEMENTS

I should like to thank many persons and institutions that have made it possible, by their contributions of advice and adequate help, for this work to be written.

In particular, I should like to express my sincere gratitude to Mr. Charles Iffland, Professor and Dean of the Ecole des hautes études commerciales de l'Université de Lausanne and the Chairman of the Dissertation Committee, for the great confidence he evinced throughout the realization of the work, benevolent support and discreet assistance, which will always be remembered.

I am deeply grateful to Mr. Gaston Gaudard, Professor at the Ecole des hautes études commerciales de l'Université de Lausanne, and at the University of Fribourg, and Director of Thesis Work. I especially wish to thank him for his invaluable advice and criticism, constant motivation, unwavering optimism and profound understanding so important that this work could be brought about, and which can never be acknowledged in full.

I am also obliged to Mr. Aurelio Mattei, Professor at the University of Lausanne, for his kindness in being a member of the Dissertation Committee, and for his valuable comments.

My special thanks are addressed to Mr. Jacque Cuttat, Commodities Division, United Nations Conference on Trade and Development (UNCTAD), for forming part of the Dissertation Committee, as well as for his encouragement and constructive criticism which were indispensable to the completion of this study.

My thanks are also directed to those who, through their personal interviews, comunication of valuable documents, recommendations to different specialists on the subject dealt with and friendly encouragements, helped to improve this work. In particular:

In the Swiss Confederation:

Mr. Heinz Hofer, le Département fédéral de l'économie publique (l'Office fédéral des affaires économiques extérieures), and Mr. Roland Burkhardt, Ministère public de la Confederation.

In the United Nations:

Mr. Duncan Ridler, Commodities Division, United Nations Conference on Trade and Development (UNCTAD).

I am particularly indebted to Mrs. Marlis Steinert, Professor at the Institut universitaire de hautes études internationales, Geneva, for her great understanding, loyal support, friendship and humanity.

My profound gratitude goes to my parents Dertad and Milica Medzikijan-Paskalj, for their special devotion, benevolent support, extreme comprehension and financial generosity throughout my studies. This will deeply be a appreciated for ever.

My deepest and particular thanks, however, go to André Schusselé, my very special friend, for his untiring assistance, encouragement, infinite care and unfaling friendship. This work is dedicated to those I owe the most.

Genève, Lausanne and Bern, January 1983 A.M.

SUMMARY OF CONTENTS

T A B L E   O F   C O N T E N T S

PART II

PART III

PROPOSALS FOR AN IMPROVEMENT IN THE BUFFER STOCK POLICY

LIST OF CHARTS

PART II

CHAPTER I:

LIST OF FIGURES

PART I

PART II

CHAPTER II.

PART III

CHAPTER II.

LIST OF TABLES

PART I

CHAPTER I.

PART III

CHAPTER I.

CHAPTER II.

A B B R E V I A T I O N S

CIPEC	-	Intergovernmental Council of Copper Exporting Countries
DC	-	Developed Countries
EEC	-	European Economic Community
FAO	-	Food and Agricultural Organization
GATT	-	General Agreement on Tariffs and Trade
IBA	-	International Bauxite Agreement
IBRD	-	International Bank for Reconstruction and Development
ICA	-	International Commodity Agreement
ICICA	-	Interim Coordinationg Committee on International Commodity Agreements
IRRC	-	International Rubber Regulation Committee
IPC	-	Integrated Programme for Commodities
ITA	-	International Tin Agreement
ITC	-	International Tin Council
ITO	-	International Trade Organization
IWA	-	International Wheat Agreement
LDC	-	Less Developed Country
OECD	-	Organization for Economic Cooperation and Development
OPEC	-	Organization of Petroleum Exporting Countries
UBEC	-	Union of Banana Exporting Countries
UNCTAD	-	United Nations Conference on Trade and Development

INTRODUCTORY NOTES

In international economic activities, trade in primary commodities has always played a large and important role. Abundant literature bears witness to the interest in regulating the commodity markets and the efforts, either successful or not, to do this.

The permanent and growing interest in possible changes and solutions in international trade policy was just as real for some years before the post-war period. The present economic situation covering the North/South Dialogue, shows the extreme importance that regulation of the primary commodity trade has today. It is a fact that the field of primary commodities has always been a mixture of economic and political factors, but never more than it is now.

The question of applying a specific measure of stabilization is a source of serious disagreements among the producing and consuming countries participating in the drafting and concluding of commodity agreements.

The measures of regulation which have been used in a number of international commodity agreements are

- export restriction schemes,
- multilateral contracts,
- buffer stocks,
- a price-compensation scheme (1) and
- indexation of export prices.

Our interest in this study will be concentrated on the evaluation of the buffer stock mechanism because, among the possible methods of primary commodities control, the buffer stock principle may be the one that

---

(1) A price-compensation scheme was suggested to UNCTAD in 1964 by Professor James Meade, see in: MEADE, James E., "International Commodity Agreements", Lloyds Bank Review, No. 3, July 1964, pp. 28-42.

a) has the longest history within the market economy and even before,

b) offers, in practice, a large number of projects that were not implemented or failed and were taken up again,

c) raises fundamental issues of economic theory (e.g. market intervention or neutrality) which cannot be given a conclusive answer due to the lack of specific studies.

Whenever the idea of the buffer stock principle appeared in the question of the regulation of primary commodities, it was applied as an instrument to fight, and to prevent, the insecurity of the availability of primary commodities. In the context of market activity, it was applied to influence the evolution of prices and, in a certain sense, of export earnings, which will be seen below in detail.

If the buffer stock was used mainly as one instrument among others, it nevertheless always revealed some specific characteristics of its own. An attempt will be made to deepen the analysis of the buffer stock mechanism, while taking into account its context, in order to make a contribution from an economist's point of view to the definition of primary commodities policy, which may be understood as the aim of our work.

As this study will deal with international buffer stocks related to market activities, they will not be covered as a national activity for strategic purposes, whatever their real importance may have been.

In the economic literature, although profuse, few concentrated developments were found that dealt, in a coherent and distinctive way, with the buffer stock principle . An attempt as such an approach may be seen as original but we leave that to the reader's judgement.

Therefore, one of the purposes of this study is to point out the objectives generally known, to reveal the practical experiences and to examine in detail the relation between them. Thus, this work is divided into three Parts.

Part I deals with the contents of the buffer stock system and the historical and theoretical facts which exist in the academic discussions concerning this matter. In the light of this, Chapter I traces the origin and development of buffer stocks in general. The historical framework is explored as briefly as possible, with the hope that this approach might elucidate general notions as a basic tool for further analysis. Chapter II refers to the theoretical functioning of the pure buffer stock mechanism. At this point only a cursory evaluation of this mechanism of control will be made. This will give us a practical introduction and some insights into its technical functioning. The final Chapter III, which is theoretical, combines concrete experiences and specific procedures created by analysed commodity agreements. A broad examination is made of different adjustments of tin and cocoa agreements, respectively. What is of importance here, is to show that the same approach in both cases underlines the importance of the buffer stock principle in application and the differences between theory and practice that emerge from it.

In the two chapters of Part II, a framework is provided for the evaluation of the buffer stock system. Chapter I puts forward a new element in the proposal for a buffer stock typology. A thorough examination of this phenomenon and the application of its criteria to the two concrete cases of tin and cocoa respectively, represent the original elements of this work which are, in particular, an elaboration of ideas concerning the stabilization programme and buffer stock as appropriate methods of control. Chapter II represents an attempt to demonstrate the advantages mentioned and their real significance, especially concerning direct effects on price fluctuations and indirect ones on export earnings.

In the framework of description and theoretical compositon a series of arguments is developed concerning the buffer stock mechanism, its policy and importance for the LDCs'and DCs' economic and political relationship under the influence of different economic circumstances. Problems in constituting the buffer stocks and of functioning as well as the problem of the buffer stock as an isolated measure of commodity control and the buffer stock concept in the time schedule are given some attention.

Part III, advances certain proposals for an improvement of the buffer stock system. This Part summarizes the proposals advanced in two chapters. The analysis in Chapter I investigates the position adopted by the UNCTAD and its principal characteristics. Further on, attention is focused primarily on those proposals which are mirrored in the choice and combination of buffer stocks with another control method. Finally Chapter II deals with revision and improvements to the financing system of the Common Fund. An examination of the attempts made and the appropriate alternative hypotheses could bring about the survival of the Integrated Programme for Commodities in spite of its imperfections.

The use of the buffer stocks in practice shows that there are a number of decisive questions to be answered before this commodity control policy can be considered secure. The intention of this study is to demonstrate that the international buffer stock mechanism has had an instructive past, and to try to evaluate what sort of answer should be given to the question which arises from common interest: Have international buffer stock a future? A sufficiently-detailed study would show it to be possible. Instead, the reader of this study should rather expect to become acquainted with the various circumstances that may affect the evolution of the buffer stock instrument.

As a final word, the ideas proposed are intended to be dynamic: they are more than analytical. The fact that we know how important and timely the chosen topic is, adds to the reasons which are at the origin of this work: its utility, originality and current relevance.

The attempt to develop empirically the points revealed in the theoretical approximation displays numerous interesting aspects worthy of concern and investigation.

PART I

THE CONTENTS OF THE SYSTEM

The work presented consists of three chapters. Chapter I gives insights into the origins and historical trend of the buffer stock policy. Chapter II deals with the pure mechanism of the buffer stocks and their functioning from a theoretical point of view. Finally, Chapter III gives information about implementation of the buffer stock in practice through particular examples.

Therefore, Part I may be qualified as a descriptive part which will permit approach through the general aspects to more particular ones, by a deductive method.

CHAPTER I

ORIGINS AND DEVELOPMENT

The purpose of taking into account cartel type agreements in this work is not to go back to their historical backgrounds and give an analysis of their consequences, but to underline their importance in market control activity. This will, in turn, show that they appear to be a basis for future methods of regulation in the International Commodity Agreements (ICAs).

A - SIGNIFICANCE IN THE CONTEXT OF CARTELS

1. International cartels in general

In view of the fact that the following analyses cartels as instruments of economic control, a brief reference to their definition will be made.

What follows will show that buffer stocks were not used by cartels as a planned method of market control, but were rather the consequence of the specific world economic evolution after World War I.

a) Extension of cartel policy

Whether voluntarily or not, when the subject of international cartels is brought up in a discussion, there is an immediate reference to the international trade regulation during the inter-war period.

As experience has shown, the international cartels rapidly increased in number and played a major rôle in the world market in the period between the two World Wars. They controlled between 40 and 60 per cent of the total amount of world trade (1), with the purpose of establishing and maintaining high monopoly prices. Nevertheless, the cartel movement has a far longer history (2) and, thus cartels should not be associated with a certain single period as they varied in their spheres of action at different times.

---

(1) MASON, Edward, Controlling World Trade, New York, MacGraw Hill, 1946, p. 26 n.

(2) "Cartel schemes are as old as business". STOCKING, George and WATKINS, Myron, Cartels or Competition?, New York, The Twentieth Century Fund 1948, p. 5.

International producer cartels existed in the past although they were short-lived. Some exist now (OPEC, IBA, CIPEC, UBEC and several others (3)) and will, in all likelihood, continue to do so in the future if certain necessary conditions are fulfilled (4).

b) Note on what a cartel is and the combination of cartel control methods

When the term "cartel" is referred to, it generally designates an arrangement between a group of producers (5) who are committed to fixing common, acceptable prices for their products, with the purpose of limiting, or eliminating, competition among themselves, and between themselves and outsiders. Cartels are either domestic or international (agreements between producers in different countries); their common feature is the reduction of competition, and, by methods of price fixing, the limiting of output (sales or exports) and market sharing, so as to bring their constituent members satisfactory predictable profits.

In order to centralize control and to restrict competition, effective cartels often used a combination of these control methods. A well-known example is the international electric lamp cartel, established in 1942 (6), which produced both the

---

(3) OPEC - Organization of Petroleum Exporting Countries
IBA - International Bauxite Association
CIPEC - International Council of Copper Exporting Countries
UBEC - Union of Banana Exporting Countries

(4) If there is an inelasticity of demand for the cartel's product, the necessary conditions are met to realize the objective of a commodity cartel: cartel members will obtain, as the result, an increase in export earnings. This statement was argued by Carl Van DUYNE in: "Commodity Cartels and the Theory of Derived Demand", KYKLOS, vol. 28, 1975, Fasc. 3, pp. 597-612.

(5) As has already been emphasized, the term "producer-seller" is used with reference to "business unites" (firms) as a matter of common usage, although "wage earners are producers". STOCKING, George and WATKINS, Myron, Cartels in Action, New York, The Twenty Century Fund 1947, p. 3, n. 1.

(6) STOCKING, George and WATKINS, Myron, Cartels or Competition?, op.cit., p. 81.

division of the market and price fixing among cartel members. The international steel cartel provided only a restriction of output, while, on the other hand, the major function of the international aluminium cartel was to limit productive capacity in different countries.

These three examples show that it is the character of cartels to use one, or to combine several, methods of control. From this point of view, they have much in common with the future ICAs' combination of control schemes.

c) Need for control

Cartel control schemes were used in the regulation of numerous commodities in nearly every branch of the economy (7) (manufacturing, raw materials and foodstuffs) in the inter-war period.

The significance that international cartels achieved in the inter-war period was due to specific economic causes and circumstances (upset in the fundamental supply and demand relationship). Not only did war create excess capacity, notably in heavy industry (8), but political pressures also led to a strengthening of the cartel movement. In the post-war period, the same movement was kept alive in the period of economic reconstruction. Cartels and open protectionism went hand in hand.

Control was necessary as well as practical (9); necessary because of the very strong economic dislocations in markets; practical because of governments' definite intervention in the market and especially in domains that had previously been considered to represent an unwarranted interference in economic affairs, and, in fact, to be impossible from the administrative point of view. The general world trade situation reinforced cartels.

---

(7) Ibid., p. 91-92.

(8) MASON, Edward, Controlling World Trade, op.cit., p. 11.

(9) What follows is, in part, derived from ROWE, J.W.F., Markets and Men, Cambridge University Press, 1936, pp.1-22.

2. International cartels, primary commodities and the relevance of the buffer stock in particular

In circumstances such as those mentioned above in subdivision c), cartels were seen as instruments of achieving sufficient strength to compete more effectively in international trade. Thus it follows that international cartels grew as a direct result of large national monopolies because those individual monopolies controlled their domestic markets to a considerable extent and began,progressively, to develop their activities outside their own countries.

Their aim was based on the desire to obtain the same overall effects as at home: the rejection of competitive markets and the assuring of satisfactory profits by methods of price fixing, market allocation and limiting output, but in the world market this time. However, they were confronted with unshakeable resistance from the monopolies of other countries. Therefore, there was a need for a solution in the form of international coordination between them, which resulted in the setting up of international cartel agreements. Through these, producers promoted their private business interests.

During this period, cartel agreements appeared in the fields of copper, tin, rubber and nitrates. A brief reference to two of them - rubber and tin - may facilitate an understanding of their organisation and spheres of action.

a) International Rubber Regulation Committee

The International Rubber Regulation Committee (IRRC) was set up in 1934 to control the rubber market. Its control instruments were designed to revitalise rubber prices which, as a result of the Great Depression, had fallen a great deal. Two of these instruments were production quotas and export quotas. The percentage of export quotas was fixed by the IRRC. Another instrument was a formal prohibition of new planting in the world's rubber producing territories (10). The IRRC established

---

(10) A rubber tree takes about seven years to reach what plantation technique considers to be tappable size", ROWE, J.W.F., Primary Commodities in International Trade, Cambridge University Press 1965, p. 123 and n. 1.

a control scheme which restricted exports to "75 per cent of capacity" (11).

Restriction of the export capacity was introduced with the purpose of reducing the existing world rubber stocks. Here it can be seen that buffer stocks did not then exist in the context of their present meaning, but were the stocks resulting from abundant production. These rubber stocks were restricted to the level IRRC designated as adequate and able to keep going a "fair and equitable price level" (12) (which, from our point of view, means to keep going high, optimal monopoly prices). This policy survived up to the middle of 1936, when the demand for rubber overtook the supply within two years (1936-1938). The result was that stocks were cut to a "sub-normal level" (13) and prices more than doubled. Although 1939 was marked by the outbreak of World War II, the rubber quota control scheme was renewed. Basically, the international rubber cartel has not practised direct control over prices.

b) International Tin Cartel

The International Tin Cartel was set up only in mid-1929 under the name of the International Tin Producers' Association, although the tin industry had been widely expanded before (14). During the period of the Great Depression, when there was a sharp decline in prices, the Tin Producers' Association advised its members to restrict production. Even though a reduction in output was realized, the resulting effects did not come up to expectations. Opposition came from the low-cost producers of the two largest tin-producing areas in the world, Malaya and Netherlands East Indies, the governments of which sponsored the Bandoeng Pool. The purpose of the pool was to keep the excess supplies of tin in the form of stocks, and to release them when market conditions were ready for them. Here the fact must be stressed that tin was the only commodity to use the buffer stock technique in that period.

---

(11) Ibid., p. 123.

(12) Ibid., p.153.

(13) Ibid., p.153.

(14) Ibid., p.124, 140 and 143.

Accordingly, with the stock releases, the pool greatly raised prices during the period 1921-1927. In 1929, stocks were a considerable 47,000 tons, compared with 15,000 in 1927. This period was marked by over-production of tin which led to a sharp fall in prices, and low-cost producers were not ready to participate in the reduction of output. From this, it can be seen that cartels, in order to exist, have to take 'outsiders' into account.

In 1929, the Anglo-Oriental Mining Company started the manipulation of the tin inventories so as to increase prices (15). Afterwards, the International Tin Producers' Agreement undertook a scheme to restrict output. The low-cost producers joind the restriction programme only when tin prices lowered to a third of the 1927 price (16), which still represented a very high level for that period.

In these two examples, an attempt has been made briefly to observe and follow the role of the cartel as an instrument of control which tries to iron out the maladjustments of supply and demand.

c) The relative importance of the cartel rôle as an instrument of economic control

How cartels are regarded and how effective they are supposed to be as stabilizing agents in the international market has best been emphasized by the following statement: "The purpose of these (international cartel) agreements is, in the main, to regulate, but not to abolish, competition. They can help to stabilize prices at a reasonable level ... They can lead to a rapid improvement in technique and a reduction in costs, which, in turn, with enlightened administration of industry, can provide the basis of lower prices to consumers ... They can provide a medium for an orderly expansion of world trade and can make a substantial contribution - and this is important - to the difficult problems of postwar readjustment of production in countries

---

(15) STOCKING, G. and WATKINS, M. Cartels or Competition?, op.cit., p. 164.

(16) Ibid., p. 164.

greatly affected by the war. They can also assist in providing much greater stability of employment" (17).

Such statements, where the virtues of cartels were pointed out, were made by the defenders of the cartels and their policy, although opinions remained devided. The antagonistic supporters focused more on the danger of cartels as regards price fixing, market allocation, restriction of output and control of technical research and development. Among other disadvantages, cartels were also responsible for disturbing international trade and reducing economic growth in general.

Whether one's view of international cartels is positive or negative, it is a fact that they exercised significant principles and methods of control, which, in turn, had a remarkable impact on world trade.

Conditions which favoured the growth of international cartels lay primarily in excess capacity (18). Besides, a natural scarcity of fundamental raw materials (sugar, nitrogen, steel, aluminium, rubber, tin, copper, and potash) represented another opportunity for the increase in number of international cartels in the world market. This was due to the fact that the source of supply of raw materials were limited and concentrated in few regions.

On the other hand, the governmental sponsorship and intervention actually contributed to a large extent to the organization of international cartels (especially in Germany in the inter-war period).

As for the buffer stocks, it must be noted that cartels were not really interested in using the stock mechanism in times of price increase. Up to that time, in the context of cartels, the buffer stock technique was not used in its generally-known concept (to reduce price fluctuations).

---

(17) Lord McGONAN, of International Chemical Industries. Speach made in the House of Lords. 5th July, 1944.

(18) In general, excess capacity arises when a company produces more than it can sell. In doing so, it will run up huge stocks of goods and will become unable to utilise its factors of production to the full.

All in all, the performance of international cartels manifested more a price maximisation than a price stabilization, policy.

B - THE ROLE OF THE GOVERNMENT-SPONSORED INTERNATIONAL CARTEL AGREEMENTS

This section will deal with the necessity for, and the objectives of, governmental sponsorship granted to the international cartel agreements, their significance in relation to the so-called "buffer stocks control technique" realized in some commodity programmes, and their efforts at stabilization.

1. Government participation

In the years of great Depression, many cartels disappeared from the market stage. This was due not only to the serious fall in the prices of specific commodities, but also to general instability caused by the much-weakened economy all along the line. In spite of the fact that these were times of risk and uncertainty, a large number of cartels overcame them, especially in commodities such as steel, non-ferrous metals, coke, cement, petroleum and fertilizers. Although among the raw-material producers (agriculture and some branches of mining industry), international cartels did exist and function, their operations were deficient in the necessary cartel cohesion as their total output was contributed by individual, small and dispersed unities.

Accordingly, business-minded raw material cartels - sugar, tin, rubber, tea - (which, in the period of the downward tendency in the demand, did not cut their prices with the purpose of increasing their individual sales) turned to the governments to seek state aid. To some extent, they saw this as a new strategy in trade, i.e. by using the power, reputation and influence of the state, they could realize their principal aims: market allocation, price increase and output control over the other countries' producers who failed to cooperate in cartel activities.

a) Governmental intervention

Government participation was needed in the cartel agreements to protect the interests of the members of cartels in particular, and national interests in general. It was extremely difficult to impose cartel restrictions, without governmental aid, on the producers who were not members of the cartel, by merely covering the common export markets.

The government reviewed the practice of effective control measures (which were completely wiped out by the Great Depression) and especially as regards certain commodities (wheat and coffee) as its producers were heading for serious economic difficulties (problem of curbing demand) which, in turn, threatened the economic situation in the country (19).

The question may be posed as to whether governmental intervention was necessary and justified? The answer may be the following: "where the prevention of new additional capacity is part of the control, legislation is, in most cases, absolutely necessary" (20). However, this does not mean that governments always agreed with total cartel policy (for example, cartels were ready to give up tariffs, but governments were not, because of the potential losses in revenue). States were ready to participate in international economy control only where dynamic and orderly marketing arrangement were concerned, that is, they were ready to support the legal concern of colective interests for cartel members only in so far as they themselves benefited from it.

It is apparent that, in the XIXth century, the approach to the problems which exist nowadays in the unequal relationship between the DCs and LDCs was not the same. This is due to the fact that there were fewer LDCs and their economies were largely under state control.

---

(19) STOCKING, G., and WATKINS, M., op.cit., p. 69.

(20) ROWE, J.W.F., op.cit., pp. 137-138.

That governments partially improved certain cartel control policies is demonstrated by the examples of Gremany and France, where the problem was one of maintaining exports (thus assuring supplies of foreign exchange) and appealing for high prices and import quotas respectively (21). However, governments did not always accept private cartels as such. Up to that time, there had existed government-sponsored schemes (tin, rubber, sugar and coffee valorization) and private cartels (copper, nitrogen and glass). However, this classification is approximate and it was always difficult to draw a distinct, limiting line between government-sponsored agreements and private cartels (22).

b) Results of governmental actions

During the 1930's, governmental participation was more or less in the second plan and, as time went on, the proportion increased and governments became official parties to international cartel agreements. It is worth noting that these were the governments of the net exporting countries (countries producing and exporting the commodity concerned). All international cartel agreements sponsored by governments reflected the same objectives and the instruments employed to attain them were of the same kind.

The objective was market stabilization and the instruments were production quotas or export quotas completed by so-called "buffer stocks". These buffer stocks were set up in the tin control scheme and, to some extent, increased in importance in sugar and coffee. These instruments were used in order to bring about a rise in prices. The question may be asked as to whether these objectives and instruments were different from those employed by international cartel agreements. Basically, they were not (23). Both of them, government-

---

(21) MASON, Edward, op.cit., p. 4.

(22) LAW, Alton D., International Commodity Agreements, Lexington Books, 1975, p. 35.

(23) This should be evident from our discussion concerning the purpose of international cartel agreements under A.2.

sponsored, and private cartels had an essential element in common - their aim, which was the stabilization of the market through the regulation of supply coming onto the market (that is, production and stockholding in the net-exporting countries). The factor that distinguished the government-sponsored schemes was the political influence of the producers and their interests.

2. The stock mechanism in particular under changing regulation objectives

The following refers to particular commodity markets in a brief outline of the significance of stocks and their meaning in the context of government-sponsored control schemes.

a) Sugar

The case of sugar market is an interesting one (see Table 1). In the period 1923-1929 there was a rapid increase in sugar production which doubled world (nationally administred) stocks and, in turn, reduced world prices by half. A need for international regulation was recognized in the 1931 agreement known as the Chadbourne Plan. The main exporters of its member nations were government-sponsored. In order to regulate this situation, its members consented to a control scheme including export quotas and general stocks release (25 per cent each year (24)) over a five-year period. Its purpose was to reduce the fall in world sugar prices.

However, the results were surprisingly different from those expected as the world sugar prices continued to fall after the intervention of the Chadbourne Plan, and were lower than before the concluding of the agreement. It was due in part, to the general, world economic situation (caused by the Great Depression). It may be noted here that a formally-provided stock regulation failed as a stabilization procedure.

(24) ROWE, J.W.F., op.cit., p. 146.

b) Coffee

In the case of coffee, the Brazilian valorization scheme attempted to control world prices in the period 1907-1940. Brazil was the largest coffee- exporting country (80% of world exports of coffee) and although the government backed the scheme to keep up the prices, it was not an international cartel agreement. It was more a national cartel that tried to influence the world market by regulating its large exports.

In 1905, the government of the State of São Paulo introduced the valorization scheme because of the inelasticity of demand, and fear of a sharp fall in prices. The purpose was to prevent the fall in prices as production was marked by a record crop. To improve its national economic policy, the government introduced the production quota and accumulated national stocks with a defined amount to be released destined for exports. The success of buffer stocks was heightened, due to the strong demand on the world market and the government decided to continue with the same policy during the following surplus periods. Between 1917 and 1929, Brazil had substantial surpluses due to large coffee crops. Nevertheless, government interference in buffer stock management to keep prices up failed in its programme during the world crisis (characterized by a general fall in prices), which resulted in surpluses being simply destroyed. In spite of its intervention, the government could not restrain the following collapse in world coffee prices.

Although those stocks were not international, and limited in too many points, which seriously complicated their management, it can be seen here that large coffee stocks were part of the Brazilian stabilization procedure. This has been pointed out as Brazil was the largest coffee supplier in the world and thus had great influence on international trade negotiations.

Besides the regulation measures in wheat, sugar, coffee, tea and rubber, governments also lent a helping hand in the form of large-scale sponsored international control to the tin cartel.

Table 1.

International Primary Commodity Agreements:
Principal Characteristics

Commodity	Entry into force	Duration (years)	Participation	Instrumants of control	Remerks
Wheat	1933	2	Major exporters and importers	export quotas; acreage restrictions	Poor compliance; outdated by bad harvests. Wheat Advisory Committee established.
	1942	0	Argentina, Australia, Canada,U.S.A. (exporters) and the U.K.	export quotas; production control; buffer pool,maximum and minimum exporter stocks; and minimum prices	Draft Convention set up an International Wheat Council
Sugar	1902	a/	Major producers (exc. Argentia and Russia)	Prohibition of beet subsidies for production or export.	U.K. to impose a counter-vailing tariff on subsidized exports.
	1931	5 b/	Major exporting interests,(particulary in Cuba and Java) accounting for less than half of world production	export quotas	undermined by expansion among non-participants
	1937	c/	Almost all sugar producing countries, including major importers	export quotas; exporters' stocks limited to a minimum of 10 per cent of quota and an end-of-season maximum of 25 per cent of production	U.K. to limit domestic production and U.S.A. to grant imports a specified share of its market. International Sugar Council set up.
Coffee	1940	4	U.S.A. and Latin American producers	export quotas	export quotas for markets other than the U.S.A. were fixed but remaind inoperative

Table 1. (continued)

Commodity	Entry into force	Duration	Participation	Instruments of control	Remarks
Tea	1933	5	Major Asian exporters; producer representation	export quotas	
	1938	5	As in 1933 but with government participation	As in 1933	
	1943	5	As in 1938	As in 1938	
Rubber	1934	5	All producing countries except Brazil and Liberia	Production and export quotas; prohibition of new planting. Export quotas fixed each quarter as a percentage of basic production quotas.	International Rubber Regulation Committee established. Representatives of rubber users as advisory members.
	1939	5	As in 1934	Ban on new planting lifted	International Rubber Study Group established.
Tin	1920		Malaya and Netherlands East Indies	Accumulation and liquidation of the Bandoeng Pool of "surplus" tin	
	1931	2	Bolivia,Malaya Netherlands East Indies, Nigeria and later Thailand	export quotas; International Tin Pool constituted	International Tin Committee set up to administer a Tin Restriction Scheme
	1933	3	As in 1931,plus Belgian Congo, Indo-China, Netherlands, Portugal and the U.K.	export quotas; buffer stock 1934-1935	Netherlands and the U.K. "consumer" delegates in consultative capacity
	1936	3	As in 1933	export quotas; buffer stock 1938-1939	As in 1933

Table 1. (continued)

Commodity	Entry into force	Duration	Participation	Instruments of control	Remarks
Tin (contd)	1942	5	As in 1936	export quotas (nominal)	U.S.A.also participated through non-voting consumer and government delegates

Source: UNCTAD, Stabilization of International Commodity Markets (measures for stabilization of primary commodity markets at equitable and renumerative prices including commodity arrangements) Doc. E/CONF.46/8, 19 March 1964, pp. 17-20.

a/ Brussels Convention, 1902-1914.

b/ Chadbourne Scheme, 1931-1935 (producers cartel agreement).

c/ First intergovernmental agreement suspended by the outbreak of war.

c) Tin

In 1931, the principal tin-producers appointed by the governments of Malaya, Netherlands East Indies, Nigeria and Bolivia set up the International Tin Control Scheme (see Table 1). The agreement was drawn up with the purpose of maintaining the steady, downward-sloping prices and declining demand in tin.

The International Tin Control Scheme was set up to work with the instruments of export quotas (supply was restricted by 78% and, afterwards, to one third of the 1929 output) and the International Pool. The forerunner of the latter was the Bandoeng Pool. The Bandoeng Pool was formed by the producers in Malaya and Netherlands East Indies, in order to meet the inelastic demand for tin, and thus to prevent a collapse in the tin prices by restrictions in surplus output and accumulations of stocks, and by releasing them gradually when market conditions were favourable (25).

Nevertheless, between 1920 and 1925, stocks were exhausted and the Pool was liquidated. After the Bandoeng Pool, the International Tin Pool represented the second effort made by producers to use the technique of so-called "buffer stocks". This was the first time that a buffer stock-pool was recognized (in 1934) as an official instrument in a control scheme. The purpose of the buffer stock was to keep prices "stable" and it was supposed to realize this by means of the release of the stocks in "accordance with a sliding scale of prices accepted by the governments" (26) which signed the agreement. Until mid-1939 buffer stocks proved to be useful, but then, with the outbreak of war, the situation in the world market entirely changed: stocks were too small to meet the increasing demand, and price boosting which, in turn, exhausted them. It proved, on one hand, that instruments of control had failed, once again, to stabilize prices of tin but, on the other hand, its liquidation assured its sponsors of a large profit.

---

(25) LAW, A.D., op.cit., p. 56-57.

(26) STOCKING, G. and WATKINS, M., op.cit., p. 75.

The problem of the buffer stock failure and its incapacity was best presented in the following statement made by K.E.Knorr: "The crux of the problem lies in the potential conflict between price-stabilization and price-boosting policies ... As long as both functions, price-boosting and price-stabilizing, are entrusted to the same institution and the same controllers, who are representative of the producers' interests, so long even the best machinery and institutional devices will not guarantee success in preventing undue price fluctuations" (27).

Besides all these criticisms, it is a fact that tin was the only commodity which, by government-sponsored agreement, exercised price control with a mechanism, to some degree, of the same kind as a buffer stocks.

d) A note on the use of the term "so-called" buffer stocks

The term "so-called" buffer stocks or "some kind" of buffer stocks has often been referred to in the text. To justify these terms, it must be emphasized that their objectives as control schemes differed from the modern buffer stock mechanism (that is, the stabilization of the short-term fluctuations of price). These control schemes were set up by government-sponsored agreements and were designed to realise their programmes and objectives: that is, to raise prices to a high market level but not to let them go too high (above it) and to encourage producers when production quotas were ordered.

Given these experiences, it can be seen that the restrictive policies which were in operation during the 1930s, including the attempts of the buffer stock scheme, were regarded by general opinion as "devices for selling a little for a lot rather than a lot for a little" (28). They were looked on as the mechanisms through which producers,

---

(27) KNORR, K.E., Tin Under Control, Food Research Institute, Stanford University 1945, p. 211.

(28) YATES, Lamartine P., Commodity Control, London, 1943, p. 14.

supported by governments, used to restrict the output and, in that way, assure high profits (for themselves), and not as measures designed to interfere at times when existing surpluses prevailed.

It is necessary to note that the cartel agreements of producers sponsored by governments largely manifested the absence of consumers. These agreements were established in order to encourage producers and their policy. Consumers (consuming countries) could not tolerate such a poicy in the long-term and they came forward with proposals for their participation which afterwards became intergovernmental agreements with the objective of stabilizing prices (eliminating excessive price fluctuations) and not of raising them. The first intergovernmental agreements which adopted both producers' and consumers' interests were concluded in the inter-war period, in respect of wheat in 1933, sugar in 1937 and coffee in 1940.

*

In this section,the purpose of our observation has been to focus thoughts on those examples (sugar, coffee, tin as well as tea, wheat and rubber) which were, to some extent, representative enough to show that some approaches to the buffer stocks as instruments of economic control were undertaken in the inter-war period by government-sponsored agreements.

As has been seen, the factor of government sponsorship and intervention, on one hand, did not have spectacular effects in the international market, but were important, on the other hand, as the roots of the future regulation of particular primary commodities.

Our analysis of the relevance of the buffer stock technique in the past reveals that it differed from today's schemes. It is obvious that the users themselves (private, governments, producers, consumers) always gave this technique its definite aspect.

C - EVOLUTION UP TO KEYNES'S RENEWAL PROPOSAL AND SUBSEQUENT PRACTICES

Following the general historical direction, commodity control activity became increasingly of interest. Since consumers joined the intergovernmental agreements (with voting rights) at the very end of the 1930's and the beginning of the 1940's with an interest in the regulation of markets for primary commodities, the fundamentals of the modern international commodity agreements were set up and with them, modern control schemes.

1. Current developments

It is noteworthy that in 1937 a League of Nations Committee covering the problem and objectives of the intergovernmental commodity agreements took the buffer stocks technique into consideration. This buffer stocks scheme was officially recommended as an instrument of market control and responsibility for its operation was to be shared by both producers and consumers.

a) The new conditions after World War II

World War II brought about a severe dislocation in world economy. Shortages were greatly accentuated and demand became extremely strong. War created new conditions (military, political, financial) which enabled most of the existing commodity agreements to work.

During the war years, the general world trade situation was an area of great interest and important discussions ensued which were aimed at preparing plans for post-war economic regulation and stability. The interests especially referred to were the reduction of trade barriers and trade discriminations and the accentuation of "commercial agreements in harmony with production and trade" (29).

---

(29) LAW, A.D., op.cit., p. 86. Those and following historical items are derived from the same book, and from YATES, Lamartine, Commodity Control, London, 1943.

b) The Hot Springs Conference and interest in buffer stocks

The United Nations Conference on Food and Agriculture at Hot Springs in May 1943, had, as its main objective, the examination of the commodity agreements problem with the aim of working out positive solutions. It is interesting to note that resolution 25 of the Conference proposes the "effective representation of consumers as well as producers" which, in general, (although not officially ratified) was accepted by most of the participants as though it were equal representation of consumers and producers. In addition, the whole spectrum of interests (production, consumption, prices, costs and profits) was presented at the Hot Springs Conference, the main objective being price stabilization. The general opinion was that if the stabilization of prices was attained and assured, such regulation would, in turn, bring about the automatic stabilization-effect in production and consumption.

It can be seen from the question of commodity control which was proposed by the British delegation that price stabilization was the centre of interest. The British proposal was presented in a form entitled "buffer stocks" and consisted in the creation of international buffer stock (for non-perishable agricultural products) the purpose of which would be not only to regulate the supply, and thus, in turn, the interests of producers and consumers, but to protect both of them from sharp fluctuations in price. It was said that the aim of the buffer stock operation should combine short and long-term stabilization of prices (30).

Although the heading "buffer stocks" appeared promising, there was no concrete solution concerning it, but it remained in the limits of divergence between representatives who were in favour of buffer stocks and those who were in favour of quotas as instruments of commodity control.

---

(30) TSOM, Stanley and BLACK, John D., "International Commodity Agreements", The Quarterly Journal of Economics, vol. LVIII, August 1944, No. 4, pp. 531-552.

c) Keynes's proposal of the international buffer stock mechanism

It may be noted that what was presented under the "buffer stock" suggestion at the Conference was essentially J.M. Keynes's renewal proposal. In order to obtain an overall idea, this requires a brief reminder of proposals and analyses made by Keynes concerning the international buffer stock device.

As far as quota policy as a measure of commodity control is concerned, Keynes was categoric in pointing out its shortcomings; "producers are too easily interested in the former (restriction); perhaps it carries with it the suggestion of higher prices" (31). This behaviour of restrictive schemes was proved by their mechanism to increase prices above a competitive level during the inter-war commodity agreements. The purpose was not to continue with the same restrictive policy, but to find a new approach by which stability in the commodity market would be assured.

Keynes argued in favour of buffer stocks. Buffer stocks have a stabilizing effect because they carry physical stocks from times of plenty (supply is large in relation to demand) to times of scarcity (supply is small in relation to demand).

Keynes saw buffer stocks as a device by means of which the possibility of controlling prices and thus attaining price stabilization, was feasible and to be recommended. The essential condition, according to Keynes, was "that prices are subject to gradual changes but are fixed within a reasonable range over short periods; ... Thus we should aim at combining a short-period stabilization of prices with a long-period price policy which balances supply and demand ..."(32), which, in turn, would bring about greater stability in export earnings both in the short-, and long-run.

---

(31) KEYNES,John Maynard, "The International Control of Raw Materials" 14th April,1942, reprinted in <u>Journal of International Economics</u>, 4, 1974, p. 299.

(32) KEYNES, J.M., <u>op.cit</u>., p. 301.

The idea of realizing the stability of export earnings was the basis of every commodity agreement in the inter-war period, but the instrument of achieving such stability was a restrictive measure in the form of production and export quotas (just the opposite of Keynes's suggestion) which proved its impracticability.

The point which Keynes also elaborated regarding buffer stocks concerned the stock level. He observed that predisposition to store had been too low in the past and, thus, he argued, a minimum level of commodities concerned in international trade should be kept on the basis of "three months minimum"(33).

His statement was supported by the analysis of the required financial resources for eight principal commodities for 1942 prices. This was not yet been "proven or disproven" (34). To analyse and evaluate the optimal stock for every commodity would demand careful estimation concerning the price range and elasticities of supply and demand.

Whatever criticisms have been advanced concerning the instruments of commodity control, either in favour of the buffer stocks or in favour of quantitative control, opinions and their economic interpretations have remained divided.

2. Subsequent practices

Attempts of the Havana Charter Chapter 6 concerning the buffer stocks

Intensive discussions on commodity control activity reached the peak of their development in Chapter 6 of the Havana Charter in 1947-48. The draft Charter elaborated the establishment of an International Trade Organization (ITO). In spite of all efforts, ITO failed, on one hand, because the Havana Charter did not come into force, but, on the other hand, the guidelines and principles of the policy of the ICAs were set up, and were regarded as being in effect.

---

(33) KEYNES, J. M., op.cit., pp. 299-315

(34) STAKHOVITCH, Alexander, "A European View of Commodity Problems: Stabilization of Prices and Stabilization of Receipts", in Stabilizing World Commodity Markets, Lexington Books, D.C. Heath,Massachusetts, 1978, p. 237.

The aim of Chapter 6 was to protect the consumer countries, as was pointed out in Article 63. Among other things, restrictive measures and price-fixing were limited and intended to be used only as temporary measures. Consumer countries were given equal voting rights with producer countries in drafting the ICAs.

Concerning buffer stocks, the achievements of the Havana Conference were not spectacular. It was specified only that buffer stocks should be dealt with as well as quotas - on the same basis.

b) Official acceptance of the establishment of ICAs

In 1947 the principles which had been set up in the Havana Charter were adopted by the Economic and Social Council and were officially recommended by them in the establishment of all new ICAs. From that time on, ICAs gained much in importance and, with them, the measures for commodity control, amongst which buffer stocks had their own place. This can best be seen from the following reference: "We know of no practicable method of reducing the international impact of short-run fluctuations in the prices and terms of trade of primary products, other than ... the negotiations of international commodity agreements; many different arrangements may be suitable for different types of commodities, including long-term contracts, multilateral quota system ... and buffer stocks, either alone or in combination" (35).

The position of quantitative control and buffer stocks as measures of the commodity control schemes continued to be regarded and "treated on the same basis" (as set up in the Havana Charter), and "any form of control may be used to the principle of adequate supplies at reasonable prices (36) - Rowe emphasises as "terms which are notoriously vague" (37).

---

(35) Measures of International Economic Stability, U.N. Department of Economic Affairs, New York 1951, p. 10,par.29.

(36) ROWE, J.W.F., op.cit., p. 161.

(37) Ibid., p. 161.

c) Operation of the first post-war buffer stock agreement - Tin

During the fifteen years after the war, only wheat, sugar and tin agreements were fully operative. They were largely based, in their construction, on their inter-war forerunners.

Among them, the Tin Agreement which came into force in 1956, was the only one which realized market control through the buffer stock mechanism, strengthened by additional export quotas when necessary.

The form of the buffer stock operation was centralized, which means that it was carried out by the Tin Council, which functioned through the buffer stock manager. The objective was to prevent the excessive price fluctuation of tin and to stabilize the tin market. The agreement defined a price range (floor and ceiling prices) and the purpose of the buffer stock was to keep the market price of tin within that range. To meet that requirement, the buffer stock manager bought the tin for the stock when prices fell below the floor-, and sold tin from the stock when prices rose above the ceiling- level. The manager might operate to sell or to buy tin when the tin market price reached the upper or lower limit of the price range. The operations of the manager depended on the funds at his disposal for buying, and/or stock of tin for selling.

The financing of the 1956 Tin Agreement was assured by the members which were exporting countries. Although the market conditions were favourable at the concluding of the Tin Agreement (production exceeded consumption), the situation changed at the end of the 1950's and the beginning of the 1960's. Such a situation brought into operation the strengthening mechanism of export quotas. Intervention had little effect as production could not meet the growing demand, which,in turn, caused a rise in tin prices. Buffer stocks operations were able to control the price by sales from stocks, but not for a long time as they were completely exhausted by mid-1961. Due to this situation of exhausted buffer stocks and the inability to increase the tin production in the short term, control of the tin market was handed over to the United States, the tin stocks of which were equivalent to more than three years' world exports and nearly one half of it was declared ready to be disposed of.

From this it can be seen that the first Tin Agreement after the war showed the buffer stock mechanism to be adequately successful. It succeeded in balancing out short-term price fluctuations on one hand, but on the other hand, it proved that its size was not sufficient to meet the vigorous and unpredictable changes in market conditions.

All in all, it was a positive and successful practical experience for the buffer stock principle.

*

In what has preceded, it has been seen that the direct objective of the operation of the buffer stock control was to stabilize the price of specific primary commodities. Keynes's renewal proposal of the buffer stock concept relied on the idea that it was the right tool to control the prices of primary products without interfering with the price trend, and thus without intervening in, or even abolishing, the commodities market. This contrasted with the scepticism expressed by the opponents of the buffer stocks (and the ICAs) concerning the fear of market disruption due to a planned economy approach. His thoughts and proposals of the buffer stock mechanism as a method of commodity control were of fundamental importance for the modern commodity trade and international economic stability.

In this part,an attempt has been made not to advocate the international buffer stocks policy but to state, by following its historical trend, that the desire to store commodities in periods of plenty in order to sell them in periods of scarcity, has existed for a long time. Additionally, our purpose was to show that buffer stocks, by their regulating mechanism, have been measures which have attempted to function as a price stabilization scheme.

CHAPTER II

THE PURE MECHANISM

As the heading of this chapter suggests, it is our intention to deal with the pure buffer stock mechanism. A definition will be given here as to what the buffer stock operation is, as such, although an isolated academic discussion appears difficult due to the complexity of reality (already described in the historic part).

Economic literature deals with the buffer stock device mainly in connection with the other regulatory methods. Thus, our aim in observing the commodity control methods is to put the stress on the buffer stock principle itself.

This instrument of commodity control will be dealt with under the series of assumptions which are explained in section A, with the primary objective of showing that "reducing variations without increasing the price level is the justification for a pure buffer stock" (1).

A - MAIN ELEMENTS AND ASSUMPTIONS

It is well known that certain economic literature about buffer stocks exists (2); nevertheless, in view of the fact that it has re-entered the present world trade interest, it is felt that it should be discussed again. Note will be taken especially of this principle, mechanism and operation.

1. Buffer stock performance

It is worth recalling, however, that the buffer stock "exercises its stabilizing influence by performing the essentially useful function of carrying physical stocks from times when they are not so much wanted to times when they are scarce and expensive" (3).

---

(1) MacAVOY, Paul W., Economic Perspective on the Politics of International Commodity Agreements, The Institute of Government Research, The University of Arizona, 1977, p. 5.

(2) The possibility of buffer stock price stabilizing operations proved of particular interest in 1942 with Keynes's proposal of international buffer stock regulation in commodity markets, which was discussed in the previous chapter.

(3) GATT, Trends in International Trade, Geneva 1958, para. (222), p. 76.

a) Principle

The stabilization function, to the extent that it was applied in former times (4), has always been more or less the same, and, as such, has long been recognized as an attractive and desirable principle of storing commodities in times of plenty (when supply is greater than demand) for use in times of insufficiency (when demand is greater than supply). Such an opperation gained special importance in the post-war period as a technique employed by commodity agreements mainly to stabilize commodity prices by regulating the supply of the commodity on the world market, which represented the fundamental aim of the control schemes. The principal objective of the buffer stock scheme was clearly defined by the statement that "the purpose of buffer stock is not to interfere with the price trend that will equate supply and demand in the long run, but to moderate violent short-term fluctuations of price around trends" (5), by buying at low prices and selling at high prices.

Those were the official wishes, but recent years revealed that the buffer stock principle has an application in modern international trade, normally in combination with other elements of control (i.e. export quotas). Its certain merits have been recognized, as well as its difficulties and problems. In order to obtain insights into its relative advantages and disadvantages, it would be useful to take into account the theoretical considerations of the buffer stocks and to see what they are, what they do, and how they work.

The international buffer stock is built up and maintained by an intergovernmental body (International Council) for the commodity concerned, to mitigate the short-term fluctuations in supply and/or demand of the commodity.

---

(4) Many hundreds of years B.C., the Chinese used the principle of product stocking.

(5) UN Department of Economic Affairs, Commodity Trade and Economic Development, submitted by a Committee Appointed by the Secretary General, New York 1963, para. 148, p. 46.

b) Mechanism and Operation

Traditionally the buffer stock mechanism has aimed at regulation of supply and/or price. To regulate demand by buffer stock is a new dimension and its efficiency must be examined in the context of the overall behaviour of the factors that influence demand, which is rather difficult and presented in section B.

With the intention of regulating commodity markets and thus avoiding sharp price fluctuations, the buffer stock agency fixes a range of prices (floor and ceiling price) for the commodity in question. Its mechanism operates as follows: the commodity is bought for the stock in the market when its supply is excessive and prices fall and reach the lower limit of the defined price range, and sold from the stock when supply is low and prices rise above the higher price range limit.

Thus the buffer stock principle appears to be logical sound in theory, and its functioning represents rather an encouraging simple device for price stabilization as, in the case of the upward swing in prices, there is a release from the stocks (selling process), and in the case of the downward swing in prices, there is an accumulation of the stocks (buying process).

The argument advanced through the commodity agreements (whether based on the buffer stock principle or not) in the post war period was, and remained for some time, that a stabilization of commodity prices will reduce instability in export earnings, which, in turn, will bring stability to the economic development as a whole. With this argument it is as well to be cautious in that it must be stressed that stability of prices does not necessarily assure stability of export earnings, as can be seen from the following Figure 1.

To simplify, we assume that the price is fixed and stabilized at the level OP, and the objective is to maintain the equilibrium point P_1. Therefore, the original situation is where the equilibrium price and quantity are P_1 and Q_1, and the total foreign exchange revenue to be maintained is OPP_1Q_1.

Figure 1.

Effect of the buffer stock
on the total foreign exchange revenue
at the stable price P

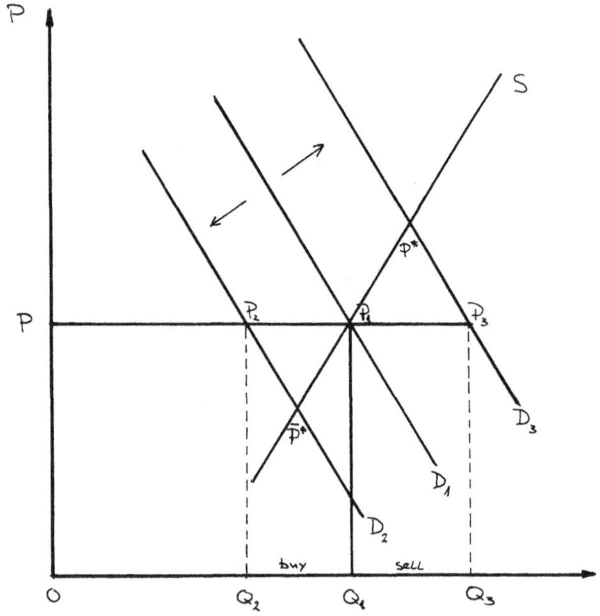

The shift in the demand D_1 (reduction) to D_2 would bring about the price change to $\overline{P}$*. This is followed by purchases for the buffer stock of quantity Q_1Q_2, which equals the decline in demand. The buffer stock regulation will give rise to the purchase of commodity, and the price will be regulated and maintained from P_2 to P_1, as well as quantity from Q_2 to Q_1. Therefore, the total foreign exchange revenue remains unchanged, given by the surface OPP_1Q_1.

To realize stability of the foreign exchange earnings, the buffer stock made the purchase represented by the surface of $Q_2P_2P_1Q_1$. If the demand curve shifts from D_1 to D_3, this will be followed by the price change to P*. Due to the buffer stock control, there is a release from the stocks and the buffer stock manager sells the quantity Q_1Q_3, which, in turn, will bring back the price and quantity from the stabilized level P_3 to P_1, (which is actually the assumed stabilized price P), and Q_3 to Q_1 respectively, and thus re-establishes the equilibrium position where the foreign exchange revenue remains OPP_1Q_1. With this operation, buffer stock realises the receipts of $Q_1P_1P_3Q_3$.

From this brief observation, it can be seen that, although the price level is kept stable and the objective of the buffer stock mechanism is to maintain the equilibrium price P_1, the quantities demanded or supplied (the variations of quantities supplied are not presented on the diagram) may fluctuate, and thus, in turn, have an effect on the total foreign exchange revenue.

It could be argued that a buffer stock scheme would have to deal not only with one element of price stabilization, but also with different price, supply and demand cycles for the relevant commodity and short-term instability caused by elements such as speculation and market disturbances (which are exeptionally difficult to predict).

2. Resources for buffer stock operation

The success of the buffer stock operation depends, from the very beginning, on several variables, among which two factors are of decisive importance: (a) the finance of the stock, and (b) the size of the stock.

a) The finance of the buffer stock

Buffer stock financing is a problem in itself. The United Nations Conference on Trade and Development (UNCTAD) (6) has tried to solve it by means of the "Common Fund" project. Current negotiations prove that this element indeed plays a key role in a future buffer stock system but, at the same time, it would be very difficult for it to become a point of general agreement.

b) The size of the buffer stock

The operation of the buffer stock scheme depends largely on the resources available. These can be in the form of cash, for buying a stock of commodity and/or for selling (7).

The resources are at the buffer stock manager's disposal. The manager intervenes at a given moment (when market prices fall below the floor price, or rise above the ceiling price) ,and uses the resources with the purpose of stabilizing the price within the agreed price range by buying for, or selling from, the stock. Therefore, "the bigger the price range, the easier the control, but the less the stability of prices" (8) and the smaller would be the amount of resources required.

c) An overall view of other factors necessary to establish a system of buffer stocks

To operate successfully, buffer stock needs a certain amount of funds and/or commodity stock. How much this quantity will be, depends not only on the size of the price

---

(6) "Consideration of Issues Relating to the Establishment and Operation of a Common Fund", Report by the Secretary General of UNCTAD, TD/B/IPC/CF/2, November 1976.

(7) MacBEAN, Alasdair, Export Instability and Economic Development, George Allen & Unwin Ltd., London 1966, p.269.

(8) ROWE, J.W.F., op.cit., p. 195.

range but also on the intensity of supply of the commodity, that is, the bigger the over-supply, the greater the quantity required. Moreover, it will depend on the degree of elasticity of supply and demand (9), that is, less resources would be required for the buffer stock if the elasticities were smaller (10).

The above are indisputably common elements which have their own influence on the quantity of the resources (funds and/or commodity stock) demanded by the buffer stock agency to maintain the prices within the defined price range. Moreover, the individual and definite characteristics of each commodity will also have an incontestable effect on the operation of the buffer stock.

According to the UNCTAD experience, the amount of resources needed to establish a system of buffer stocks is determined by, and depends on, certain common factors.

Besides the ones already mentioned, there is an extensive list of other factors (11) which are related to the natural characteristics of the commodities, the margin of the price range, demand and supply responses to changes in prices and some others.

As has already been said, another main factor for a favourable stabilizing policy is that in order for buffer stock to operate successfully (to mitigate the short-term fluctuations in supply and demand), such a stock has to be of a size large enough to absorb the average fall or rise in demand and supply within the given commodity price

---

(9) It is right and useful to add that in fixing buffer stock quantity, due regard must also be paid to the potential risk created by substitute commodities (e.g. for primary commodities, synthetics).

(10) Radetzki explains this effect graphically by the steepness of the demand and supply schedules. The steeper the schedules, the less resources required, in: RADETZKI, Marian, International Commodity Market Arrangements, C. Hurst & Co., London 1970, p. 83.

(11) An Integrated Programme for Commodities: The role of international commodity stocks, TD/B/C.1/166/Supp.1, December 1974, p. 20, para. 44.

stabilization range. A buffer stock requires special provisions regarding its periodical renewal (development bank fund, for example) in order to be successful. Furthermore, the size of the buffer stock depends on the price range defined (floor and ceiling prices) as well as on "the extent to which the equilibrium price, in the absence of stabilization, would persistently fall above or below that range" (12). If it happens that the equilibrium price is situated outside the defined price range, above or below, the buffer stock will exhaust either its fund or commodity stocks. This is what happened to the buffer stock of tin in mid- 1961 as it was not large enough to meet the rising demand and was thus completely exhausted. "If the selected price range is too low, the stock will end its phase of stabilization with a profit and can be reconstructed to stabilize prices within a higher price range. If on the other hand the selected price range is too high, the stock will end its stabilization phase with a stock of the commodity bought at prices above the current market price and hence will have suffered a capital loss. The risk of such a loss, which might well be substantial, is a major deterrent to the participation of consuming countries in the buffer schemes" (13).

Although the maintenance of buffer stock involves some serious difficulties and problems, it is indubitable that this stabilization scheme has certain great merits. "... It can be operated even if some importers and exporters are not members. It does not require extensive governmental control of trade in the product, and it allows competition in the market as between low-cost and high-cost producers.

---

(12) JOHNSON, Harry G., Economic Policies Towards Less Developed Countries, George Allen & Unwin Ltd., 1976, p. 146.

(13) JOHNSON, Harry G., ibid., p. 146.

It exercises its stabilizing influence by performing the essentially useful function of carrying physical stocks from times when they are not so much wanted to times when they are scarce and expensive" (14).

In addition, it does not interfere with the ordinary market transactions (dealers are free to buy from, and sell to, whomever they like and in whatever quantities they want at what prices they wish (15)); nor does it influence changes in taste for commodities. Therefore, the process of buying for, and selling from, the buffer stocks, smooths the year-to-year variations in demand resulting from trade recessions.

Finally, a positive point for the buffer stock procedure is that it offsets severe price fluctuations in the short-run, although this has a rather negligible effect in the long-run.

B - THE SYSTEM WITH THE CHANGE IN DEMAND

It is agreed in general that, observing the price instability in the primary products market, it is very difficult to distinguish to what degree fluctuations are due to the action of market forces and to what degree they are due to autonomous factors.

Instability in demand (as demand for most primary products is relatively unresponsive to price, low-price-elasticity of demand) for primary products - influenced by the development of synthetic substitutes, or changes in protection policies, particularly as regards agriculture - can be the cause of great instability in the supply of primary products (16).

---

(14) Trends in International Trade, GATT, Geneva, 1958, p. 76. para. (222).

(15) YATES, Lamartin, op.cit., p. 225.

(16) O'NEILL, Helen, A Common Interest in a Common Fund, UNCTAD, New York, 1977, p. 9.

It may be said that price fluctuations in the primary commodities are due to short-term inelasticity of demand and supply.

It is well known that the conditions which justify operating the commodity control schemes in general, and buffer stock in particular, lie in the price instability (17) of the world market. It may be said that the source of the wide price fluctuations in primary products lies in the changing forces of both supply and demand conditions.

Such forces have combined effects and, after some remarks pertaining to the objective of stabilization through the buffer stock mechanism and certain specific assumptions, the change in the demand market will be dealt with.

1. The two objectives of stabilization through the buffer stock mechanism

What is meant here by price stabilization is that by using the instrument of buffer stocks through the buy-sell-process, the price of the commodity concerned is maintained within the price range around the defined price trend. This is the first objective of the buffer stock mechanism. The second objective, is that price stabilization through buffer stock mechanism and its management can also stabilize export earnings(18).

---

(17) It is not our intention to analyse here the various approaches to the problem of welfare gains and losses from price stabilization. (The result of this, in brief, is that by using price stabilization via buffer stocks, a net welfare gain can be realized as an overall effect on the society, that is, the gains obtained through the price stabilization policy will always neutralize the losses.) The literature on this topic is abundant, and for nearly forty years (starting with Waugh in 1944), the most eminent economists have dealt with the subject (Oi, Massell, Samuelson, Bieri and Schmitz, Turnovsky and others) taking into consideration the changes in the world market caused by the demand and supply and their respective elasticities, as well as other basic economic variables.

(18)MICHALOPOULOS, Constantin, PEREZ,Lorenzo L.,"Commodity Trade Policy Initiatives and Issues", in: Stabilizing World Commodity Markets, ed.,by ADAMS,Gerard F., KLEIN,Sonia A., Lexington Books, D.C. Heath & Co. Lexington 1978,p. 248.

a) Delimitation of what to stabilize

Given the above information regarding stabilization, it may be said that importance must be attached to what is to be stabilized. Here a careful note should be taken of the fact that price stabilization does not directly mean stabilization of export earnings, nor vice versa.

From a practical point of view, it could be said that the effect on price stabilization of buffer stock action can be measured at once, whereas the reaction in revenue to a buffer stock action can be measured only after some time and, moreover, a buffer stock action can be only one element among many influencing export earnings.

b) The complexity of the relationship of price stabilization and export earnings stabilization

The extent of the complexity of the relationship between these two forms of stabilization, is well illustrated by Stakhovitch in his statement: "The two systems are neither symmetrical nor alternative. They may,however, be complementary. ... Price stabilization, at least through the mechanism of buffer stocks, has very limited applicability. The flexibility of receipts stabilization, which can be utilized for any commodity a priori, makes the scheme very tempting. However, price stabilization is a much more powerful tool. Theoretically, it is symmetrical in benefits to producers and consumers. Receipts stabilization is clearly a form of transfer, a form of aid that is commodity-linked. The choice between the two objectives or, conceivably, a combination of the two, depends clearly on the purpose we are pursuing and on the structure of the demand and supply of the commodities involved" (19).

---

(19) STAKHOVITCH, Alexandre, "A European View of Commodity Problems: Stabilization of Prices and Stabilization of Receipts", in: Stabilizing World Commodity Markets, ed., by ADAMS, Gerard F., and KLEIN, Sonia A., Lexington 1978, p. 240.

2. Buffer stock operation in the demand shift market

Although the two systems of stabilization mentioned are of incontestable complexity, an attempt will be made, using a simplified market analysis under certain assumptions, to express their behaviour through the means of geometry, taking into consideration the demand and supply forces.

Thus the effect of the buffer stock and its operating problems on the demand shift market will be discussed first and then the indirect effects on export earnings with price stabilization by the buffer stock will be presented.

a) Assumptions for the simplified market analysis

The following assumptions will be considered (20):

- demand and supply curves are linear;
- the shift of demand and supply curves are parallel

(the supply shift market will be dealt with in Section C below). Further, it will be supposed that the price of a particular commodity manifests the fluctuations around its real trend. To attempt to stabilize the price through the buffer stock mechanism, it is assumed that the price range (floor price P_f and ceiling price P_c) for the commodity concerned is given and is symmetrical to the market equilibrium prices (P_1 and P_2). It is presumed that the buffer stock manager who operates the buffer stock has sufficient resources (funds for buying and/or stock of commodity for selling). To effect the price stabilization within the price range, the quantity of commodity bought or sold for the stock must correspond to the quantity demanded or supplied ($\bar{Q}_1Q_1' = Q_2'\bar{Q}_2$) at the range limits ($P_fP_c$). Thus, in order to avoid excess stocks, the quantity bought in one period at the lower range limit corresponds to the quantity sold in the second period at the upper range limit. In addition, it is our supposition that demand and supply do not vary considerably with the level of prices.

---

(20) What follows is partly derived from BROWN, C.P., Primary Commodity Control, Oxford University Press, 1975, p. 135-136; and RADETZKI, Marian, International Commodity Arrangements, London 1970, pp. 82-85.

b) Case of shift only in demand-elastic curve

The buffer stock mechanism should be brought into operation when the commodity market price reaches the upper or lower limit of the price range . This can be seen by means of the following Figure 2.

From the diagram it can be seen that the buffer stock manager neither buys for, nor sells from, the stock when the market price is within the price range, that is between P_f and P_c. In the first period, demand shift to D_1 leads to the temporary decrease in price to P_1, and the price falls below the floor price P_f. To support the floor price P_f, the buffer stock manager must buy quantity $\bar{Q}_1 Q_1'$ from the market and this will cause the market supply to be reduced when the market price tends to fall. If, in the second period, the price exceeds the upper limit of the price range, the ceiling price P_c, and rises to P_2, a temporary demand leads to D_2. To defend the ceiling price P_c, the buffer stock manager must sell $Q_2'\bar{Q}_2$ quantity of the commodity concerned from the stock. Thus the quantity released from the stock will have the effect of increasing the market supply when the market price tends to rise. It is assumed that the buffer- stock manager has enough resources at his disposal to operate in such a way.

c) Case of shift only in demand-inelastic curve

The following Figure 3 demonstrates how the quantity of resources needed for the operation of the buffer stock can vary with the degree of elasticity of demand (21).

It will be noticed that the more inelastic the demand schedule is, the less resources are required to level temporary price fluctuations in the commodity market concerned.

From the point of view of the operating problems of the buffer stock instrument, the role of the demand and supply elasticities is of considerable importance, as they directly determine the amount of resources needed for the realization of its price stabilization working principle.

---

(21) Supply behaviour will be observed in the following section.

Figure 2.

The buffer stock operation effect
in the market with the shift in demand only
elastic demand curve

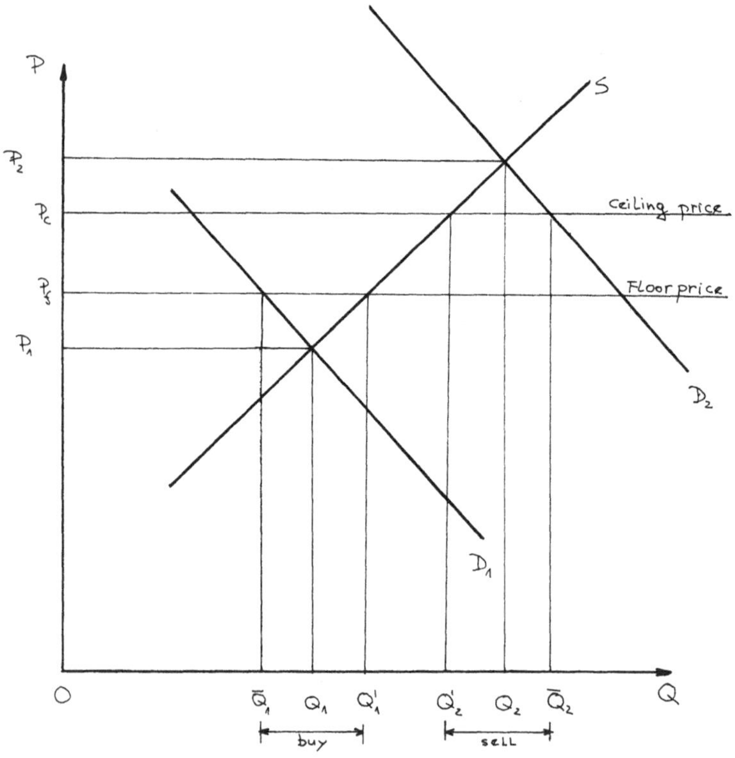

Figure 3.

The buffer stock operation effect
in the market with the shift in demand only
inelastic demand curve

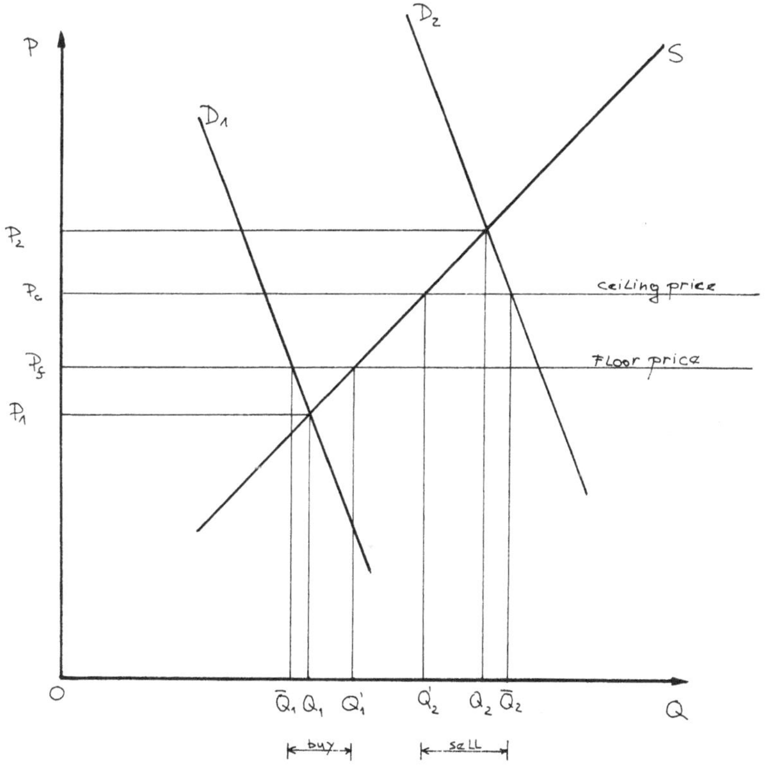

d) Effects on the price revenue of the shift in demand curve caused by the price stabilization policy by means of buffer stock

So far it has been shown that the use of the buffer stock succeeded in maintaining the price fluctuations within the given range. An attempt will now be made to follow the effects on the revenue caused by the price stabilization policy by means of the buffer stock, under the assumptions made. The following geometrical diagram represents the analysis of Professor H. Johnson (22) and his argument that there is an impact of price stabilization policies on the stabilization of export earnings (23).

In period 1 the export earnings of producers are $OP_1R_1Q_1$ and in period 2, $OP_2R_2Q_2$. The average value of export earnings of producers is $(OP_1R_1Q_1 + OP_2R_2Q_2)/2$ when there is no buffer stock price stabilization operation.

With the buffer stock price stabilization, producers' export revenue corresponds to OP_oRQ_o. "In summary, price stabilization through buffer stocks stabilizes producer income at the expense of reducing its average level, in the case of instability due to demand shifts"(24). This is given in Figure 4, by

$$\frac{(OP_1R_1Q_1) + (OP_2R_2Q_2)}{2} > OP_oRQ_o$$

So far it has been shown that schemes have always dealt with the market price stabilization even when the objective has been the stability of producers' revenue. In the next step the system with a change in the supply will be attentively followed.

---

(22) JOHNSON, Harry G., "Commodities: Less Developed Countries' Demands and Developed Countries' Responses", in: The New International Economic Order: The North-South Debate (ed., by BHAGWATI, N.), Cambridge, The Massachusetts Institute of Technology Press, 1977.

(23) This effect was proved in 1964, by H.G.Grubel, who analysed only the demand shift market with the non-parallel shifts in the demand schedule, but took into consideration the demand elasticity in period 2. GRUBEL,Herbert G.,"Foreign Exchange Earnings and Price Stabilization Schemes",The American Economic Review, vol. LIV,1964, pp. 378-385.

(24) JOHNSON, Harry G., loc.cit., p.251.

Figure 4.

Effects on the revenue of shift in demand only with and without price stabilization by a buffer stock

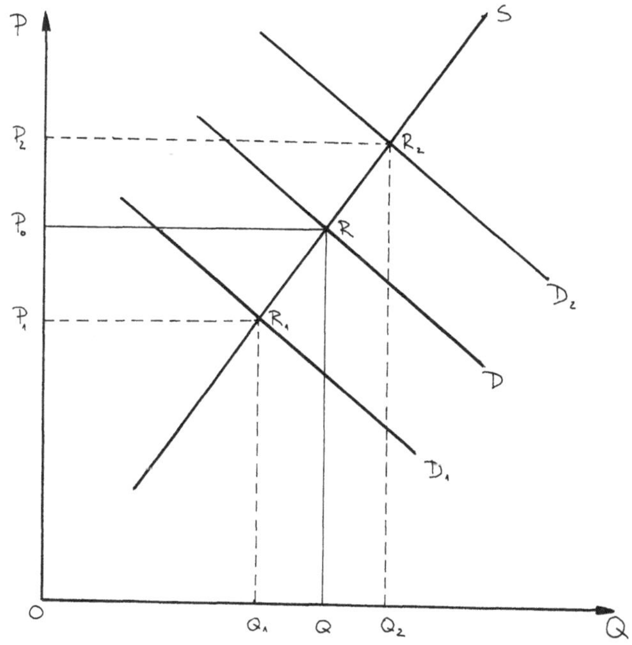

C - THE SYSTEM UNDER A CHANGE IN THE SUPPLY

Primary (mostly agricultural) commodities are largely subject to the effects of autonomous factors, such as plant and animal diseases or changes in climatic conditions resulting in short-run supply instability (25). Therefore, the low supply elasticity (response of output to price changes), which is characteristic of primary commodities (although there is a net difference between agricultural and mining products, where the latter has a higher supply elasticity than the former), means that any increase or decrease in demand will bring about considerable instability in prices (26).

So far, only the price stabilization effects of the buffer stock instrument and the policy designed to influence demand in the primary commodities market have been considered. As the fluctuations of prices in the world market are due to changes in both demand and supply conditions, our interest in this section will be to continue our consideration of what the buffer stock mechanism accomplishes in its price stabilization policy, but now in the supply shift market.

1. The buffer stock operation in the supply shift market

With regard to the assumptions made for the simplified market model in the preceding section, the consequences of the buffer stock mechanism and its price stabilization effect on the supply shift market only will now be considered followed by a presentation of its indirect impact on the export earnings in the same market.

---

(25) STERN, Robert, "World Market Instability in Primary Commodities", Banca Nazionale del Lavoro, Quarterly Review, Rome 1976, no. 117, pp.177-178.

(26) MacBEAN, Alasdair I., Export Instability and Economic Development, London 1966, p. 25.

a) Case of shift only in supply-elastic curve

Figure 5 corresponds to Figure 2, with the difference that demand is stable and supply shifts, with the given price range $P_f P_c$(floor and ceiling price, respectively). It is assumed that in period 1, supply is OQ_1 and price OP_1 as there is no buffer stock action. To support the floor price OP_f, the buffer stock manager must buy $Q_1'\overline{Q}_1$ quantity from the market for the stock. In turn, the effect will be a reduction in the market demand as at the price OP_f, the market is ready to buy only the quantity OQ_1' since the price has gone up from P_1 to P_f.

In period 2 it is assumed that the supply is OQ_2 at the price OP_2 without the intervention of the buffer stock manager. To support the ceiling price OP_c of the given price range, the buffer stock manager will sell the commodity from stock. The quantity released from the stock is $\overline{Q}_2Q_2'$. The effect of this intervention will be a fall in price to the ceiling level OP_c; at that price, the quantity bought by the market would be OQ_2', thus the buffer stock manager would have to sell $\overline{Q}_2Q_2'$ quantity. It is assumed that the buffer stock manager has sufficient resources (funds for buying and/or commodity for selling) for this operation to be possible.

b) Case of shift only in supply-inelastic curve

Our next figure concerns the operating problems of the buffer stock instrument in the inelastic supply shift market. Figure 6. points out that the more inelastic (steeper) the supply schedule is, the less resources the buffer stock manager needs to have at his disposal for it to function as a means of price stabilization.

Case 1 : Assuming that the price range is given as in Figure 6, the first case to be taken up is where, if the quantity bought for the stock $\overline{Q}_1Q_1'$ continues to be greater than the quantity released from the stock $\overline{Q}_2Q_2'$, the price will fall below the range floor and will continue to fall far below the OP_1. It

Figure 5.

The buffer stock operation effect
in the market with the shift in supply only
elastic supply curve

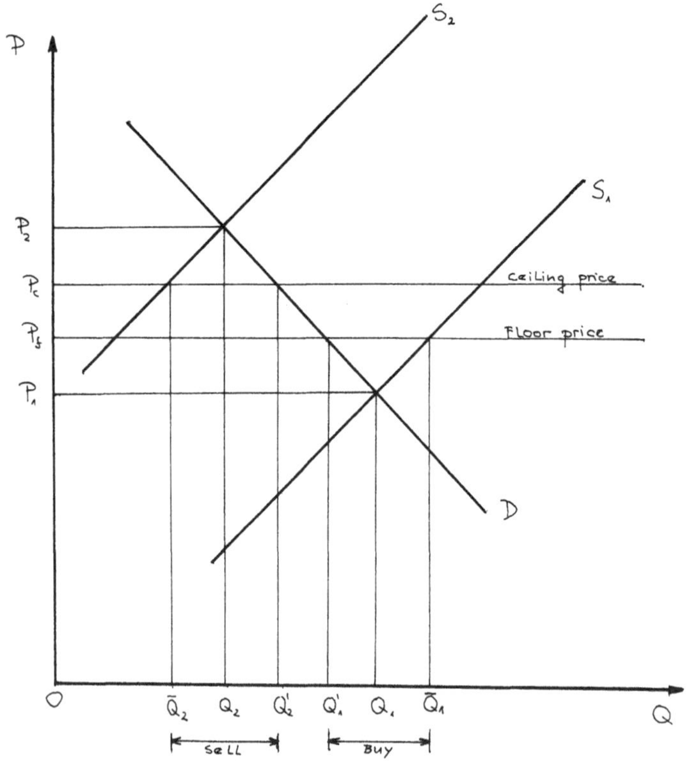

Figure 6.

The buffer stock operation effect in the market with the shift in supply only inelastic supply curve

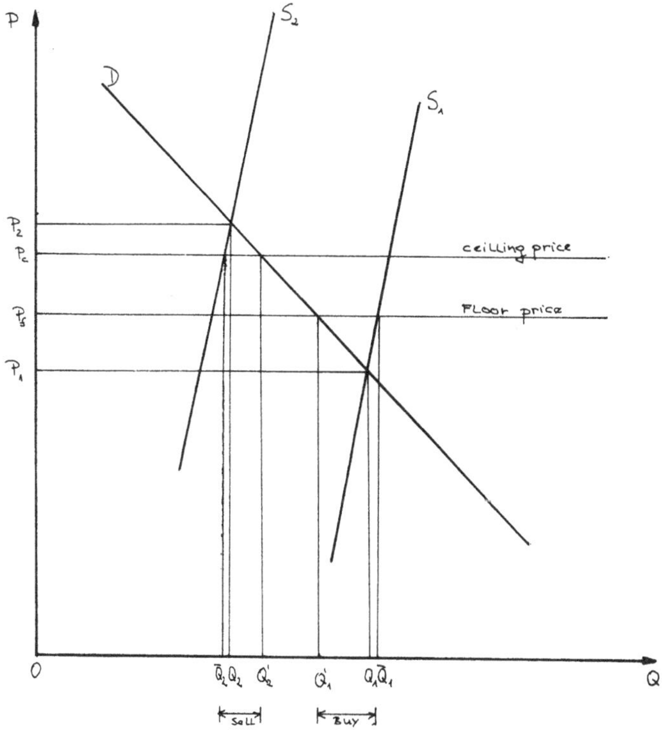

will result either in an exhaustion of the available storage space through amassing too large stocks, or exhausting the total funds, which have been made available, for buying the commodity. In either case, the result will be the same. The buffer stock will lose control over the market and the scheme will break down.

Case 2: In the second case, with the same price range, if the quantity released from the $\overline{Q}_2Q_2'$ continues to be greater than the quantity bought for the stock $\overline{Q}_1Q_1'$, the price will pass the upper limit OP_c, the ceiling price, and will exceed OP_2, as the manager will not have a large enough quantity stockpiled, i.e. the buffer stock will be of insufficient size to supply the commodity demanded due to the sudden changes in the market situation. The excess of demand over supply and the considerable rise in prices would exhaust the buffer stock and the scheme would become inoperative.

It can be seen that the size of the price range determines the resources needed for the buffer stock scheme to operate. If the price trend is given, then the larger the price range, the smaller the amount of resources needed for the functioning of the mechanism.

Such considerations of the operating problems of the buffer stock point to the conclusion, which is well known and too often repeated, that the financial and storing capacities are the vital conditions for the adequate realization of the buffer stock technique.

c) Effects on the price revenue of shifts in supply curves caused by the price stabilization policy by means of a buffer stock

The next point that concerns us is to explain the impact on revenue of shifts in supply curves appearing from the price stabilization policy by means of a buffer stock. Further, the assumptions made must be considered. Figure 7, below, corresponds to Figure 4 and represents Professor Johnson's argument that price stabilization via buffer stock instrument will have effects on the export revenue stabilization.

Figure 7.

Effects on the revenue of shift in supply alone with and without price stabilization by a buffer stock

Case 1: elastic curve

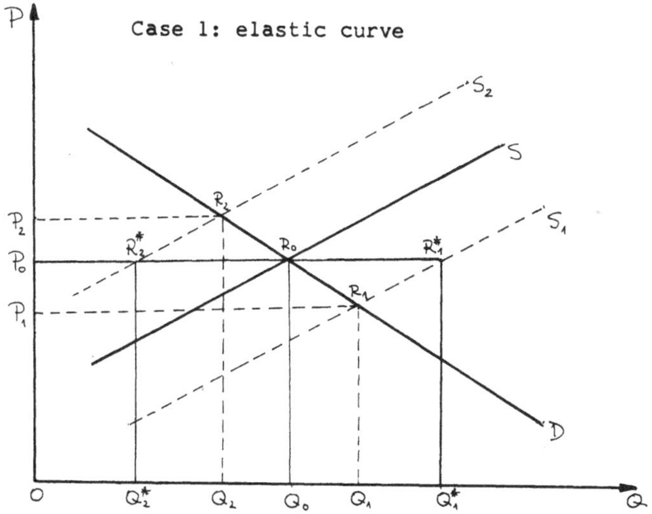

Case 2: inelastic curve

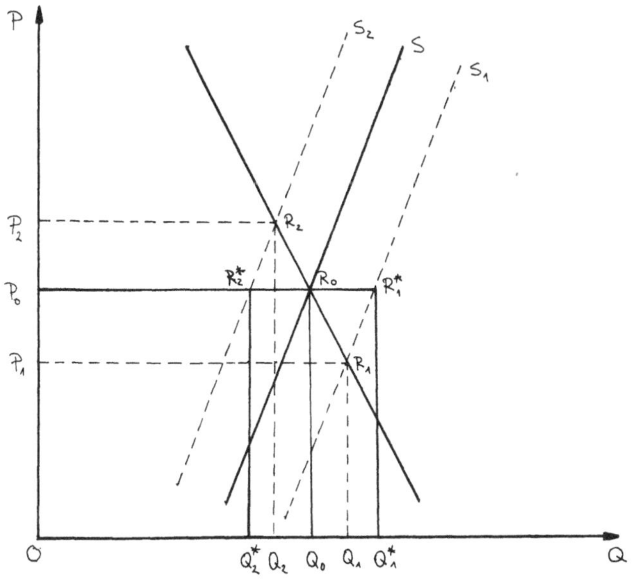

Case 1: case of supply elastic curve
Figure 7, case 1, shows graphically that "in the case of instability due to supply shifts, it* (* price stabilization through buffer stocks)(normally) increases instability of producer income, while increasing its average level" (27).

With the price stabilization through a buffer stock, the producers' average revenue is $(OP_oR_2^*Q_2^* + OP_oR_1^*Q_1^*)/2$. This means that the buffer stock manager, in period 1, buys $Q_1^*Q_o$ of the commodity concerned (expenditure $Q_1^*Q_oR_oR_1^*$) and sells, in period 2, $Q_oQ_2^*$ of the same commodity (revenue $Q_oQ_2^*R_2^*R_o$).

Without buffer stock intervention the average producers' income is $(OP_2R_2Q_2 + OP_1R_1Q_1)/2$.

Accordingly, the total value of the producers' stabilized and increased revenue is

$$(OP_2R_2Q_2 + OP_1R_1Q_1) < 2\ OP_oR_oQ_o$$

Case 2: case of supply inelastic curve
In Figure 7, case, 2, with inelastic supply curve, the effect would be the same: price stabilization increases the instability of the producers' revenue, but not if both curves (supply and demand) are sufficiently inelastic (28), because in such conditions, "stabilization of earnings cannot go further than the remaining fluctuations in quantities" (29).

This suggests that, regarding our simplified market model, which represents a hypothetical situation in the market, the buffer stock mechanism has a principal objective in the stabilisation of the commodity price and, indirectly, it can give rise to, remarkable effects as regards the producers' revenue. Here the operation of the buffer stock has been presented from a theoretical point of view.

---

(27) JOHNSON, Harry G., op.cit., p. 251.

(28) BEHRMAN, J.R., International Commodity Agreements,1977, p.11.

(29) MICHALOPOULOS, Constantin, PEREZ, Lorenz,L., op.cit., p. 248.

In practice,its operation is much more complex, as it depends on the specific characteristics - technical and commercial - of different commodity markets (30). Thus, in a discussion of the use of the buffer stock as a mechanism of commodity control, it is extremely important to try to verify which commodities are stockable and, thus, which commodities could be dealt with by the buffer stock instrument (31).

---

(30) ADAMS, Gerard F., "Commodity Stabilization Policy and Econometric Models", in: Econometric Modeling of World Commodity Policy, (ed.,by ADAMS, Gerard F., BEHRMAN, Jere R.), Lexington Books 1978, p. 4.

(31) An eligibility list indicating which commodities could be classified as stockable is presented by STAKHOVITCH, Alexandre,"A European View of Commodity Problems: Stabilization of Prices and Stabilization of Receipts",op.cit., p. 236.

CHAPTER III

CONCRETE EXPERIENCES

As this heading indicates, the following is a brief evaluation of concrete experiences of ICAs. The previous chapter informed us that the primary objective of the pure buffer stock mechanism, its stabilization function by means of moderating strong fluctuations in commodity supply and/or price, is theoretically feasible. Therefore, this should facilitate the attempt to follow and understand the success or failure, if any, of several characteristic ICAs.

Tracing the recent history of ICAs, a glimpse can be caught of the need for them (particularly associated with the LDCs and their patterns of output and trade, which were especially vulnerable to fluctuations in the international markets for primary commodities) (1), as well as attempts made to establish them as possible problem-solving instruments of control and regulation of the instability in commodity markets.

The reasons why the primary commodity trade is subject to great instability are numerous and complex (2). The background of the instability problem was the subject of the lavish analysis offered by the report of the United Nations Committee of experts as early as 1951, and then again in 1953 (3)(4).

---

(1) Most primary commodity producing countries, which are, in general, LDCs, are largely dependent on the export trade of even one primary commodity. Table 2 indicates, for each of several individual commodities, which is the part of the market shares of the LDCs in the primary commodity export. A list of commodities given in Table 3 provides information about the total export earnings of LDCs, that is, how far they depend on export of several individual primary commodities.

(2) As such,they require to be dealt with in depth.Within the scope of this work, the direct examination of these instabilities has not been considered. Nevertheless, it is assumed to be of considerable importance to refer to them whenever this seems relevant to the question at issue.

(3) Measures for International Economic Stability, U.N.,New York 1951, sales No. 51.II.A.2.

(4) Commodity Trade and Economic Development,U.N.,New York, 1953, Sales No. 54.II.B.1.

Table 2.

Primary Commodity Export Markets Shares of the LDCs

(1974/1975 and 1978/1980, percentages)

Commodity	LDCs share in world exports 1974/1975	1978/1980
Cocoa	99	96
Sisal	98	98
Rubber	98	98
Coffee	97	97
Jute	96	87
Bananas	93	94
Tin	85	86
Tea	82	77
Sugar	70	63
Vegetable oils	66	72
Cotton	58	47
Copper	55	63
Iron ore	38	44
Rice	39	46

Source: U.N. , F.A.O. Trade Yearbook, 1981.
I.B.R.D. Commodity Trade and Price Trends, 1979.

Table 3.

Commodity Exports from Developing Countries Accounting for more than 20% of Total Export earnings, 1981

Commodity	20%-50%	50%-80%	80%-100%
Bananas	Guyana 37	Jamaica 76	Suriname 81 (1980)
Bauxite and Alumina	Cameron 21 Grenada 46 Ivory Coast 22	Ghana 63	
Coffee	Cameron 22 Costa Rica 24 Guatemala 23 Haiti 20 Honduras 25 Ivory Coast 31 (1979) Kenya 21 Nicaragua 38	Columbia 57 (1980) El Salvador 58 Ethiopia 61 Madagascar 53 (1980)	Burundi 88
Copper	Chile 43 Zaire 47	Papua New Guinea 53 Peru 63	Zambia 95
Cotton	Mali 48 Paraguay 44 Upper Volat 44 Yemen Arab. Rep. 49 (1977)	Chad 54 (1976)	
Jute	Bangladesh 42		
Phosphates	Jordan 21 Morocco 32 Senegal 20 Togo 40		
Sugar	Dominican Rep. 45 Guyana 31 (1980) Malawi 21 Swaziland 49	Fiji 53 Mauritanius 68	
Tea	Sri Lanka 31		

./.

(Table 3, continued)

Commodity	20%-50%	50%-80%	80%-100%
Tin	Bolivia 38		
Rice	Burma 50		
Petroleum	Indonesia 59 Kenya 26 Malaysia 27 Syrian Arab. Rep. 49 Singapore 38	Congo 63 (1979) Gabon 62 Ecuador 61 Mexico 63 Tunisia 54	Alger 92 Bahamas 95 Bahrain 91 Iran 94 Iraq 98 Kuwait 86 Lybia 100 Nigeria 94 Netherland Antilles 94 Saudi Arabia 100 Oman 100 Quatar 94 United Arab. Emirates 93 Venezuela 95
Diamonds	Bostwana 42	Siera Leone 53	
Groundnuts	Israel 25	Gambia 54	
Uranium			Niger 74

Source: International Financial Statistics, International Monetary Fund, Vol. XXXV. No. 8, August 1982, pp. 60-455.

It is relevant to recall some of the primary causes of the instability situation. Briefly summarized, although it is difficult to generalize, they were mainly due to the:

- cyclical variations in the economic activity of industrial DCs,
- trade conditions created by wars,
- technological progress and competition of substitutes (synthetics),
- violent and frequent price fluctuations,
- deterioration in the relation of LDCs and DCs as regards exports and imports,
- inelasticity of demand and supply,
- speculation (5).

None of these elements has lost any relevance. In the search for solutions to such problems, the importance of this subject is proved and emphasized by the abundant literature, permanent international commoditiy negotiations (especially after the 1973-75 boom in commodity prices) and rapidly-growing interest in international trade for primary commodities (more LDCs participation in North-South relations) and the recent creation of the Common Fund (adopted on 27th June, 1980, in Geneva) - regulating the financial side of buffer stock agreements.

Therefore, in order to guide our interest in the desired direction, this chapter will briefly inquire into the actual experiences gathered from some representative examples of ICAs and their methods of regulation, particularly in respect of the role of the buffer stock instrument, if existing.

In section A of this chapter, a reference will be made to ICAs functioning without buffer stock regulation, where our interest will be focused on the wheat, sugar, coffee and olive oil agreements. This will give an insight into two

---

(5) More detailed examination of those points can be found in United Nations reports cited in notes (3) and (4) respectively, and LAW, Alton, International Commodity Agreements, op.cit., pp. 2-17.

other kinds of techniques of commodity price stabilization: export quotas and multilateral agreements, which used them as tools of stabilization in the post-war years.

In the second part of the same section, particular attention will be paid to the informal agreements where buffer stock has been suggested to operate as an instrument of control. Our example is based on tea and jute. They are two of the commodities forming the group of "ten core" proposed by UNCTAD's Integrated Programme for Commodities (IPC). In this respect a reference will be made to the UNCTAD's proposal for the establishment of the multiple commodity buffer stock programme.

Tin and cocoa ICAs where buffer stock played a remarkable role will be mentioned only in passing, as each of them will be dealt with in more detail in sections B and C respectively.

In this part of the work, the fact has been taken into account that, of all the commodities which are important from the international point of view, only about fifteen have been considered in detail as to their general consequences in the commodity trade. Formal international agreements have been concluded for only few of them. Some have been drawn up as informal arrangements, as shown in Table 4.

Table 4.

International Commodity Agreements and Informal Arrangements

ICAs	Informal Arrangements
1. Tin	1. Tea
2. Cocoa	2. Hard fibres (FAO)
3. Rubber	3. Kenaf (FAO)
4. Jute	4. Skimmed milk powder and butter fat (GATT)
5. Coffee	
6. Sugar	5. Whole milk powder (GATT)
7. Wheat	
8. Olive Oil	

In spite of the fact that ICAs have had more failures than successes in control activity in the commodity markets, the very optimistic prospects concerning ICAs continue to improve; but how desirable and necessary are they? (6).

A - BUFFER STOCKS AND ICAs

Historical observations of experiences with ICAs in 1945 and during the following thirty-five years show that international buffer stocks were used as a technique of commodity price stabilization in only one commodity - tin (6a). This, of course, represents a sort of paradox, as an abundance of literature was devoted to its theoretical analysis during the period indicated and the presentation of which was introduced in the previous Chapter.

Before turning to an individual commodity analysis referring to the theoretical key issues in Chapter II, it can be positively said that when an international commodity agreement is established and it is agreed that the measure of control shall be a buffer stock, then the buffer stock operation must stay within the structural limits of the agreement in question.

This means that once the price range, with its ceiling and floor price, is fixed, buffer stock control cannot make it wider or smaller, but the buying and selling activity is not limited within the range and can be adjusted according to market trends. Such an operation is valid for a regularly-functioning ICA.

In the case where the regular functioning of the ICA is called into question because of the exhausting of the existing stocks or unexpected accumulation of stocks, a modification should be made in the agreement.

---

(6) This means that the establishment of ICAs must be preceded by detailed economic analysis, including policy objectives. The question is not only to know if the ICA can help to attain certain objectives, but also if the fixed objectives can be realised from the economic point of view.

(6a) The cocoa buffer stock mechanism, although officially established in 1973 had never been put into operation. The particularities of this problem will be described in Section C of this Chapter, which has been specially reserved for Cocoa Agreement analysis.

1. Reference to ICAs without buffer stock regulation

The fact that only five international commodity agreements were established in the post-war period up to the end of the 1960's is due to different economic factors such as quite strong demand, post-war shortages, depleted stocks and favourable market conditions characterised by high prices.

A list of average percent price changes per year given in Table 5 for ten individual commodities provides some insights into how prices changed during that period.

Table 5.

Year-to-year fluctuations in market prices 1901-1950 and 1960-1980. Average percent price change per year.

Commodity	1901-1950 % a/	1960-1980 % b/
Rubber	20.6	12.3
Coffee	17.2	23.96
Sugar	17.1	20.57
Cocoa	16.7	12.42
Cotton	15.4	6.45
Wool	14.2	3.19
Copper	13.3	1.24
Tin	13.3	7.28
Wheat	11.9	8.66
Tea	7.1	3.70

Source: a/ U.N., Instability in Export Markets of Underdeveloped Countries, U.N., New York, 1952, p. 10.

b/ Own computation. Data from: Monthly Commodity Price Bulletin, UNCTAD, 1960-1980, April 1981, TD/B.1/CPB/L.1/Add.1

This shows that, exporters of the primary commodities, in what, for them, were suitable conditions, were not particularly attracted by the idea of risking their position in concluding the numerous international agreements in the commodity markets where their interests were not compatible with those of the imports. The formal agreements concluded were in only five commodities: wheat, sugar, tin, olive oil (7) and coffee, and were based on the principles and procedures laid down in the Havana Charter (8). The agreements reached were based on any, or all, of three basic techniques of commodity price stabilization:

- multilateral contracts,
- quota restrictions and
- buffer stocks.

These methods of regulation were applied on an individual basis or in combination with each other, with the purpose of influencing the volume of supply of the primary commodities.

The International Wheat Agreement illustrated the multilateral contract principle, while the Sugar Agreement and the Coffee Agreement worked on the quota-fixing principle. The Tin Agreement used the buffer stock technique reinforced, where necessary, by quota restrictions (export).

---

(7) The International Olive Oil Agreement is an example of an agreement which did not have an entirely ordinary form of market regulation. There were successful negotiations concerning the Olive Oil Agreement in the post-war period (after 1955) and it had more of an advisory character in so far as it did not include any means of market regulation such as buffer stocks, quotas or any other. Its objective was more to ensure a quality standard for olive oil (and thus encourage consumption) than to interfere with the evolution of world prices and trade.

(8) Although the Charter never came into effect, the aims and objectives of these ICAs were:
- to prevent, or moderate, cyclical variations in primary commodity prices as temporary disturbances (without interfering in long-term trends), and
- to prevent a tendency towards overproduction as well as more permanent disturbances (securing the long-term equilibrium between production and consumption).

This reference, in brief terms, to each of them as a standard type of agreement, will give a rough, but useful, picture of the improvement made by them, if any, and their classical difficulties.

a) Wheat

A fully-operative post-war International Wheat Agreement (IWA) came into force in 1949. It was of the multilateral contract type of ageement.

The objective of the multilateral purchase and sales commitment (MPSC) is to specify maximum and minimum prices at which producing and consuming countries are obliged to sell and to buy, respectively, the stipulated, guaranteed quantities (i.e. export and import quotas) of the given commodity. The trade within the price range agreed to in the contract is free, and as long as the price oscillates within the settled limits, the agreement mechanism does not interfere with the market.

The establishment of the price range represents one of the essential points of this control technique, as the interests of the importing and exporting member countries, although a compromise is aimed at, are directly opposed. Another decisive factor as far as the guaranteed quantities are concerned, is that the multilateral contract agreement stipulates that the total export quota must be equal to the import quota. Therefore, it is of vital importance for the success of the MPSC type of agreement to accumulate the stocks with which to intervene in times of supply shortages. With the operating IWA's, it was always the tendency of the major wheat exporters (the United States and Canada) to maintain decision-making stocks and thus play the dominant role in price-maintaining policies.

The 1949, 1953 and 1956 IWAs involved obligations to buy and sell stipulated quantities (specified by the IWAs and covering two-thirds of the total world trade in wheat) at certain prices, but called for no production or export quotas nor for central accumulation stocks (9).

---

(9) See also ROWE,J.W.F., Primary Commodities... op.cit., pp. 163-169.

The 1959, 1962 and 1965 Wheat Agreements (extended from year to year until 1967) had some modifications. The system of guaranteed quotas was replaced by a specific percentage purchase. With this percentage purchase method, the importing member countries were obliged to buy the agreed quantity of their annual import requirements from the exporting member countries, which, in turn, were obliged to sell the equivalent quantities at the current price (10). This specified percentage purchase was, on average, 80 per cent of their commercial purchases (11).

From 1967 to 1971, the International Grains Agreement, which consisted of two conventions - the Wheat Trade Convention (WTC) and the Food Aid Convention (FAC) raised the price range in order to protect the minimum prices, which prevented purchases of wheat at prices below the settled minimum from countries that were not members of the WTC. As not all major exporters were willing to respect the establishment of such a minimum price, the WTC faced failure. From that time up to 1978 (when preparations were begun to draw up an International Agreement to replace the 1971 IWA (12)), because of the shortages on the supply side (crop failures), prices reached dramatically high levels.

It would be an exaggeration to say that the outcome of these agreements was a success as they had no noticeable influence on the stabilization of wheat prices. It would be more appropriate merely to confirm their existence. Whether it was due to a failure of the exporters' internal agricultural policies, or the method of regulation, or the inability of exporters and importers to co-operate, is difficult to determine.

Observation of the way the IWAs have operated since World War II could result in the following question being posed: If the IWAs were based on the international buffer

---

(10) and (11) BARANYAI, L., op.cit., p. 26 and RANGARAJAN, L.N., op.cit., p. 236.

(12) UNCTAD, TD/WHEAT.6/EX/R.2, 21st March 1978.

stock principle or a combination of international buffer stock and multilateral contracts, would results be more encouraging as regards the price stabilization of such a vital staple food?

The answer to this question may be provided by practical experience, probably in the very near future, as it figures as one of the UNCTAD's suggestions in the context of IPC for use in the wheat control scheme in the form of international buffer stock reinforced by multilateral contracts as a supply management (see Table 5). Finally, it is a fact that this combination of two techniques already existed in the regulation of the international wheat market, although it occurred unintentionally due to the specific position of the United States and Canada as major wheat exporters. Their large national buffer stocks were notably successful in stabilizing prices on the international wheat market during the period of the 1956 IWA.

From a theoretical point of view, multilateral contracts differ from buffer stocks in that (13)

- the former are not specifically designed to keep the world price at the level at which it is set in advance,
- their strength does not depend on wide price support,and
- they can be introduced in periods of high, as well as low, prices (buffer stocks can be brought into operation only in those periods when prices are low) (14).

b) Sugar

The means of regulation which were employed in the four post-war International Sugar Agreements (ISA) were of the export-quota type. This method implies a global control of exports from supplying countries (in order to maintain the price) and assures the market shares allocation between the participating countries for the agreed period. From the

(13) BROWN, C.P., Primary Commodity Control, Kuala Lumpur, Oxford University Press London, New York,1975,p. 167.

(14) BROWN, C.P., ibid., p. 167.

experience gained from the previous ISAs (1953,1958,1968 and 1978), it was considered to be the most adequate and desirable technique for price stabilization that had been employed in the regulation of the extremely complex world sugar market (15). None of these ISAs (1953, 1958 and 1968) had any significant effect on price levels (16) although the sugar market was subject to violent price fluctuations due to the narrowness of the market and lack of supply and demand elasticity.

The ISAs became inoperative when member importing and exporting countries were not able to agree on mutually satisfactory quotas.

Interest in the establishment of the international buffer stock mechanism in sugar gained in momentum after the world shortages and extremely high prices of 1973-74. This indicates that the buffer stock facility for sugar has never been fully utilized although many points can be found that would qualify sugar for an international buffer stock scheme. Thus, stocking measures were accepted (17) in the last 1978 ISA in the form of special stocks along with export quotas. The result of this is that these special stocks are manageable in the short-term (the duration of the Agreement is five years) and the financial cost is regulated and bearable).

The physical problem of holding sugar as a stock should not be exaggerated, as it has at least two valuable

---

(15) The so-called "world sugar market" was composed of domestic markets (among the producing countries), special arrangements between the biggest importers and exporters (i.e. imports into USA, USSR and UK) and the residual, so-called "free market"which accounted for about one ninth of total world production and consumption and had, at times, been regulated by various ISAs. The complexity of the sugar market is due to the fact that this commodity is produced in both DCs and LDCs and is derived from two different plants: sugar cane (which is a perennial crop) and sugar beet (an annual crop).

(16) JUNZ, Helen B., and MacAVOY, Paul, "A Hard Look at Prospects for Commodity Agreements", in ed., ADAMS,G., and KLEIN,S., op.cit., p. 281.

(17) UNCTAD, TD/SUGAR.9/10, 17th October, 1977, International Sugar Agreement, Article 46 p. 36.

characteristics:

- it is a relatively non-perishable (18) and hence storable, and
- it is produced by developed, as well as developing, countries.

Moreover, sugar is already included on the list of the stockable commodities drawn up by UNCTAD (19). Another work (20) was dedicated to the analysis of the possible maximum levels of sugar stores which an international stocking agency might acquire for the stabilization policy.

These brief observations and other, developed estimates of the costs of storing, holding and maintaining stocks of sugar (which are the key points in determining its suitability for stocking) indicate that there are many good reasons why sugar would be suitable for an international buffer stock mechanism. The probability exists that buffer stocks held and operated internationally are likely to be more effective in stabilizing the world sugar market than national stocks are.

The special stocks designated under the last ISA (1978) already represented one approach, however tentative, to the problem. Fixed at the maximum global level of 2.5 million tons, the buffer stock will stabilize sugar prices as well as protect the consuming countries from the risk of shortage.

It is certain that, with the recent proposition of the Common Fund, a solution can be found to the problem of financing the international sugar buffer stock, especially as sugar is amongst the ten "core" commodities suggested for the IPC (see Table 6.)

---

(18) IMF/IBRD, The Problem of Stabilization of Prices of Primary Products, 1969, p. 71.

Although it is said that "... perishable commodities are not usually regarded as suitable for buffer stock schemes", yet there is no hard - and - fast criteria of perishability in this sense.

(19) UNCTAD document TD/B/C.1/166/Supp.1, p. 22, Table 4.

(20) UNCTAD document TD/B/C.1/186.

Table 6.

Groupings and measures for sixteen individual commodities relevant to the IPC (Integrated Programme for Commodities) presented by the UNCTAD Secretariat

Commodity	Major storable commodities(a)	Common Fund "core"commodities (b)	Buffer stock	Supply managemant
1. Cocoa	+	+	Yes	export quota
2. Coffee	+	+	Yes	export quota
3. Tea	+	+	Yes	
4. Sugar	+	+	Yes	MPSC (c)
5. Bananas	-	-	No	export quota and MPSC
6. Wheat	+	-	Yes	MPSC
7. Rice	+	-	Yes	MPSC
8. Cotton	+	+	Yes	
9. Rubber	+	+	Yes	export quota and MPSC
10. Jute	+	+	Yes	export and production quota
11. Wool	+	-	Yes	export quotas
12. Hard fibres	+	+	Yes	export and production quotas
13. Copper	+	+	Yes	export quota and MPSC
14. Iron Ore	+	-	No	MPSC
15. Tin	+	+	Yes	export quotas and MPSC
16. Bauxite	+	-	No	MPSC

(a) UNCTAD, TD/B/C.1/166, 9 December 1974

(b) UNCTAD, TD/B/C.1/184,24 June 1975

(c) Multilateral Purchase and Sales Commitments

Source: UNCTAD, "An Integrated Programme for Commodities: Measures for Individual Commodities", TD/B/C.1/194, 1 October 1975, pp. 19-63.

c) Coffee

Coffee was, and still is, the most important agricultural commodity (21) (in financial terms) produced exclusively by LDCs and for most of these it is a major source of export earnings (22). Although coffee has no close substitutes and is subject to a relatively inelastic demand, protracted negotiations were necessary before the first International Coffee Agreement was at last signed in 1962. It was concluded between the major exporting and major importing (23) countries and entered into force in 1964. The method of regulation of the coffee market was a set of export quotas (basic, annual and quarterly) the principal aim of which was to ensure that "the general level of coffee prices does not decline below the general level of such prices in 1962" (24), though it did not establish any price range. Not until 1965 was the Agreement ameliorated by the addition of a price range defining the floor and the ceiling price.

Considered as successful in reducing coffee price fluctuations and maintaining them at relatively stable levels (25), this Agreement had a positive effect on the LDCs major exporters' earnings, which largely depended on coffee exports.

---

(21) In the world commodity trade, coffee ranks second after petroleum.

(22) FORD, Gerald R., "International Coffee Agreement Transmitted to the State", Message from President Ford, The Department of State Bulletin, vol. LXXIV, No. 1924, 10th May 1976, pp. 614-616.

(23) Of world coffee consumption the United States and the EEC countries account for one half and one quarter, respectively. See also "The International Coffee Organization", J.W.T.L., No.1, 1967, p. 360.

(24) ROWE, J.W.F., "Primary Commodities...", op.cit., p. 180.

(25) Law remarks that especially from 1964 to 1966, when there was a 20 percent rise in coffee prices, "the 1964 price jump (to nearly 50 ¢) must be considered the direct result of the coffee agreement, with only minor, if any, assistance from the weather", LAW, A.,"International...",op.cit., p. 44. The aim was to keep up the price level with the purpose of safeguarding sufficient investments for future supplies, the consequence of which was a conflict between exporting and importing countries. See as well RANGARAJAN, L.N.,op.cit., pp. 107-111.

Its successor, the Coffee Agreement of 1968, based on a system of variable export quotas in combination with a multilateral contract, broke down in 1972, before the expiry of the five-year agreement. The problem was in reaching a mutual agreement between exporters and importers as regards the fixing of export quotas, which represents the most important and vulnerable aspect of any international agreement operated by the system of export restrictions.

Once again, there was a conflict between exporting and importing countries which meant that a consensus could not be reached on an adequate price level after the instability of the dollar (devaluation).

The Third International Coffee Agreement came into existence only eight years later, in 1976. When the Agreement entered into force, the coffee prices exceeded the upper limit of the price range settled by the agreement by a margin twice as large as expected.

The main instrument of price stabilization was still (as in the previous agreements) export quota regulation with the determination of the members' share of the world market. The new element was in favour of international stock holding, which represented an effort to protect the world coffee market from production variations similar to those that resulted from the catastrophic 1975 frost damages.

It appears that the need for internationally-held buffer stocks is felt only after periods of great difficulty and never under normal circumstances. This is surprising as such stocks seem to be an important element in the stability of the coffee market as they can offset the risk of tight supply and price fluctuations due to weather changes or speculation.

From the point of view of attaining their objectives, the 1962 and 1968 Agreements, operating in conditions of coffee surpluses, were sufficiently important to keep supply in reasonable balance with the estimated demand. The Agreements achieved a situation of price stability (export quotas had some influence on the coffee prices in the world market), but were not designed to deal with short-term fluctuations. An international buffer stock can influence the short-term oscillations on both

- the supply and demand side, and as well as
- the price trend.

Concerning the first point, in the UNCTAD proposal for the IPC, international buffer stocks (see Table 6.), are suggested in combination with the supply management measures (26) in the following term: "the stock (an internationally managed stock of coffee) could be expected to function ... both as a short-term buffer stock and as a medium-term assurance of supplies" (27).

This assurance of supplies has to be understood in the context of the functioning of the buffer stocks and not as a separate new function. On the other hand, a purely national buffer stock approach would not offer a consistent solution either. Experience gained in the holding of large international stocks in specific, individual exporting countries (like Brazil - the major coffee exporter), has not provided a satisfactory solution to the problem of supply and price instability.

There is evidence to suppose that if many exporting countries that are in possession of considerable national buffer stocks succed in co-operating and co-ordinating their stocks, this will certainly produce a desirable, positive effect on the stabilization of the international coffee market (27 a).

---

(26) As defined by a document from the UNCTAD, supply management measures are presented as a means which will, in the long-term, tend to bring supply and demand into an equilibrium. See UNCTAD, Trade and Development Board, An Integrated Programme for Commodities: Measures for Individual Commodities, TD/B/C.1/194, 1 October 1975,p.7,par.18.

(27) Ibid., para 69 (a), p. 22.

(27a) And not what happened in the case of so-called "tourist" coffee (African coffee) when, in the period of the first International Coffee Agreement from 1962 to 1968, member countries exported coffee illegally via non-member countries and were thus outside the quota scheme set by the Agreement (e.g. Liberia's export capacity in 1966 was 60.000 bags, but the actual export was 798.000 bags,i.e. all issuing from Ivory Coast).

Concerning the second point, the price trend, one other matter of very considerable importance is that, since 1962 the price trend of coffee has been upward with a tendency to remain high or even rise more.

This represents a serious problem which is relatively difficult to overcome, and it is therefore inexplicable that the UNCTAD document contains the following proposal: "Acquisition of stocks to deal with fluctuations in an upward price trend will require pricing provisions that allow some proportion of output to be set aside in relatively good crop seasons over the next few years, taking account of the reduced world supply potential"; just as the buffer stock mechanism cannot be brought into operation in periods of high prices and supply shortages, nor can a price range be set when the price trend has an upward swing. This is so because any price range that is set at an unrealistic, high level will lead to curtailment of demand for coffee, which, in turn, will greatly complicate the operation of the agreement and render it inoperative (cause it to break down). Assuming this to be so, what is the purpose of establishing a range on such a high price trend?

2. ICAs with buffer stock regulation

What follows will underline the fact that ICAs with international buffer stock regulation were amongst a number of projects and drafts as well as operating agreements.

The cases of tea and jute will be evaluated in a brief examination of each of them covering the principal difficulties, objectives and their possible solutions, respectively.

The attempts made to propose tea and jute for International Agreements of the buffer stock type, had to stress the necessity of intervention to stabilize these markets.

Informal agreements which might in the near future become ICAs with a buffer stock regulation will, therefore, be dealt with.

a) Reference to tin and cocoa

The International Tin Agreement (ITA) was the first to make use of the buffer stock principle as a control scheme.

It goes without saying that there was more discussion of buffer stock as a technique than practical application. This situation was due to operational problems arising from the specific circumstances which were characterised by the varying supply and demand of different commodities.

Nevertheless, when it came into force in 1973, the Cocoa Agreement was based on the buffer stock method and thus represented another acceptable step, which, however small, proves that fruitful negotiations have become possible as regards recognising the theoretical merits of this technique. The Cocoa Agreement never came into operation because the price range was set far below the world cocoa prices.

These two agreements will be dealt with below.

b) Tea

The first post-war International Tea Agreement (28) was established in 1950 with a five-year duration. The only participants were the major producing-exporting countries - Ceylon, India, Indonesia and Pakistan. The Agreement was based on the system of export quotas. Restrictions were set on new plantings, production and tea exports (29). The mechanism was not fully operated due to the discrepancy on the demand side when prices showed a constant downward tendency, which, in turn, resulted in the International Tea Agreement not being renewed in 1955. The outcome of this was an unregulated market.

---

(28) It was preceded by the experience of International Tea Agreements set up in 1935, 1938, 1943 and 1948 which were also based on the export quota formula.

(29) DAVIS, Joseph S., "Experience Under Intergovernmental Commodity Agreements, 1902-45". The Journal of Political Economy, vol. LIV, June 1946, No. 3, pp. 199-202.

After these events, India (the largest producer and consumer) and Sri Lanka tacitly divided the world tea market to ensure their exports, which can be considered an informal cartel agreement, and thus there was no interest from their side in bringing about a new International Tea Agreement.

The period 1950-60 was marked by an upward trend in tea prices, which encouraged tea production. Since 1960, new producers in East African countries have begun to compete with the major tea producers.

This has resulted in demand being overtaken by large supplies, which, in turn, has caused a considerable decline in prices. The difficulties that arose in the tea market were of the usual type exporters-importers, as in other commodities, but this time exporters-exporters. In the search for a solution to the problem of regulation in the tea market, exporters were ready in 1969 to conclude a new agreement (export quotas type) in collaboration, for the first time, with importers. This is how the International Informal Agreement for Stabilization of Tea prices (realized by the FAO Committee on Commodity Problems) was born (30).

Today tea is one of the subjects of the UNCTAD's proposal for IPC, and there exists a real likelihood that producing and consuming countries will try to find a solution by setting up an International Agreement for tea. The problem is that opinions are divided on the setting up of the new International Tea Agreement regulating mechanism (31):

- Producing countries' proposal: international buffer stock operating alone;
- Importing countries' proposal: international buffer stock and export quotas.

Here, disagreement between producers and consumers once again comes into play because of a conflict of interest.

---

(30) FAO, Draft Economic Articles of an Export Quota Type Agreement for Tea, CCP: Tah./1A/69-5.

(31) UNCTAD V, Review of implementation and follow-up action, including the on-going preparatory work and negotiations TD/228, UNCTAD V Manila, May 1979, p. 16.

To make the right choice in the stabilization measures, two principal elements, in particular, need to be examined:

- the nature of price fluctuations, and
- the evaluation of the cost of storage.

In general, the price trend in tea has been on the decline. (Even the 1972-74 boom in commodity prices had no significant effect on tea).

The unusually high prices prevailing in 1977 have been replaced by a continuous decline. In view of the fact that tea is also subject to strong annual price fluctuations, intervention is really required (32).

On the other hand, tea is subject to a secular decrease in demand (price inelastic demand over the long period) and, as such, could be a commodity that would respond to price stabilization. When it comes to the question of evaluating the cost of storage, tea (like coffee) represents a special case for international buffer stock. The reason lies in its different quality sorts. These, of course, make storage more complicated (humidity, temperature etc.) and different storage costs are to be covered. Therefore, tea could be examined as a general classification and might possibly be divided into groups of only a few types or qualities, which are easier to handle and might then be subject to international buffer stock regulation.

Tea accounts for a large percentage of the export market shares of the producing LDCs (see Table 1), which is a good motive for better co-operation between the tea exporting and importing countries.

c) Jute

One of the most unstable commodities in the post-war period has been jute. Considerable fluctuations in supply, as well as in prices and exports have been noticeable on the jute market along with the repercussions of this in the exporting countries (LDCs). Exports of jute (excluding synthetics represent 95.6 percent of the exports of LDCs.

---

(32) KEBSCHULL, Dietrich, KUNNE, Wilfred and MENCK Karl Wolfgang, Das integrierte Rohstoffprogramm, Verlag Weltarchiv GmbH, Hamburg 1977, p.81.

The period between 1950 and 1960 was marked by an expansion of jute consumption. Since then, the jute market has been faced with strong competition from synthetic products, which has seriously affected the demand for jute, with the result that in the ten-year period 1964-1974, total world demand was only at approximately the same level.

Since jute was the object of competition from synthetics (produced mainly in DCs) the interest in this commodity suffered a decline in the DCs'consumption of 16% for the same ten-year period.

During the 1972-74 period of boom prices in most commodities, jute prices doubled but were immediately levelled by the large supplies of the previous two years (see Table 7).

The case of jute also shows us that, in the face of strong competition from substitutes, attention in the market devoted to a primary commodity is directed mainly to the price movements.

With its strongly fluctuating prices, jute is a very unstable product, and since 1968, there have existed different proposals and desires for the creation of an international buffer stock, which reflects the desire for intervention in the jute market.

When the buffer stock is used as an instrument of price stabilization, the first step is to consider whether any commodity is suitable for it, and a set of factors should point out the feasibility of stabilization will be dealt with below.

According to some economists, such as Stakhovitch, it appears that jute, along with a number of other commodities does not satisfy certain conditions required from an economic and technical point of view (33).

---

(33) STAKHOVITCH, Alexander, "A European View of...", op.cit., p. 236.

Table 7.

Fluctuations in Jute Prices - Bangladesh[a/]

Year	P	%	Year	P	%
1960	329.33	-	1971	271.84	- 0.3
1961	413.66	25.6	1972	280.58	3.2
1962	283.31	-31.6	1973	278.40	- 0.8
1963	283.86	0.1	1974	353.04	26.8
1964	273.66	- 3.6	1975	377.31	6.8
1965	264.84	- 3.3	1976	295.74	-21.7
1966	305.36	15.2	1977	319.91	8.1
1967	294.96	- 3.5	1978	397.46	24.2
1968	269.29	- 8.8	1979	384.72	- 3.3
1969	286.54	6.4	1980	314.30	-18.4
1970	272.60	- 4.9	1981	268.87	-14.5
Average					11.0

a/ Bangladesh White D, BWD, $ U.S. per metric tons.

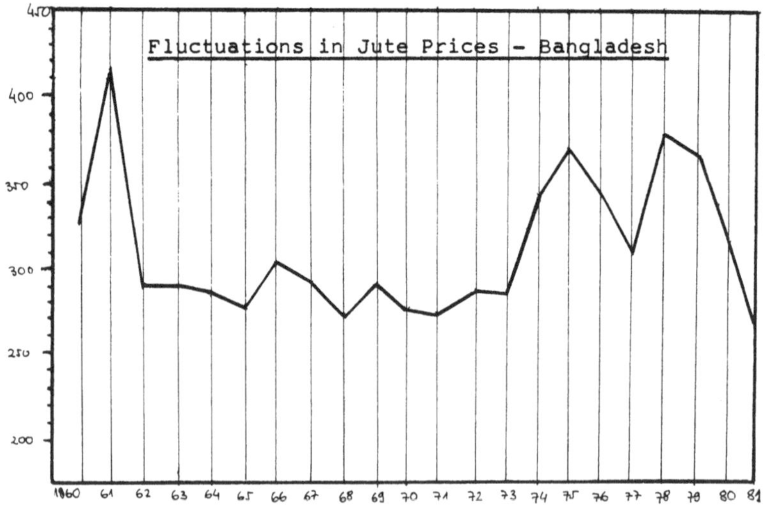

Source: FAO, Raport et perspectives sur les produits, 1981-1982, Rome 1982, No.22, Quarterly Summary of Jute Goods Statistics, 1975/76.

Jute belongs to a commodity group with close synthetic substitutes (demand elasticity in the short-run is low), which can be considered as by-products. This has the consequence that their price is, to a great extent, arbitrary (34). Therefore, an international buffer stock for raw jute is exposed to price reduction by the competitive price of synthetic substitutes, which threatens to render the stabilizing mechanism inoperative. It may be said that due to the synthetic substitutes, the position of raw jute in the market is seriously threatened.

On the other hand, an examination of the nature of the price fluctuations, shows that jute, with its oscillations not only in prices but also in supply and exports, satisfies that important criterion for the use of international buffer stock.

Points which should be evaluated in addition are whether jute has the characteristic of a storable commodity, and how large the stocks should be. Here the problem of different qualities (as in the case of coffee and tea) should be solved. Raw jute and jute products should be classified in a few, similar quality groups, which could be subjects of a buffer stock stabilization scheme.

UNCTAD in its IPC proposal has recognized the price instability of jute and has proposed the implementation of adequate international measures: buffer stocks intervention in combination with export quotas (see Table 6). So far the agreement concerning the measures has not satisfied the claims of the producing countries.

Another criterion for setting up an International Jute Agreement, or an International Jute Arrangement, can be identified as the need to increase the productivity and competitiveness of jute.

This represents - together with a downward tendency in the market share of jute (in the past five years), the threat of synthetics in the jute market, and the general instability

(34) Ibid.,p. 236.

in the jute market (35) - an appeal for prompt intervention on behalf of jute and jute products (35a).

Producers and consumers have reached an agreement concerning the major aspects of the problem, but have not yet decided on the stabilization measures.

- Exporting countries' proposal: international buffer stock
- Importing countries' proposal: no stabilization scheme for jute (in view of the fact that jute goods exclude all possibilities of stabilization).

The above illustration shows the traditional discord that exists between producing and consuming countries on the subject of stabilization measures, which is complicated, as far as the jute market is concerned, by the combination of exports of raw jute and of jute products. Whatever the disagreements, it seems that there is an urgent need for jute prices to be stabilized, if the price evolution of this commodity is taken into account.

This rough outline of the situation on the jute market gives us reason to suppose that the adoption of a stabilization scheme alone for jute would not constitute a successful remedy for price oscillations. Instead of pure restrictions in supply (fixed in an Agreement), the solution could be found in development of the market and improved supply conditions.

B - THE CASE OF THE TIN AGREEMENT REGULATION

In the light of some historical specifications made about tin in Chapter I, it can be seen that the main features of pre-war regulation were

- lack of co-operation between producers,

(35) UNCTAD V, "Review of ...", <u>op.cit.</u>, pp. 12-13.

(35a) After long discussions, the First ICA for Jute and Jute Products was drawn up in 1982 for a five-year duration (see: UNCTAD/TD/JUTE/11,5th October,1982). It will enter into force on 1st July, 1983 after its ratification. Its purpose is to ameliorate structural characteristics of the jute market,reinforce its competitiveness and enlarge its production. Its finacial facilities are to be regulated through the Common Fund for primary products, as soon as the latter has been ratified.

- absence of substitutes for tin and demand proving to be inelastic,
- coercive methods which were used in the regulation of production and export quotas,
- efforts to assure regularity and continuity of supply, and
- buffer stocks which displayed their role in regulating sharp price fluctuations (in two cases).

Taken as whole, the regulation arising from the tin agreement is regarded as having been relatively successful. Moreover, it proved to be advantageous in preventing a fall in tin prices.

Below, the post-war period will be dealt with in a somewhat more extensive study of the operating experiences of the International Tin Agreements (ITA). An attempt will later be made to analyse the role of the buffer stock mechanism (which is its main feature) formally. Finally, several remarks will be made concerning the experience gained from the use of buffer stocks, and their future prospects.

1. Evolution of practice

The fact is that the only post-war agreement with a continuous working schedule - regularly renewed after the five year duration - was the tin agreement. As such, the period from 1956 to 1980 was referred to as an example and, even more, as a model to be used for certain primary commodities - especially among minerals.

Although considered a success, the uninterrupted existence of the International Tin Agreement should be regarded as relative as it manifested certain special, unpromising features (36), and from the very beginning was "sponsored" by the U.S. "strategic stockpile".

---

(36) Mc NICOL, David L., Commodity Agreements and Price Stabilization, Lexington Books, D.C., Heath & Co., Lexington, Massachusetts, Toronto, 1978, p. 76-77.

a) Supply, Demand and Price Characteristics

As far as production and consumption are concerned, it could be said that the tin market is practically (37) divisible into two aspects:

- tin is produced almost exclusively by LDCs,
- it is consumed almost exclusively by DCs.

This approximate market share presentation does not mean that DCs are absolutely dependent upon the LDCs tin exports, especially when there are factors which have slowed down the normal growth in overall demand (see Table 8), for example

- the appearance of substitutes (aluminium, cellophane),
- or technological improvements.

Since 1956, when the first ITA was put into operation (see Table 8), prices have displayed a steady increase except for the price drop in 1957/58 due to the depletion of the U.S. stockpiles. In the period of the general price boom in commodity prices in 1973-74, tin prices enjoyed an extraordinary rise and reached a level four times higher than in 1956. After a slight pause in 1976, prices continued to rise sharply to such an extent that 1979 saw the highest price level ever noted in tin, reaching 707 U.S. cents per pound, i. e. a level six times greater than that of ten years earlier, in 1969.

Up to the 1973-74 price boom, demand was, more often than not, greater than supply, and in 1969 reached an equal level. It reached its highest level between 1972 and 1974 and, since then, demand has overtaken supply.

After that, world tin production fell short of demand and tin prices continued to rise. The problems in the major producing countries were heavy taxation and a lack of natural availability.

---

(37) 85.5 per cent of tin is exported by LDCs (see Table 1) and the total world tin production of DCs is only 3 per cent. Thus they are the exclusive importers.

Table 8.

Tin World Production, Consumption and Price

Year	Production '000 metric tons	Consumption '000 metric tons	Price U.S. c/lb
1956	167	150	104.0
1957	158	143	98.8
1958	121	136	97.6
1959	114	148	104.8
1960	146	162	104.1
1961	139	159	116.3
1962	144	159	117.7
1963	141	160	116.7
1964	147	166	157.8
1965	152	163	176.3
1966	157	173	162.4
1967	177	172	153.6
1968	188	176	147.8
1969	184	184	163.7
1970	184	182	174.4
1971	186	189	167.2
1972	191	192	177.6
1973	187	214	227.2
1974	181	200	396.3
1975	178	174	339.5
1976	182	194	374.7
1977	180	185	553.3
1978	193	186	589.3
1979	204	188	707.3
1980	190	176	785.7

Sources: InternationalTin Council, Statistical Bulletin, June 1980 no.6 vol. XXIV.

(Due to these conditions, Malaysia lowered its tax on profits from 15% to 12.5%, to relieve the tax burden to some extent) (38).

The supply, demand and price characteristics (Figure 7a) were influential in bringing about permanent changes in the levels of the price ranges of the tin buffer stock during the period of operation of the first ITA. Figures 7b and 8 show how the ceiling and floor prices were permanently resettled during the operation of the four ITAs (39).

From the above interpretation of the development on the tin market, it can be seen that the problems of fluctuation in prices are directly related to changes in supply and/or demand. In the case of tin, supply and demand have both proved to be inelastic.

b) Continuity of evolution of the Tin Agreements

For a period of twenty-four consecutive years, International Tin Agreements were officially concluded on five successive occasions, each time for a duration of five years. The first ITA (signed in 1954) entered into force only in 1956 because of the economic situation which was not favourable, for concluding the agreement (price rose sharply due to the Korean War boom and U.S. purchases for strategic stocks).

Membership of the Agreement comprised (40) producing (41) and consuming (42) countries.

---

(38) Commodity Year Book 1980, New York 1980.

(39) Data for the fifth ITA, 1975-80, are not available for the moment.

(40) This was in accordance with the principle and objectives of the Havana Charter.

(41) Bolivia, Malaysia, Thailand, Indonesia, Nigeria and Congo (Zaire).

(42) Among the consumers, the number of which rose to 22 in the fifth Agreement, it is important to note the case of Australia (which was a consumer until 1964, when it became a significant producer) and of the USSR (which, despite its huge production (data unavailable) is accepted as a consumer); FOX, William, Tin: The Working of a Commodity Agreement, Mining Journal Books Ltd., London 1974, Chapter XII.

Figure 7a.

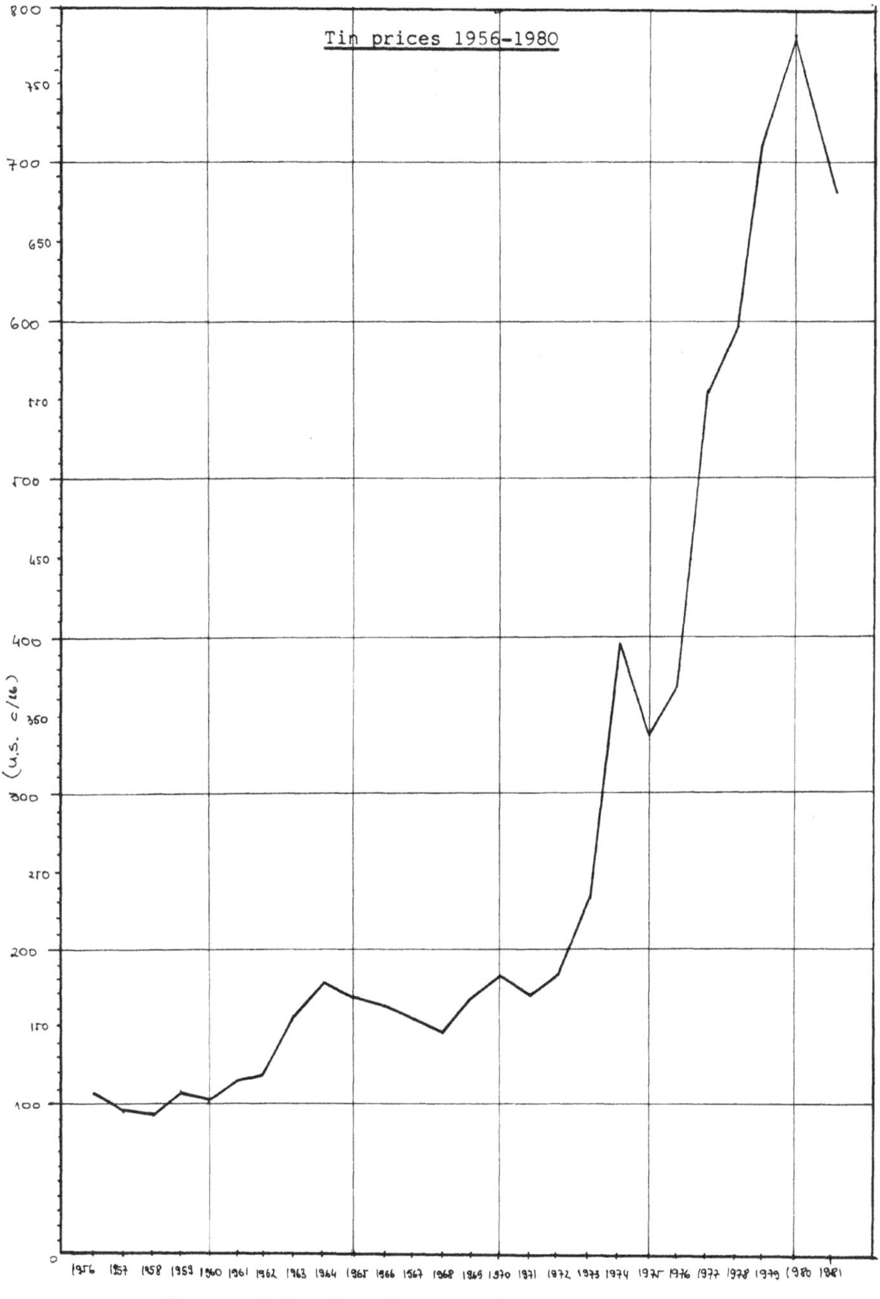

Source: Data given in Table 8, p.89.

Figure 7b.

Tin Price ranges 1972-1981

Period of operation				Floor price	Ceiling price
4 July 1972	-21	September	1973	583 a/	718
21 Sept. 1973	-30	May	1974	635	760
30 May 1974	-31	January	1975	850	1050
31 Lan. 1975	-12	March	1976	900	1100
12 Mar. 1976	- 7	May	1976	950	1100
7 May 1976	- 9	December	1976	1000	1200
9 Dec. 1976	-15	July	1977	1075	1325
15 Jul. 1977	-14	July	1978	1200	1500
14 Jul. 1978	-20	July	1979	1350	1700
20 Jul. 1979	-13	March	1980	1500	1950
13 Mar. 1980	-13	January	1981	1650	2145
13 Jan. 1981	-17	October	1981	27.28 b/	35.47

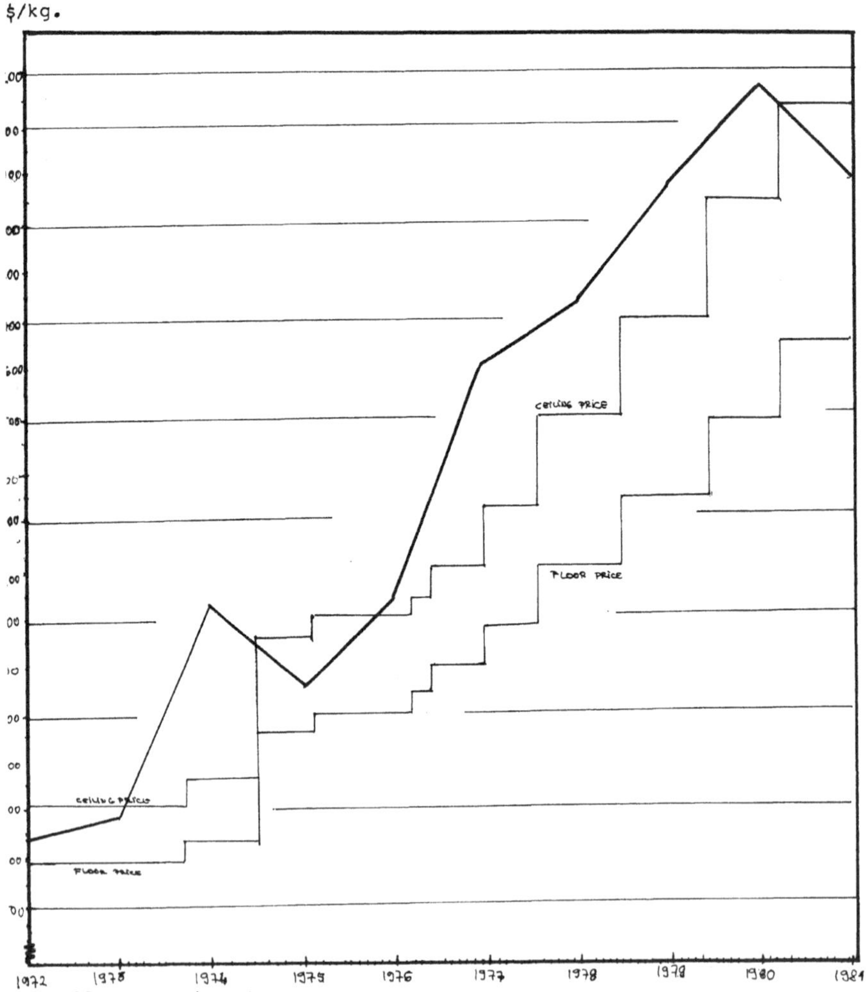

a/ M$/ pikul
b/M$/ kg.

Source: Monthly Statistical Bulletin, ITC, No. 11, vol.XXVI. November 1982.

Figure 8.

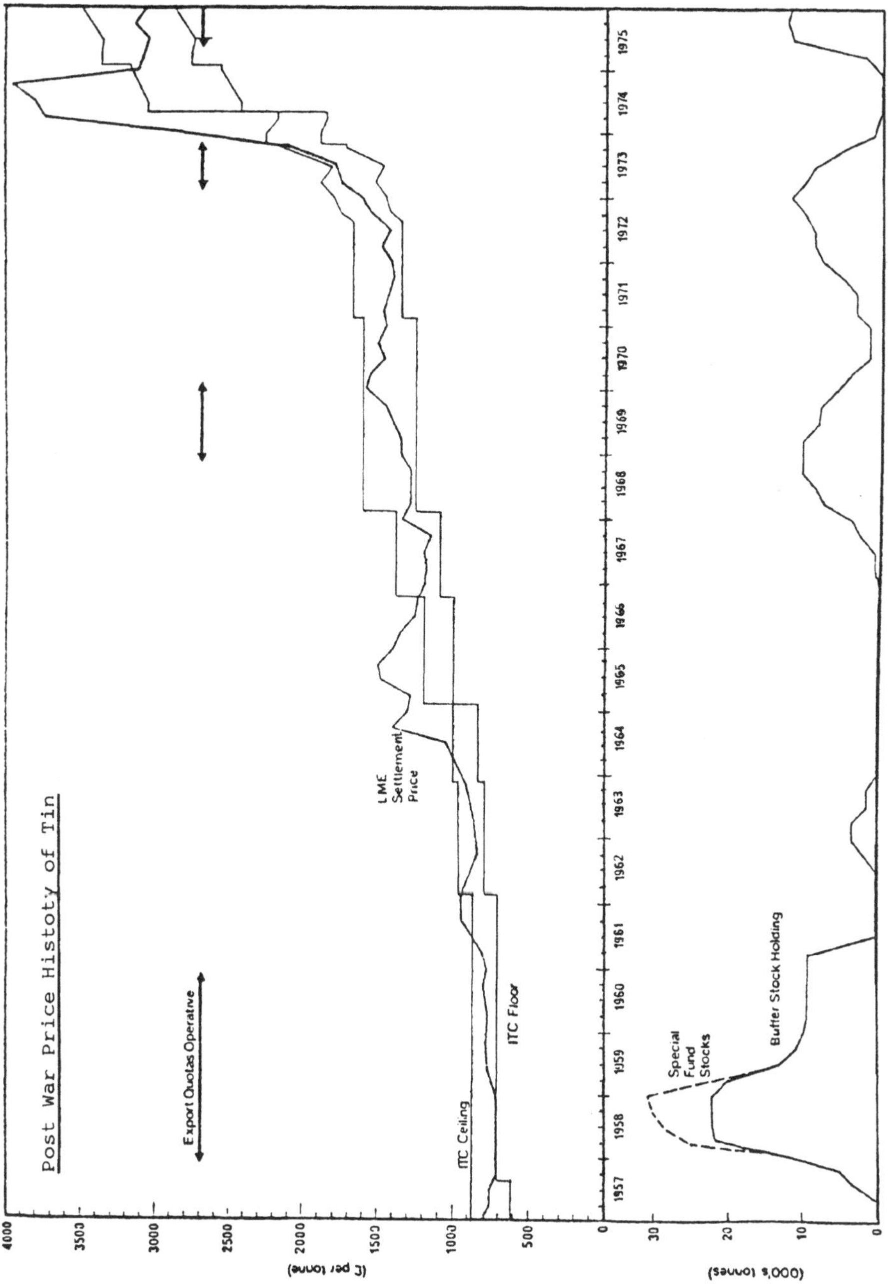

Source: Commodity Year Book, 1979, published by Commodity Research Bureau Inc. N.Y.

Amongst the member-countries, the United States - the largest consumer - was notably absent. The U.S. stayed out of the Tin Agreement until the fifth ITA in 1976, when they finally joined. Both producing and consuming countries are represented with equal voting rights in the International Tin Council (ITC), which is the administrative governing body of the agreement (43).

The operating mechanism of all ITAs was an international buffer stock, reinforced by export quotas when it was found to be necessary. The objectives, as presented in the First Agreement, remained almost the same throughout and were

- to prevent a maladjustment between supply and demand of tin,
- to prevent excessive fluctuations in the price of tin,
- to ensure adequate production of tin at reasonable and "fair" prices (44) at all times.

In addition to these, the Fifth Agreement put the emphasis on the following objectives

- helping to increase export earnings from tin, which was an additional element to those set up by the Third and Fourth Agreement,
- to increase economic growth in LDCs (45).

The relative success (opinions are divided) of the five international agreements, especially in reducing price fluctuations (through the buffer stocks control scheme) is, in comparison to other commodities, basically due to a very important element: the co-operation that existed between major exporting and importing countries.

---

(43) Ibid., and BURGER, Sharon R., "The Fifth International Tin Agreement", Law and Policy in International Business, vol. 9, No. 2, 1977, pp. 581-583.

(44) Reasonable and "fair" prices, were defined as those that would be remunerative to producers and acceptable to consumers, according to the U.N.'s terminology.

(45) BARKMAN, Kerstin, "The International Tin Agreement", J.W.T.L, vol. 9, 1975, pp.495-542.

c) Agreement valid at present

The Fifth ITA came into force in July 1976 for a five-year duration (up to June 1981). The objectives remained mainly the same as those formulated in the one preceding it. Membership covered producing and consuming countries, as before. The new, extraordinary element was that the United States officially joined the Tin Agreement, for the first time (46), as the world's largest tin consumer. Whether the decision was more politically then economically backed, gives rise to various speculations (47).

Like the four preceding Tin Agreements, the Fifth was based on the operating control scheme of using the buffer stocks (reinforced only on a temporary basis by export quotas) to maintain the tin price within the agreed price range. The support of the buffer stock was assured mainly by the producers. Only a few consumers participated in the donation and the reply from the United States, from whom most was expected, was negative. The U.S.A. refused to contribute to the buffer stock of the ITC (International Tin Council) (48). From a formal point of view, the United States did not have to obtain the consent of the ITC when they wanted - as intended - to supply the market direct with tin from the American strategic reserves.

The last, Sixth International Tin Agreement came into force in 1981, for a five-year duration. Its conclusion was brought about under the UNCTAD's Integrated Programme for Commodities.

---

(46) In the previous four Agreements, the United States never took the oportunity of joining the ITA because of the role of their strategic stocks, which could always be used at any given moment and which they did not want to place under the influence of the ITC, or at its disposal.

(47) As commented by the Wall Street Journal, on 21st April, 1976, on page 1, col.6, this act on the part of the United States was basically due to the effect of the anxious strengthening of commodity cartels and the constraining influence of the Third World.

(48) This action was said to be political, being part of the overall U.S. policy concerning primary commodities. See RAMGARAJAN, L.N., op.cit., p. 259.

2. Significance of the buffer stock principle

We have seen that the principle of the pure buffer stock mechanism lies in action which purports to establish the price range - the floor and the ceiling price (the vital point of the mechanism) - within which the price can oscillate. According to the oscillations the buffer stock manager will act as follows:

- when the market price reaches or falls below the floor price (agreed minimum), he buys the commodity for the stock as long as his financial funds are sufficient;
- when the market price reaches or exceeds the ceiling price (agreed maximum), he sells commodity from the stock as long as the stocks last.

The Tin Agreement, although it was the only one functioning on the lines of the international buffer stock scheme, was not of the pure form (see c) below).

a) Preconditions of the Tin buffer stocks

There were several factors which contributed in Tin Agreements to the operations of the buffer stock control schemes: first, producers and consumers were able to bring about a degree of co-operation with each other (this was the aim in other commodities, too). The restricted number of producers was in favour of this. Moreover, tin also had the feature that nearly all the world trade in this commodity was covered by the Tin Agreement (which has not been the case for many other commodities, like sugar). Then again, the tin market was the object of considerable, but not exaggerated, price fluctuations (which were quite successfully reduced, in comparison with other commodities). However, it must be added that this stabilization became possible because the Tin Agreement was backed by the international buffer stock mechanism and the United States' strategic stocks) (49).

---

(49) This can be seen from the Table which summarizes the fluctuations in prices, volume and earnings for some primary commodities, developed by RAMGARAJAN, L.N., op.cit., Table 7.5, p. 191.

It might be interesting to note that tin is an easily-storable commodity of uniform quality, which is a great advantage, especially in organizing its storage. (This is not the case with iron ore and bauxite (see Table 6), which,in view of the fact that there are several different qualities to deal with, have not been proposed for an international buffer stock regulation in the Integarated Programme for Commodities).

All in all, supply, demand and price instability for tin, as mentioned above, complete the factors required for an Agreement based on international buffer stock intervention.

b) Functioning and effectiveness of the Tin buffer stocks

In the first three Tin Agreements, the functioning of the buffer stocks was realized in the same way. The price range (between the floor and ceiling price) was specified on three levels (50). According to where the market price was, the buffer stock manager operated as follows:

- upper level: if the price was at this level, he could sell tin from the stock, but he could not buy it for the stock (and if the price rose above the ceiling price he had to sell tin);
- middle level: if the price was at this level, he could neither buy for, nor sell from, the stock;
- lower level: if the price was at this level, he could buy tin for the stock, but he could not sell from it (and if the price fell below the floor price, he had to buy tin).

The Fourth and the Fifth Tin Agreements brought further simplification in so far as only floor and ceiling prices were valid and the manager's activities were made easier.

However, in spite of all the emphasis put on the buffer stock mechanism as incorporated in the Tin Agreement, a question can be raised: could ITA's buffer stock control scheme be regarded as a perfect and successful example?

(50) MacAVOY, Paul, op.cit., p. 20.

If we come back to the price range, the role of the buffer stock was partially successful. When it was defending the floor price, it proved to be very effective. True, the task of protecting the minimum price was facilitated by reinforcement by means of export quotas. On the other hand, buffer stock failed to protect the ceiling price on several occasions when it could have been really useful. To be able to carry out this function, the buffer stock of tin ought to have adequate financial resources in addition to its own adequate supply of tin, so its size should be sufficiently assured before successful performance can be expected of it.

In the light of historical events, the tin buffer stock has almost been of an inadequate size as it was exhausted in 1961 and again in the period 1970 to 1976. During 1961, 1963-66 and 1973-74, buffer stock failed to defend the ceiling prices. Therefore, the regulation achieved by the Tin Agreements in the given periods (First and Second Tin Agreements) was not effective enought to meet high demand and regulated prices. (Of course producers gained, due to the rise in prices). It was not a question of something being wrong with the buffer stock principle itself, but simply that stocks were too small in size to respond effectively.

c) In combination with export quotas

All ITAs were, in principle, international buffer stock type agreements. The export control mechanism in the ITAs had a supporting character and it intervened when necessary to defend the floor price of the buffer stocks' price range. In periods of large supplies of tin, the market price tends to fall, and falls below the floor price. The buffer stock must then make its purchases. Its purchases stop when its financial resources are exhausted. From this moment on, the floor price can no longer be defended by the buffer stock mechanism. That is the moment when the export quota mechanism comes into play by putting restrictions on the exports coming from producing countries.

This combined mechanism indeed worked on several occasions. The functioning of ITAs proved to be very successful when it came to the question of supporting the floor price in periods of low prices.

3. Concluding remarks

One of the primary objectives of the ICAs is price stabilization. The International Tin Agreement was based mainly on this objective, but also proved to be a model of an efficient price-increasing agreement.

a) An appraisal of the experience gained

Although the ITAs have the long experience of twenty-four years behind them, it would br reckless to take them as a good model of international buffer stock regulation to be directly applicable in the case of any other primary commodity (even with similar basic characteristics).

Nevertheless, the points where it failed or succeeded can give some insights into its experiences and even facilitate an appraisal of the new possibilities for the amelioration of its performance in the tin market.

The existence of the first four Tin Agreements was largely marked by the absence of the U.S. as a member and the need to accord with the policy of the General Service Administration (GSA) (responsible for the U.S. stockpile management), which represented the main force in the tin market. (The magnitude of the GSA can be seen from the fact that in 1961 world supply was 136,000 tons and U.S. reserve stocks 350,000 tons from which 164,000 tons were declared to be surplus. Currently, 205,000 tons of tin are contained in the U.S. stocks, which represents nearly a four-year supply (51)). Although these stocks have been of a national character, their buying for, and releasing of, surpluses have had remarkable effects on the international demand for tin.

---

(51) BURGER, Sharon R., op.cit., p. 589.

Therefore, the U.S. membership (less threat from GSA) and a greater buffer stock potential were two new dimensions realised in the Fifth International Tin Agreement.

b) Prospects for an integrated approach

The buffer stock control scheme suggested for tin and developed by UNCTAD's IPC for ten "core" commodities is in favour of a link with export quotas. The reason behind such a decision lies in the problem that there are too many difficulties in the operation of a pure buffer stock mechanism, which is determined by the specific differences of the demand and supply elasticities necessary to stabilize and/or raise the producers' export earnings.

Those in favour of this approach suggest that the tin market has been regulated for many years and, in spite of the agreement, tin prices have shown considerable fluctuations. Therefore, this situation cannot be attributed simply to purely economic developments that could be regulated by "pure" buying for, and selling from,the buffer stock.

c) Prospects for an individual approach

Criticisms of the functioning of the buffer stock have been directed at its failure to maintain ceiling prices and if there had not been export quotas (although their intervention has been occasional), the success in defending the floor prices would not have been so great.

Our opinion is that this was due, not to failure in the buffer stock principle, but to the lack of a large stock provision. The problem of the size of the buffer stock therefore goes hand in hand with that of financing.

The fact that past ITAs buffer stock operations were not financed adequately proves that a perfect agreement between the producers and consumers was not reached concerning their contribution, as only producers financed the buffer stocks.

Some time ago (52), another round of negotiations concerning the Sixth International Tin Agreement was opened, and was prepared in collaboration with both producers and consumers. As regards the Agreement mechanism (up to now a combination of buffer stocks and flexible export quotas has been practised), the differences of opinion were rather greater than could be foreseen (because up to that time the administrative organ - ITC - had been responsible for fixing the maximum and minimum price and this was not to be changed until the conclusion of the Sixth ITC).

The United States, pleaded among other things, for a pure buffer stock system without export quotas. The opinion of the U.S. was negative towards export quotas and they insisted on considerably-increased buffer stocks. This proposal was not met with positive acceptance because it was in opposition to the proposal of the buffer stock plus export quota combination (EEC proposal). At the same time, the attitude of the producer countries was disapproved of because they rejected new concepts in the new agreement (U.S. concepts) as well as the position of the European Communities. The divergencies of opinion were serious.

On the other hand, the functioning of the buffer stock as regards producers and consumers seems to be uncontroversal. Again, a regulation is aimed at that will assure that operations of the large non-commercial U.S. reserve stockpiles will not conflict with the Agreement objectives.

A pure international buffer stock established for tin would be effective in regulating short-term supply. As can be imagined, a buffer stock of "sufficient size" need not to be achieved at once or in the initial stages, but it could be adjusted periodically. There would, therefore, be no need for the export quota request.

---

(52) From February to April 1980.

C - THE CASE OF COCOA MARKET REGULATION

Cocoa represents a very interesting case, apart from its natural features, from the point of view of its regulation and, as such, is worth being presented.

Theoretically, the First International Cocoa Agreement was based on the buffer stock type agreement, but it never operated because world prices were always above the ceiling price.

On the other hand, the case of this commodity illustrates the extreme length of negotiations that were necessary before the First International Cocoa Agreement entered into force. It took a total of seventeen years, and then turned out to be inoperative.

After a short presentation of the history of the cocoa market, the objective of the following will be to discuss why the buffer stock mechanism was inoperative. As to the prospects for future cocoa market regulation, several general remarks can be made.

1. Evolution of practice

With the recent fall in the price of cocoa, producers became extremely interested in finding a basis for a price stabilization programme through a new Cocoa Agreement - not without profound regret at letting the Second International Cocoa Agreement collapse at the end of March 1980.

a) Supply, Demand and Price Characteristics

Export market shares of LDCs for raw cocoa represent 99.2 percent (see Table 2) of the total world trade for this commodity.

Cocoa therefore represents a vital source of export earnings (see Table 3) for a certain number of LDCs.

Table 9.

Market Shares of the Four Largest Exporters of Cocoa
(in thousand metric tons)

Country	1975/76	1976/77	1977/78	1978/79	1979/80
Ghana	343.0	270.2	213.9	206.8	195.8
Ivory Coast	163.2	193.9	212.2	267.9	232.4
Nigeria	223.7	169.7	197.7	124.5	138.0
Brazil	142.3	107.2	118.1	145.9	135.6

Source: International Cocoa Organization, vol.VII, No.2,March 1981, London.

In view of the export shares, the interest in the price stabilization is essential for cocoa as, in general, the Third World covers 96% of the total world production of cocoa (where Africa's contribution is 62% and Latin America's 34%).

As in the case of other agricultural commodities, production in cocoa is subject to important fluctuations due to climatic conditions and/or plant illness, or, being a tree crop, to time lag for harvesting (53). It follows, therefore, that supply and prices are subject to severe fluctuations in their turn.

Severe fluctuations in prices of cocoa have been due, not only to supply inelasticity(owing to considerable variations in yield), but also to inelasticity of demand (see Table 10).

b) Periods of cocoa world market regulation

High prices in cocoa in 1953-54 were the background for negotiations between the consumers. These obtained the establishment of the official forum of the Cocoa Study Group, which prepared a draft of an ICA on cocoa at the first session held in 1956 (54).

(53) Time lag between planting and harvesting of cocoa is 8-12 years; BROWN, C.P., op.cit., p.8.

(54) KOFI, Tetteh A., "The International Cocoa Agreements", J.W.T.L., vol. 11, 1977, p.43.

Table 10.

World Production, Consumption and Prices of Cocoa

Crop Year	Production '000 of mt	Year	Consumption '000 of mt	Prices US ¢ per lb
1963/64	1,212	1963	1,039	25.05
1964/65	1,525	1964	1,035	22.85
1965/66	1,260	1965	1,260	16.57
1966/67	1,336	1966	1,367	23.48
1967/68	1,352	1967	1,366	27.13
1968/69	1,236	1968	1,410	32.70
1969/70	1,424	1969	1,353	40.97
1970/71	1,493	1970	1,357	30.57
1971/72	1,589	1971	1,439	24.43
1972/73	1,410	1972	1,567	29.15
1973/74	1,447	1973	1,557	51.29
1974/75	1,550	1974	1,478	70.77
1975/76	1,502	1975	1,463	56.51
1976/77	1,348	1976	1,519	92.79
1977/78	1,503	1977	1,366	171.92
1978/79	1,499	1978	1,367	154.32
1979/80	1,623	1979	1,422	149.32
1980/81	1,629	1980	1,493	118.06

Source: Quarterly Bulletin of Cocoa Statistics, International Cocoa Organization, vol. VII, No. 3, June 1981.

The same failure was repeated at the U.N. conferences in 1966 and 1967 (55).Producers were not insensitive to the consumers' action to find a way of combating the strong price fluctuations. The result was the creation of the Cocoa Producers' Alliance in 1962 involving Ghana, Ivory Coast, Brazil, Nigeria and Cameroon - the five major producers -, with the purpose of retaining part of the 1964-65 crop.

Several abortive negotiations preceded the coming into force of the First International Cocoa Agreement in 1973. It was to have a duration of three years, in the course of which it remained inoperative due to the high cocoa prices, which were above the agreement objectives. Declaring the Agreement too rigid and unable to accomplish its aims, the U.S. refused to sign it in spite of being the largest consumer.

After the re-negotiations during 1975, the Second International Cocoa Agreement replaced the first one in 1976, with the aim of stabilizing prices on the uncertain cocoa market. In spite of having participated in the negotiations, the U.S. did not ratify it again. The main objectives of both Cocoa Agreements, to adjust production to meet consumption, and to prevent excessive price fluctuations by means of the mechanism of export quotas and buffer stocks, were not attained. The operating mechanism was too rigid and the Second Agreement failed to make it more flexible.

c) Latest development

On 31st March,1980 (56) the Second ICA on Cocoa expired without the prospect of re-negotiations for a new Agreement. This decision was taken subsequent to a number of negotiations between producers and consumers, which had been conducted without success since 1978 and which ended in total disagreement as to the setting (i.e. increasing)the minimum

---

(55) Ibid.

(56) In the sub-division c), the latest data are quoted from various issues of the Neue Zürcher Zeitung (from March and April 1980).

price of 120 ¢ lb. proposed by the producers. The latter argued that the price had already been estimated at too high a level due to the refusal of important producing countries to sell cocoa under 150 ¢ lb.

The end of the theoretically perfect Cocoa Agreement marked another immediate failure to renew or even to extend the Cocoa ICA and this represents a serious disturbance in the North-South Dialogue.

Thus March 1980 ended with the definitive disruption of the negotiations. During June and July 1980, prices fell so low and continued to decrease so much that it created a new, urgent situation in the world cocoa market because the world supply may increase by 20 percent by 1985.

Therefore, producers and consumers agreed to take part in a series of negotiations (57) and tried, in spite of their divergent interests, to find a means of ensuring cocoa price stabilization and short-term export policy.

2. Significance of the buffer stock principle

Defined as being among the most unstable (58) of primary commodities, due to its severe supply, demand and price fluctuations, cocoa made a price stabilization scheme imperative.

The solution was developed through the cocoa ICAs' control mechanism, relying on export quotas and the buffer stock principle.

a) Introduction in practice

The combination of buffer stock and the instrument of export quotas has had similar objectives in both ICAs for cocoa.

---

(57) Starting on 28th July, 1980.

(58) UNCTAD, TD/B/C.1/194, loc.cit., p. 19.

This combination was designed to prevent excessive price fluctuations, to stabilize and increase export earnings, to facilitate expansion of consumption and to assure adequate supplies of cocoa at reasonable prices(59).

The combination of the two instruments was to operate in order to defend a price range, set up with a minimum price of 39, and maximum price of 55, cents per pound. It is worth noting that this price range (set up in 1975) was established for much higher prices (1973, minimum of 23, and maximum of 32, cents per pound) and also that it considerably increased the range between them (from 9, to 16, cents per pound) (60).

The Cocoa Council was given greater authority (than in the First ICA on Cocoa) to periodically review and adjust the price range for buffer stock purchases. Nevertheless, the price range was found to be too inflexible as the buffer stock was supposed to buy only what would have been allowed by the imposition of the quota and, therefore, the U.S. refused to join the agreement.

The storage problem (61) was solved by locating the buffer stock in suitable conditions and the buffer stock maximum capacity was to be 250,000 tons.

b) Application of the technique

When the Cocoa Agreement entered into force in 1976, everything was planned from the theoretical and technical point of view except for one important point: the heavy increase in the current price. The result was that the Agreement was inoperative. This was due to the fact that

---

(59) U.N.Doc. TD/COCOA.4/8, 10th November 1975, International Cocoa Agreement, art. 1 .

(60) Ibid., art. 28.

(61) The storage of cocoa in producing countries represents an important problem because of climatic conditions (heat and humidity) which, in a short time, can cause deterioration.

- the current price increased far above the ceiling limit (shortage of cocoa supply), and the high prices stayed above the unrealistic price range that had been agreed on during the three-year duration of the ICA, and
- the buffer stock of the Cocoa Agreement was not accumulated and therefore never came into operation.

In situations where prices unpredictably rose so high above the price range, the buffer stock was not able to play a part in the price-stabilization policy. This was not because of its conceptual incapacity, but because of the inflexibility of the Agreement mechanism and its ensuing inability to face the evolution of the market trend. The Cocoa Agreement was unable to provide an answer to

- the price increase in cocoa, and
- the fact that cocoa was in short supply.

c) Combination of the buffer stock with export quotas

Given the price range, the basis of the combination of buffer stock and export quotas is as follows:

- when the market price approaches, and rises above, the ceiling price:
  a. sales are made from the buffer stock, which expands supply, and
  b. quotas are suspended;
- when the market price approaches, and falls below, the floor price:
  a. purchases are made for the buffer stock, and
  b. an appropriate reduction is made in export quotas.

From this general basis, a whole variety of combinations can be developed, depending on what role the agreement dictates for the buffer stock and export quotas.

The Second International Cocoa Agreement, of 1976, established a price range divided into seven sectors, where the action of the buffer stock and the export quotas was set off automatically (see Table 11).

Table 11.

The Second International Cocoa Agreement (1976) price of 39 to 55 ¢ per lb. and the trigger action of the buffer stock and export quoats

Mechanism of action	Price is in the lower part of the range [a]				middle range	Price is in the upper part of the range	
	below 39	39 - 42	42 - 45	45 -47 (marking period)	47 -53	53 -55	above 55
Buffer Stock Action	Buffer Stock will keep on buying till it is exhausted	buffer stock will buy up to 4% of annual export quotas	buffer stock buys the 3% of the annual export quotas	no regulatory action	no regulatory action	buffer stock will sell up to 7% of annual export quotas	buffer stock continues selling until it is exhausted
Export Quotas Action	Substantial cuts in export quotas are made	Substantial cuts in export quotas are made	97% of annual export quotas	100% of annual export quotas are effective (but quota cut besome possible if price decline further)	no regulatory action	quotas are suspended	quotas are suspended

a/ price is in cents per pound

Source: International Coca Agreement, 1975, UNCTAD; TD/COCOA.4/8, 1975. Agreement entered into force on 1st. October 1976.

3. Concluding remarks

a) An appraisal of the experience gained

In view of past experience, it is difficult to believe that a perfect, solution can be found to the problems of the price stabilization policy in the cocoa market, unless the weak points and those responsible for failure are reviewed with the aim of eliminating, in advance, the repetition of past mistakes, and thus avoiding future ones.

Therefore, if preparations are to be made for a new buffer stock project that can play a part in price stabilization policy, several basic and crucial factors should be realistically examined, such as:

- price range (a higher, wider one)
- financing of the buffer stock (sufficient funds)
- size of the funds (those needed for the operation, i.e. financial,and the quantity of the cocoa in the stock), and
- existence of substitutes.

Cocoa has no direct substitutes. However, in periods where prices are too high, demand may suffer a sharp fall as interest in direct substitutes (like fats and oils) will increase. Therefore, this point should not be neglected.

b) Prospects for a new regulation

Cocoa has been proposed for UNCTAD's IPC and its agreements would be built around a buffer stock instrument reinforced by export quotas, as a regulator of supply (see Table 5). This means that the scope of the operating mechanism will stay the same but, in view of promises made by the Cocoa Organization, a change will be made in the floor price to make it more realistic.

The problems go further in the sense that the price range will be wider, and instead of the 9-16 cents per pound in the last Agreement, it should be, perhaps, 40 cents per pound.

The extent to which these promises will be kept depends, among other factors, on whether disagreement among producers and consumers disappears, or at least, decreases.

It is difficult to believe in miracles, and to believe that there are prospects of regulation of commodity markets within the UNCTAD's IPC after the recent failure of the Cocoa Agreement is too optimistic.

c) General context for future cocoa market regulation

The cocoa market is very sensitive to the strengthening pressure of supply, and not without reason. Market observers expect an additional, vigorous increase in the Brazilian supply in the medium term. According to estimations, by 1984/85 Brazil's cocoa production alone will be almost 450,000 tons, which represents nearly double the amount in 1977/78. Since Brazil has announced the "Prococoa" programme, which aims to increase production, the prospects for 1990 are around 700,000 tons. The burden of a common price policy on the producers under pressure to maintain the level of quality is therefore impressive. On the other hand, there seems to be little prospect of demand matching this rising supply. The extent of demand is not of great importance because of different substitution possibilities.

Therefore, it is clear that efforts to stabilize cocoa prices on the most recent registered level above 120 cents per pound have little chance of success.

The question may be raised as to whether a stabilization policy, in order to be successful, should not be supplemented by efforts to introduce a quantity policy. However, the difficulty of reaching an agreement in this field on the international level cannot be overlooked. Nevertheless, considering the specific case of cocoa, it seems quite evident that a pure buffer stock instrument will not be enough to provide the regulation required in the market for this commodity, and that it would be better to combine it with export quotas, determining the role of each of them very precisely.

How far future negotiations between producers and consumers will be able to meet the real situation will be seen after the July and September meetings, if they do not end in the usual disagreement.

This brief look at the five formal ICAs and several informal arrangements, has shown that, besides the instability problem, which represents nothing new in the commodity market, one of the ICAs' problems was that they always fell into a confusion between two crucial aims:

- the stabilization of prices, and
- the raising of prices.

Whether or not ICAs were successful, their principal objective in using the buffer stock method of control and others, was to restrict the supply - directly or indirectly - and to manage surpluses.

Additionally, it has been shown that the production of the commodities dealt with takes place mainly in LDCs and consumption occurs for the most part, in DCs. Thus, disagreement among producers and consumers caused the failure of many post-war agreements, especially in the settlement of problems such as concerning

- the price range and/or
- export quotas.

Admittedly, our discussion has been limited to only a few basic problems of the buffer stock policy. The financial implications of alternative buffer stock policies have not been covered and were mentioned only in order to draw attention to their vital importance. This subject will be analysed later in the work.

The aim was to discover, by means of specific commodities, whether there have been examples of the operation of the pure buffer stock scheme. In the light of the information regarding the different control mechanisms, it may be said that the theoretically "pure" buffer stock scheme is feasible but in concrete cases, it turned out to be very difficult to operate, as buffer stocks were usually backed by the export quotas system. It appeared that

- the financing of the buffer stock, and
- the amount of resources needed (financial and commodity in stock)

are two vital elements of the buffer stock mechanism in bringing about price stabilization of a commodity within the established price range.

* * *

This Part has made it clear that in view of the experiences gained with buffer stocks incorporated in ICAs, it may be said in conclusion that, besides certain basic common factors (price range, financing, amount of resources) and a number of purely practical issues yet to be settled (pure buffer stock, its combination with the export quota), buffer stock operation depends on, and varies according to, specific characteristics of the commodity market.

(*) Note should be taken that while this work was being written, the ICA on Natural Rubber was concluded, in October 1979, under the UNCTAD IPC. Although adequate attention should be given to this commodity, it will not receive detailed consideration within the scope of this study. Some relevant points, however, must be presented in brief. (See in Part II, Chapter I, Section C, note (39), page 186).

PART II

EVALUATION OF THE SYSTEM

Various aspects of an evaluation of the advantages and an indication of the problems of the buffer stock scheme which have been recorded will be considered in this part, which is divided into two chapters. Chapter I is concerned with the proposals and application of the buffer stock typology. Chapter II deals with the advantages and disadvantages of this system of commodity control.

Part II may therefore be considered as an empirical attempt to apply the typology hypothesis to the general aspects and principal features of the buffer stock control method.

CHAPTER I

PROPOSALS FOR A BUFFER STOCK TYPOLOGY

In the present chapter, before the proposals for a buffer stock typology are discussed the term "typology" needs to be defined in general. In the attempt to define this term, the importance of the suggested typology will become clearer, thereby showing the value of spending time finding a worthwhile definition for the systematic and orderly insights that will then be provided.

Generally, typology is a method of models which incorporate certain essential elements of all phenomena or subjects,all of the same nature and having the same importance in their relationships and characteristics. Here, "type" is understood in the sense of "average". However, the object of our inquiry will be the type understood as an ideal model corresponding to theoretically-developed criteria.

It must be taken into account that when a reference is made to the possibility of proposals for establishing a buffer stock typology, the buffer stock operations under consideration are acknowledged to be the means, and not the aim, of regulating the primary commodity markets.

A - THEORETICAL CRITERIA SUGGESTED FOR THE ESTABLISHMENT OF TYPES OF BUFFER STOCKS

In this section, attempts will be made to focus the analysis on the question of which criteria, i.e. which groups of common elements, are to be referred to in the regulation of different buffer stocks and which theoretical principles are to be taken as standard in judging the essential aspects of the economic problems leading to the establishment of international buffer stocks.

In short, the position taken here, in accepting the importance of reference to theoretical criteria, has to include the formation of the general observation and a comment should be made about the general aim: - the point is, not only to find common elements determining buffer stock action, but also to characterize the objectives or effects of those elements for buffer stock action.

As has been indicated, it should be clear that the buffer stock operation seeks to attain certain objectives. It is therefore important to develop an equitable framework of theoretical criteria which, in turn, will help us, later on, to find out how to use the typology.

For this reason, and for our present purpose, the first stage of the analysis will consist in distinguishing between intrinsic and extrinsic criteria.

1. Intrinsic criteria

Intrinsic criteria refer to those characteristics which are essential for, and inherent in, primary commodities from the economic and technical (1) point of view. Such criteria may determine the typology formation with certainty and can be viewed under the following headings:

a - natural qualities
b - nature of production and
c - stockability

a) Natural qualities

One of the criteria for determining if a primary commodity is suitable for stocking is based on its physical characteristics, which will, in turn, reveal whether the commodity can be stocked without appreciable deterioration in quality. Basically, this is determined by distinguishing whether the primary product is

- durable or
- perishable

Due to its purpose (to smooth the price fluctuations), the buffer stock mechanism can be established only for durable primary commodities (2) and cannot be set up for the perishable ones (3).

---

(1) Terminology is very flexible when it is a question of the term "technical". Here, it is taken to mean the type of product, its nature of production and its stability.

(2) Minerals and metals (tin, copper, rubber, lead).

(3) Fresh fruit (bananas and citrus fruits).

However, the physical problem of holding certain commodities in stock should not be exaggerated by these two classifications, for the reason that certain primary products are relatively non-perishable goods and hence storable. How far some commodities are relatively non-perishable depends on the degree of deterioration of the commodities if the storage period is exceeded. This suggests that, for certain commodities (the storage of which takes place in temperate and tropical climatic regions), storage periods are limited to only a few years due to the factors which influence the deterioration and loss in quality. These commodities require a series of special treatments during the storage period, such as careful temperature control, corresponding humidity or adequate storing time.

Table 12 reveals the fact that, for some primary commodities, certain elements are of vital importance in judging the feasibility and profitability of keeping the commodity in stock.

<u>Table 12.</u>

<u>Natural elements which influence the deterioration of certain commodities in the temperate and tropical regions</u>

Coffee	temperature and humidity (control)
Cocoa	time of storage (weight loss after a certain time of storage)
Sugar	fermentation (due to high humidity)
Tea	loss in value if not manufactured under optimum temperature and humidity conditions (value for use in quality)

Source: Explanations extracted from UNCTAD: <u>An Integrated Programme for Commodities.</u> Progress report on storage costs and warehouse facilities, Geneva, 1975, TD/B/C.1/187,Annex I, p. 3.

Here, as far as the non-perishable goods are concerned, our interest was concentrated on those commodities which are important for the export earnings of developing countries, and include, principally, the commodities from temperate and tropical regions.

It follows that, for some primary commodities (from the point of view of natural elements) (4),deterioration in storage can be gradual and, therefore, a systematic turnover of stocks is required in adequate proportion. It can be brought about through the

- recycling (turnover inside the storage surface), and
- rotation (moving out of the storage surface and replacing by a new output).

This is especially true for the agricultural products in tropical and temperate regions.

It is,perhaps,worth pointing out that the "perishable commodities are not usually regarded as suitable for buffer stock schemes; yet there is no hard-and-fast criterion of perishability in this sense. While there are some products, such as bananas, for which buffer stocks are, at present, technically impossible, and others, such as tin, for which storage is relatively cheap, there are a large number of "grey area" commodities ... for which the technical-economic factors, including some loss due to deterioration, would have to be balanced against the benefits. These factors would include the alternative forms in which commodities could be stored" (5).

Hence, for the so-called "grey-area" commodities or, as we prefer to call them, the "relatively non-perishable" ones, there are ways of influencing their perishability to a certain degree, by observing special storing conditions which differ from one commodity to another.

---

(4) Coffee, cocoa, sugar, tea.

(5) IMF/IBRD, The problem of stabilization of prices of primary products, A Joint Staff Study, Part I,Washington D.C., 1969, p. 71.

In conclusion, it may be noted that a delimited classification of commodities according to their natural qualities can be set up in three classes, as follows:

- perishable goods
- relatively non-perishable and
- durable goods.

Therefore, every primary commodity must be examined carefully and a decision reached as to which of these three categories it may be included in. We suggest this grouping of three categories as a criterion for the typology relating to the natural qualities, for all primary commodities. This criterion may be considered rather general, but it must be borne in mind that the primary commodities are largely predetermined by a whole variety of natural qualities (only in the third category the perishability may be artificially influenced, as was mentioned above).

b) Nature of production

Yet another element has its importance as being one of the technical characteristics of primary commodities - the nature of production.

The volume of production of primary commodities can be influenced by two factors:

- natural conditions, and
- elasticity of supply.

With regard to the former - natural conditions, the volume of production of most agricultural commodities can be exposed, especially in the short-run, to elements such as variations in climatic conditions, plant and/or animal diseases, and pests, all of which, in one way or another, lead to considerable variations in the seasons' yields. Variations in weather (frost, rains, etc.) can have bad repercussions on the harvests of certain agricultural commodities (especially vulnerable are wheat and coffee) which, in turn, will give rise to a considerable reduction, or increase, in the world stocks of the commodity concerned.

Therefore, it would be as well to point out that natural conditions have a direct effect on the production cycles, as, from time to time, they cause unforeseen overshortages of certain agricultural commodities.

As for minerals and metals, the variations in the production cycles are due more to progressive exhaustion of the known reserves than great political and social changes. There is still evidence to show that they can be regarded as rare from an absolute, or from a relative, point of view.

Those who argue for absolute scarcity foresee future shortages due to the exhaustion of non-renewable minerals and metals. It has been argued, on the other hand, that they are rare from the relative point of view because, with new technologies, substitution possibilities have increased greatly, and natural resources have been explored enough for an absolute statement to be made.

The second factor which influences the volume of production of primary commodities is - elasticity of supply. In general, the price elasticity of supply for most primary commodities is rather low. The term "rather" has been used here intentionally, as the degree of elasticity of supply between agricultural, and mineral and metal primary products registers a net difference due to major costs, which are fixed overheads, for the mining products, as reported by MacBean (6).

Therefore, agricultural products have a lower supply elasticity than the latter. Table 13 is a general summary of the price elasticities of supply, and demand for selected commodities which are representative of three main groups of primary products: food and tropical beverages, agricultural raw materials, and minerals and metals.

---

(6) MacBEAN, A., op.cit., p. 24.

Table 13.

Price elasticities[a/] for certain primary commodities, 1980

Commodity	Elasticity of supply	Elasticity of demand
Cocoa	0.32	-0.23
Coffee	0.28	-0.32
Tea	0.25	-0.23
Cotton[b/]	0.04	-0.17
Sugar[c/]	0.04	-0.02
Jute	0.36	-0.35
Copper	0.12	-0.32
Rubber[d/]	0.09	-0.17
Tin	0.19	-0.62
Wheat	0.70	-0.66
Rice	0.20	-0.18

a/ Own computation. Production and consumption prices are data for 1979 and 1980.

b/ Cotton elasticity of supply is 0.037. Despite the increase in the area planted there is fall in production due to the low yields.

c/ Sugar elasticity of supply is 0.034 and of demand -0.014. Sharped reduced crops in the Caribbeans'.

d/ Rubber elasticity of supply is 0.085. There is a fall in production, due to the switch to palm oil cultivation.

Source: FAO Production Yearbook, FAO, Rome 1982.

Raport et perspectives sur les produit, 1981-82, FAO, Rome 1982.

Monthly Bulletin of Statistics, UN, ST/ESA/STAT/SER.G/118, vol.XXXVI, No. 10, October 1982.

The figures given in the above table indicate the price elasticities of supply for a certain number of agricultural products. Cotton, sugar and rubber show a rather low value of 0.037, 0.034 and 0.085 respectively, in comparison with metal such as tin, the value of which is 0.19. In the certain cases, price elasticities of supply are shown to be higher than price elasticities of demand, which is lower in value. It can be seen in the case of cocoa, 0.32 to -0.23. With regard to supply, the low price elasticity of certain commodities will cause a change in their demand, which will then, as a result, bring about an oscillation in price.

With regard to demand, the low price elasticity will bring about an oscillation in price, due to the change in supply induced by natural conditions (disasters). As the responses of supply and demand to the price changes are interdependent causing price instability in the world market, there is no need to discuss them separately.

Furthermore, it should be noted that demand for natural commodities in domestic markets is quite stable over a certain period of time. Nevertheless, the variations in domestic supply will have an important influence on the import demand, i.e. in the international market. Table 14 shows the price elasticities of domestic demand and supply, and imports for a number of selected primary commodities.

Table 14 also provides statistics which indicate that the elasticity of demand is, to a great extent, low in value, ranging from -0.2 to -0.5. When compared with the values of the elasticity of supply, it is clear that the latter, although somewhat low, is still greater in comparison with the former. In Tables 13 and 14 the objective was to present the price elasticities of supply and demand and their effect on the domestic and international market. From a general point of view, it can be seen from Figure 9 that both these factors have definite effects on prices.

Table 14.

Price elasticities for certain grouped primary commodities

Commodity	Elasticity of demand		Elasticity of supply	
	D	M	D	M
Food and beverages				
Vegetable oils	-0.2	--	0.7	--
Coffee	-0.5	-0.2	0.4	--
Sugar	-0.4	--	--	--
Rice	-0.3	--	--	--
Tea	-0.15	--	0.7	--
Agricultural raw materials				
Wool	-0.25	--	--	--
Rubber	--	-0.8	--	--
Minerals and Metals				
Cooper	-0.3	--	0.4	--
Zinc	-0.15	--	--	--
Tungsten	-0.1	--	0.8	--

Source: Extracted out from the Survey of Commodity Demand and Supply Elasticities, UNCTAD Research Memorandum No.48, March 1974.

D = domestic demand

M = imports

-- = data not available

Figure 9.

Oscillation in price due to the supply and demand changes

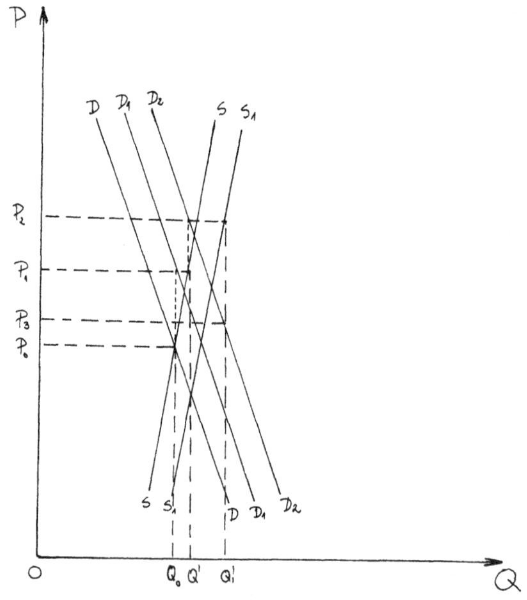

Figure 9 demonstrates the fact that supply and demand curves are both to be found in the basic period S and D, and the quantity supplied, Q_o, is offered at the price P_o. In the second period, there is no change in the quantity offered, i.e. production stays at Q_o, but demand changes, which is manifested in the shift of the demand schedule from D to D_1. Quantity Q_o is now in demand at the price P_1, which is rather high in comparison with P_o. This, in turn, will influence production and the quantity supplied will change to Q'. Let us now suppose that demand changes. The situation will change with the shift of demand curve from D_1 to D_2. The production of Q' will be in demand at the price P_2 which is higher than P_1. Due to the situation in the following period, supply will increase to S_1 which, with the quantity supplied of Q_1', will result in a much lower new price, P_3.

This presentation traces what happens if both inelastic supply and demand change. The result is a considerable oscillation in price.

From the above points, it should be clear that the general notion of elasticity is one of the efficient instruments applied in the analysis of international trade. Therefore, a well-informed approach to elasticities is important to evaluate the effects of price changes and instability. Although it is difficult to separate the analysis of elasticity of supply and elasticity of demand, these factors should be regarded, and adopted, as a criterion for typology. We suggest that supply and demand should therefore be regarded as two groups.

With regard to supply, bearing in mind the above considerations, it may be noted that export supply affects price variation on the world market, and this concerns primary products without particular distinction and without grouping them.

With regard to demand, commodities could be split into three groups: those from temperate zones, tropical baverages, and those used as inputs in industrial production - minerals metals (7).

---

(7) - Temperate zone: cereals, vegetable oils, sugar;
- tropical beverages: coffee, cocoa, tea, and also tobacco, rubber, textile fibres;
- industrial input: copper, iron ore, zinc, tin, lead, tungsten, phosphate, manganese.

This criterion may be regarded as essential, as the factors enumerated above influence the volume of production of primary commodities, and therefore bring about (a considerable influence on the) price fluctuations in the commodity markets.

c) Stockability

The suitability (for storage) of commodities depends, amongst others, on two dominant factors:

- time dimension, that is to say, the period during which commodities are properly stored and can be preserved without disproportionate deterioration, and
- costs of storage.

The suitability of different commodities for storage varies and, therefore, it should first of all be decided which commodities are suitable for storing. Here we refer to the beginning of this section. There, one of the basic approaches adopted as an intrinsic criterion, was the natural qualities of primary products. A better illustration of the fact that, for certain commodities, storage periods can be rather short, especially in the tropical and temperate zones, before deterioration sets in, is provided by Table 15.

This UNCTAD analysis is only an example as it covers only five out of the thirty-five primary commodities which are internationally traded. Neverthless, this sample shows the possible consequences as a percentage of deterioration in the commodities if the storage period is exceeded. Therefore, in order to preserve the quality of the product, the quantity stored must be determined by the time-lag of storing. The optimum storage period varies from one commodity to another (due to its own characteristics) under different storage conditions.

The agricultural commodities are more sensitive to the time dimension as their quality decreases through the stocking process far more quickly than that of commodities from the mining sector, and varies from one year for the former, to an unlimited period of conservation for the latter.

Table 15

Storage periods for selected commodities in temperate and tropical zones

	Storage period	Percentage deterioration if period exceeded
Coffee	Beans (a) 2 months tropical belt without temperature/humidity control (b) In temperate zone Ambicas 1 year; Robustas 2-3 years.	With proper temperature and humidity control, 2-3 per cent weight loss after one year's storage. Under normal market conditions there is a 10 per cent discount for all coffee stored for periods exceeding one year.
	Parchment (a) Cannot be stored in tropical zone (b) Approximately 2-3 years in temperate zone	
Cocoa	Beans With proper temperature and humidity control can be stored 3-4 years a/	2 per cent weight loss after 3-4 years
Tea	Manufactured Tea If manufactured under optimum conditions will keep up to a maximum of 12 months with strict humidity and temperature controls combined with free flow of air around chests. If poorly manufactured lower limit is about 3 months.	Tea will assume zero value for use in quality blends after limits are exceeded. Only suitable for instant and similar teas.
Sugar	Raw (a) In tropical zone 3 years plus, without deterioration	If high humidity, possible fermentation and weight loss.
	(b) Virtually unlimited storage period in temperate zone	None
	Refined Can be stored only if temperature and humidity are rigorously controlled	None
Rubber	Raw (a) Under tropical conditions, very short	Raw rubber will decompose if attacked by mould; deterioration approaches 100 per cent.
	(b) In temperate zone can be stored virtually indefinitely	-----
	Crumb rubber (a) Crumb rubber is normally packaged in polyethylene bags and can be stored only in tropical zones if temperature and humidity are rigorously controlled.	
	(b) No problem with length of storage in temperate-zone warehouse.	None

Source: An Integrated programme for commodities: Progress report on storage costs and warehouse facilities, UNCTAD, TD/B/C.1/187 3rd June, 1975, Annex I, p.3

a/ one source suggests that the storage period can be substantially longer than 3-4 years.

Furthermore, the region where, and the conditions under which, commodities are stored, are of considerable importance in preserving the commercial value of commodities. The difference can be seen if the same commodity is stored under the same conditions in two different regions, i.e. temperate and tropical regions. Table 16 illustrates the nature of this fact for commodities, classified in four groups: minerals and metals, food, agricultural raw materials and tropical beverages.

From the table provided (as an example only a few commodities are referred to), it can be seen which commodities can be kept safe without disproportionate deterioration if stored under proper conditions. Disproportionate physical deterioration means that during the optimum storage period, although commodities safeguard their natural features, they undergo a certain percentage of quality change (quality loss) which does not influence their commercial value. It may be said that maximum conservation during the storage periods, in both temperate and tropical regions, favours minerals and metals most, as they are practically unaffected.

With regard to food, agricultural raw materials and tropical beverages, variations in their deterioration are of great importance as it varies from 3 to 36 months. Most of them are prone to disproportionate physical deterioration in tropical zones, but keep longer in temperate ones.

It is apparent, therefore, that the stockability of each commodity demands maximum conservation during its optimal storage period, which depends directly on the cost of storage.

<u>Costs of storage</u> for primary commodities represent a very important component as they determine the length of the optimum storage period and depend on the storage technology which exists at a particular point in time. Costs of storage correspond to those costs which arise during the holding of commodities in stocks and their maintenance. On one hand, they comprise costs such as insurance, transport and prevention of physical deterioration of commodities in different places of

Table 16.

Maximum conservation and storage periods in temperate and tropical zones

	Maximum conservation a/		Maximum storage b/	
Minerals and metals	Temperate zone	Tropical zone	Temperate zone	Tropical zone
Copper concentrates c/	12	6	--	--
Copper metal	unlimited	unlimited	unlimited	unlimited
Tin concentrates	unlimited	unlimited	unlimited	unlimited
Tin metal	unlimited	unlimited	unlimited	unlimited
Food				
Sugar(refined) d/	unlimited	4	--	--
Vegetable oil seeds e/	24	12	6	3
Vegetable oil (crude) f/	12	12	--	--
Agricultural raw materials				
Jute g/	unlimited	12	--	--
Cotton h/	36	36	--	--
Rubber (crumb) i/	unlimited	6	--	--
Tropical beverages				
Coffee j/	36	12	--	6
Tea k/	12	12	--	--
Cocoa l/	24	2	--	--

Source: An Integrated Programme for Commodities: Second Progress Report on storage costs and warehouse facilities, UNCTAD, TD/B/C.1/198, 29 September 1975. Table composed on the basis of Tables given in Annexes I, II, III and IV.

a/ Period for which the commodity will keep its commercial values.

b/ Maximum period for which the commodity may be stored without internal cycling.

c/ If the maximum storage periods indicated are exceeded, the risk of oxidation increases.

d/ In temperate zones, refined sugar can be kept indefinitely provided packaging and warehouse facilities are of high standard. In tropical zones, sugar cannot be stored longer than approximately four months without transformation to a sirup consistency. Information is presently incomplete with regard to the storage of raw sugar in both temperate and tropical zones.

e/ If maximum conservation periods are exceeded infestation by insects is possible and rancidity problems may occur. Internal cycling will be necessary to avoid heat build up and physical deterioration. The internal cycling cost in the case of vegetable oil seeds has been assessed as 66 ¢ MT for temperate zone storage. Full in-and-out costs have been changed in the case of tropical storage, except for Brazil where modern temperate zone conveyor systems are in operation.

f/ Free fatty acids and proxide values can become excessively high if storage periods exceed 12 months.

g/ Jute may still be merchantable after 24 months of storage in tropical areas but after 12 months, the risk of weight loss and attack by termites and moths increases.

h/ In principle cotton is not perishable but after three years discoloration may occur.

i/ If rubber is sufficiently dried, storage is unlimited in temperate zones, the risk of decomposition is high if storage periods exceed six months.

j/ Depending on the world supply and demand for coffee, green beans can be held up to 36 months in temperate zones without being discounted at time of sale, although 12 months is the more usual period. In tropical areas only parchment coffee is stored and must be internally cycled every six months to preserve quality. The normal-holding period is 12 months.

k/ Providing tea is adequately packed and kept under normal conditions, it can be stored for periods up to 24 months without chemical deterioration. However, under normal market conditions, tea will command a lower price after 12 months due to purported flavour deterioration.

l/ Cocoa can be stored two years in temperate zone warehouses but not more than 2 months in tropical zones, because of the risk of fermentation.

storage location, which depend on the quantity stored. On the other hand, the general administrative costs of storing primary commodities are also an element of the costs of storage but are quite independent of the quantity stored.

One may ask whether this second component of costs of storage - the administrative one - is an extrinsic product criterion, and may therefore impose the same conditions on each commodity. However, we are of opinion that this component cannot be dissociated from the costs of storage in general.

The costs of storage can be grouped in three classes all of which are linked by their interaction (8)

- costs of management,
- costs of physical operations, and
- interest costs on the capital employed in the operation.

At this point, the necessity for all costs relative to storage known in practice to be covered by a coherent cost concept should be emphasized. Here some of the major categories of storage costs can be dealt with; detailed calculations have been made by UNCTAD, especially detailed analysis of the "core commodities".

Costs of storage are complex and a decisive factor in determining the suitability of primary commodities for stocking. Therefore, it can be added here that minerals and metals have a great advantage over agricultural products as they demand fewer specific conditions (such as temperature, humidity, etc.) than the latter. These tend to loss of weight and quality due to their degree of perishability. It should be remembered that perishability is not completely excluded in the case of metals (oxidation).

It is generally accepted that one of the criteria for determining the suitability of buffer stock operations is whether the commodity can be stored at relatively low costs.

---

(8) COLEBROOK, Jay, "The Cost of Storing Primary Commodities", Journal of World Trade Law ,vol.II, no.4, July:August 1977, p. 369.

Accordingly, the criterion suggested above - stockability - has to be examined in detail as it represents a vital technical-factor-criterion for the typology. Nevertheless, it cannot be isolated in a definite individual analysis, but rather approached as an important part linked to the natural qualities and nature of production of primary commodities.

2. Extrinsic criteria

Extrinsic criteria refer to those characteristics of primary commodities which are of external origin and do not naturally belong to them. How they determine the typology formation is less certain and only profiled determined analysis can provide or reject this information. Extrinsic criteria appear in a similar, or equivalent, way in all cases of primary products.

Therefore, having already provided an insight into intrinsic criteria, we shall now proceed with a study of major extrinsic criteria (9). We suggest here that such a study has a three-fold aspect as follows

- financing of the buffer stocks
- criterion of degree of instability in prices
- natural, vis-à-vis synthetic, substitutes.

a) Financing of the buffer stocks

In general, the key problem in the buffer stocks operation is mirrored in its financial conditions. Therefore, it may be considered as the most serious criterion for the buffer stock typology.

---

(9) It is an open question whether this three-fold division corresponds to some more general observations. The literature shows that the extrinsic characteristics of commodities are grouped under - institutional factors (those that are sensitive to change by government actions, for example spread of technology, spread of capital etc.) and - market factors (those that are related to economic factors which)determine the price of the commodity in the market. (As regards this classification, refer to RAMGARAJAN, op.cit.,pp. 56-59). It appears to some extent, that this is the broadest way to approach the characteristics of commodities. In spite of what scientists have told us, we suggest that the whole purpose of our grouping is to present the criteria of these commodities, either intrinsic or extrinsic, in a way which may determine the buffer stock typology.

From this point of view, the financing of the buffer stocks could be regarded as an action which has two requirements

- a certain amount of funds to make the purchase of commodity stock possible, and
- certain regular capital investments necessary to cover the costs of storage, including the interest costs on the capital employed in the operation.

In order to attain these objectives, the sums required for both financial actions have to be examined with regard to the interest of the countries involved in the operation of the buffer stock scheme, i.e. by both importing and exporting countries. Therefore, the two groups of countries must provide sufficient capital financial resources for running a buffer stock scheme, as their common interest lies in the smoothing of the price fluctuations, which, in turn, will ensure greater economic stability.

To ensure the purchase of commodity stock, the buffer stock agency has to have adequate foreign exchange at its disposal. As exporting countries are usually LDCs and therefore too few in number to provide the sum required themselves, financial participation should be sought from importing countries. This should be obtained in the form of membership participation, which would provide the basic conditions for the buffer stock agency for purchase of commodity for stock.

The question as to why the membership participation of both exporters and importers should be required can be answered as follows. In the case where the exporting countries provide most of the required financial funds and importing countries do not participate, a relatively small amount of foreign exchange will still be represented. This situation means that, over a certain period of time, the buffer stock agency has to effect purchases and sales of the given commodity before it can accumulate enough financial resources to have a significant effect upon the circulation of foreign exchange to the exporting countries. It follows, therefore, that, if the importing countries also take part in the membership participation in order to meet financial requirements, the period during which the effect of the money market to the exporting countries would be felt, should definitely be made shorter, which, in turn, will provide them with more benefits.

All that has been stated in brief above shows that the participation of the two groups of countries will be of adequate importance in the realization of the quantitative financial dimension. When the estimates for the financial requirements are analysed, the series of factors must not be neglected on which the amount needed depends.

To judge its importance, the fact must be considered that, for different commodities, financing of the buffer stocks would depend on the initial buying price, the size of the buffer stock, the price range and the costs of storing. The extent of the financial funds required could, in part, depend on the appropriate and equitable estimates of the commodity experts, but this alone can hardly be determined, as it depends on the willingness of governments to grant the financial resources needed.

Our reflections may underline the degree of difficulty involved in characterizeing buffer stock financing with a number of generally-applicable criteria. There is no doubt that financing is a factor which overlaps many others, all of which determine buffer stock constitution and operations.

It can be stated in general, however, that buffer stocks need great financial means and this calls for the financial participation of both producing and consuming countries. The greater the participation, the sooner the buffer stock operations can effectively start. This shows the direct interest that producing and consuming countries have in financial participation. Our conclusion is that financing does not represent an independent condition, but rather the result of several other constitutive factors such as the size of the buffer stock, the price range, the costs of storing, and, in addition, the potential decisions of governments with regard to their financial participation.

These comments may therefore be said to provide a brief characterization of the importance of the influence of the participation of both exporting and importing countries on the financing of the buffer stocks.

b) Criterion of the degree of instability in prices

The next step in the analysis of factors preponderant in the establishment of the buffer stock typology is to consider the criterion of the degree of instability in prices. A knowledge of this will make it possible to discuss, at a later stage, the size of the buffer stock, which should be large enough to meet the needs of variations in both supply and demand and to even out fluctuations in prices. The nature of fluctuations in commodity prices and the volume of products that enter international trade, reflect how unstable supply and demand conditions are.

Price instability can be regarded as a two-fold phenomenon

- annual average fluctuations, and
- year-to-year fluctuations.

According to the nature of the price fluctuations, primary commodities can be classified in two groups: those with

- strong price fluctuations , and those with
- price fluctuations that are not excessive, relatively speaking (10).

Attention has to be paid to the fact that certain commodities reveal the need for stabilization measures, for they manifest strong monthly price fluctuations, although their annual average oscillation could be classified as moderate.

Therefore, it may be said that the UNCTAD's commodity classification concept concerning strongly fluctuating prices and relatively stable prices, is rather rigid. There are a great number of primary commodities that are traded internationally and reveal their unstable features either through the annual

(10) The observations of UNCTAD revealed that strong price fluctuations are measured in sugar, copper, rice, cocoa, palm oil, tungsten, lead metal, bananas, rubber, copra, and price fluctuations which are not excessive, relatively speaking are to be seen in coffee, groundnut oil, coconut oil, sisal (until 1972), tea and cotton (until 1972).

average prices or through the monthly prices, and it should be realised that there are difficulties in expressing the price evolution simply through two categories. If the commodity classification is considered as follows

- tropical foodstuffs and beverages (including wheat, corn, rice, coffee, cocoa, tea, bananas and pepper),
- vegetable oils and seeds (soya beans, groundnuts, copra, palm oils, coconut oil, olive oil, linseed oil)
- ores and metals (phosphate, manganese, iron ore, aluminium, copper, lead, zinc, tin and tungsten)

on the basis of the statistical data for these groups of commodities, a figure can be established which represents their average annual price evolution (see Figure 10).

However, it has to be kept in mind that the figure given is only meant to make it easier for the reader to understand the approach to the general overview of the price fluctuations during the period between 1970 and 1980, which reveals the annual price situation as well. This does not mean that all the commodities presented, although they show price instability, need the stabilization measure through the buffer stocking policy. Neither does it mean that they are suitable for stocking. (This can be examined only by applying all the relevant criteria to the establishment of the buffer stock.

For this reason, despite the fact that commodity price fluctuations can be regarded as being either strong or relatively not excessive, the sub-category of the moderate price oscillations should also be taken into account. In order for the nature of the price oscillations to be appreciated, it must be pointed out that relatively not excessive price fluctuations do not mean moderate ones. The former are those which reveal fluctuations and therefore require a stabilization measure through the buffer stock operation, like tin, and the latter are those which manifest price fluctuations which are not necessarily great enough to justify such intervention.

Figure 10.

Annual average prices index for certain primary commodities, 1970-1980

(1975-1977=100)

Source: Figure is plotted on the basis of data calculated from: Monthly Bulletin of Commodity Prices, UNCTAD, various issues, 1970-1980, Geneva.

c) Natural commodities vis-à-vis synthetic substitutes

From our point of view, it seems worthwhile elaborating on the possible extrinsic criteria of the theoretical proposal for a buffer stock typology from the competitive relationship between natural commodities and their synthetic substitutes (11).

It should be recalled that the number of primary commodities (12) which are mainly produced in the LDCs are being challenged more and more by the competitive production of synthetic (13) substitutes made in the DCs.

The need for synthetic substitutes appears in developed countries where technological possibilities are developed. The research for their development is initiated in the first place by the strong fluctuations in the prices of natural commodities, and by the superior quality and ensured supply of the synthetic product.

When the prices of certain natural products tend to be relatively high, the necessity for synthetic substitutes becomes important, and is justified in commodities where changes and development of technology are provided.

Usually synthetics do not compete with natural commodities in the small time-schedule, due to the costs of production.

---

(11) Here, it may be remembered that two goods are substitutes if a rise in the price of one results in an increase in the demand for the other.

(12) Rubber, cotton, wool, jute, hard fibres, lauric oils, hides and skins, and even sugar.

(13) The possibility of substitution of natural products by other natural products should not be omitted. This substitution will not be the same as in the case of the synthetics. (The direct competition of a synthetic product to a natural one will probably start only after the optimum market price of the natural product has been given up. On the other hand, the relevant natural products may compete with each other from their initial supply). Only in the case where one LDC production is based on one monoculture, does substitution of another natural product risk creating special problems. However, there are no major obstacles that should prevent a solution to problems arising from this substitution, as it is generally accepted today that the problems of natural products should be solved by a global approach.

Therefore, price elasticity of demand for natural products tends to be rather low. However, when the price tends to be unstable, shown by a rising trend in the longer time-schedule, synthetics overtake the natural commodities because their costs of production become lower due to the investments made in production. The natural ones, in this case, start to manifest rather high price inelasticity of demand (14).

The extent to which synthetic substitutes will endanger natural products depends on a series of factors which are of financial, economic and technical origin. This, on the whole, aggravates the situation of the primary commodity producers, i.e. mainly LDCs, and, in turn, has a considerable effects on their price stabilization policy and their export earnings.

In our view, therefore, the problem we have considered regarding synthetic substitutes as a rival to natural products, shows that it not only influences the price of the commodity in the short-run, but also has marked effects on it in the long-run. It should be remembered that price instability can be manifested in the strong oscillations, which are more characteristic of the short-run, and in a secular decline of the price trend in real terms, which is more characteristic of the long-run. Whatever the aspect of the price instability, it causes negative repercussions on the countries which export as well as import the primary commodities. Thus, their common interest is to adopt the appropriate commodity control scheme to combat the price instability. On one hand, it is not self-evident that the buffer stock policy may be the best solution, but on the other hand, the criteria provided by the competition of synthetics argues in its favour, suggesting that something could be hoped for and realized with this type of stabilization policy. The buffer stock will become an efficient instrument when it can provide the natural product with factors similar to those of the synthetic product (in particular price stability, supply security and quality level).

3. Summary of the theoretical criteria

In Tables 17, 18 and 19 respectively, an attempt has been made to provide a general view of the theoretical intrinsic and extrinsic criteria for establishing different types of buffer stocks. The purpose was not to develop different commodity characteristics in order to get to a commodity typology, but to depict the criteria leading to the establishment of different types of buffer stocks. The question is justified as to whether buffer stock operations do not represent a clearly-defined mechanism and therefore could not even be taken into consideration for typology. However, on the other hand, the important point is whether it can be argued that different types of buffer stocks can be proposed on the basis of divers qualities registered in two groups of proposed criteria.

Table 18 shows that our choice was limited to the hypothetical commodities X, Y and Z. Here, delimitation has not been made, not in order to set up a commodity classification as such, but to show that intrinsic criteria purporting to group buffer stocks into different categories, appear in a different manner in commodities. Three broad categories of commodities have therefore been developed and it is assumed that all thirty-five internationally-traded commodities may be dealt with in one of these three.

If commodity X is a durable commodity, then it can be assumed that it belongs to the category of metals and minerals. If commodity Y is perishable, the assumption is that it could be classified in the group of food and tropical beverages; and if commodity Z is shown to be relatively non-perishable it could perhaps be identified as an agricultural product.

Table 19 shows that other qualities for buffer stocks, grouped under extrinsic criteria, concern those commodities that have no specific distinction. Being necessary, like intrinsic ones, the extrinsic criteria determine the creation of buffer stock typology in a rather uniform way.

This does not exclude the existence of differences from one analysed buffer stock to the other, but it will be a question of degree and of quantitative aspects.

It may be taken into account therefore, that all indispensable qualities and elements required for the implementation of one buffer stock operation for a specified commodity, will not necessarily correspond to those required for another one; this, in turn, determines the particular type of commodity control. In the manner indicated, it may be assumed that this approach to the buffer stock typology can be accepted.

Table 1.7.

SYNOPTIC TABLE

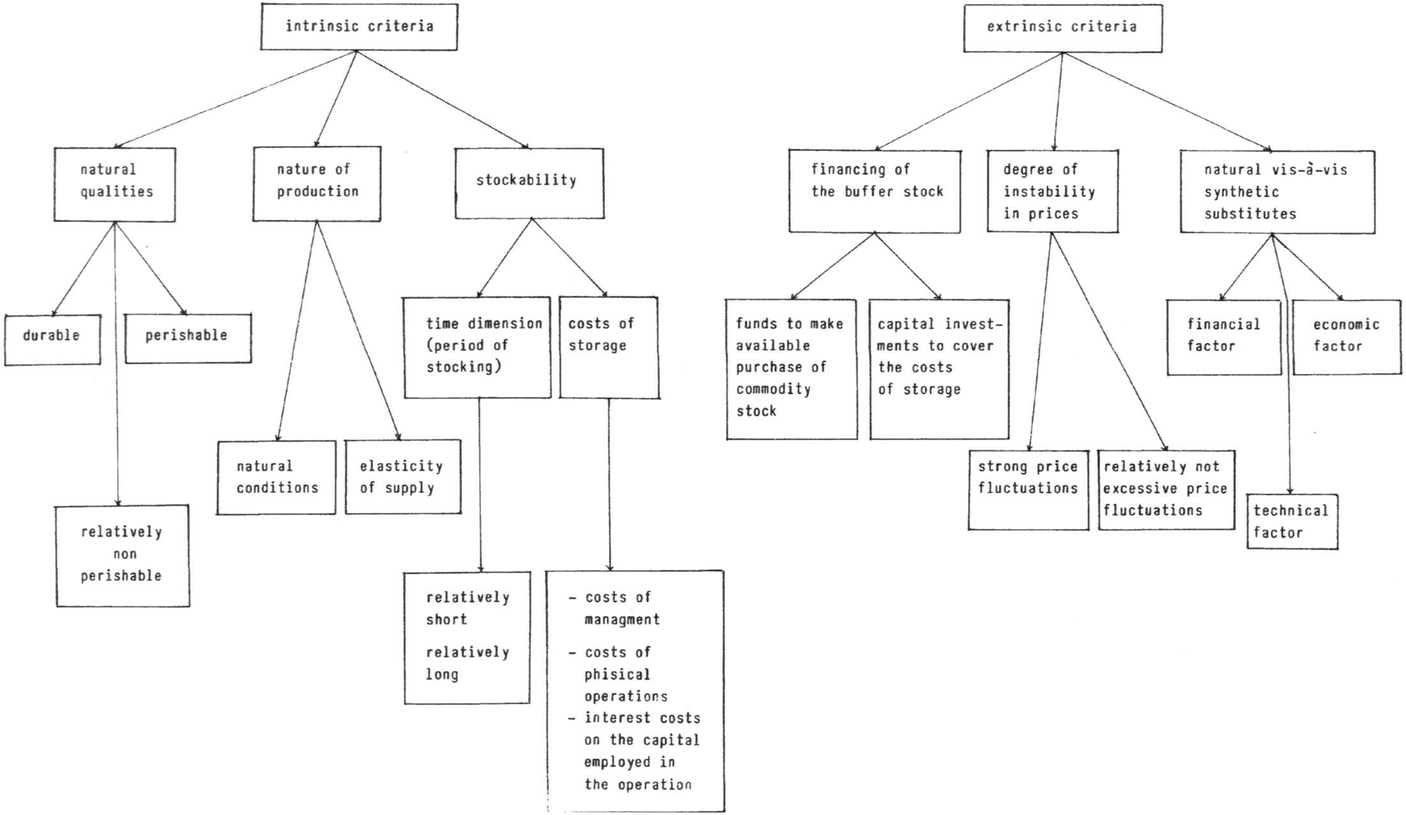

Table 18.

	Commodity		
	X	Y	Z
Intrinsic criteria			
(1) Natural qualities (if commodity is suitable for storing)			
(a) durable (storable)	Yes	No	No
(b) perishable (non storable)	No	Yes	No
(c) relatively non-peri-perishable (storable during limited time to avoid deterioration in quality)	No	No	Yes
(2) Nature of production			
(a) natural disasters (bring to shoratges of yields what in turn brings reduction into stocks)	No	Yes	No
(b) elasticity of supply - low	Yes	Yes	Yes
(3) Stockability (suitability for stocking)	Yes	No	Yes
(a) time dimension (period of storing			
a_1 unlimited	Yes	No	No
a_2 limited	No	No	Yes
a_3 short	No	Yes	No
(b) costs of storage (if they are relatively low)			
b_1 costs of management	Yes	Yes	Yes
b_2 costs of physical operations	Yes	Yes	Yes
b_3 interest costs on the capital employed in the operation	Yes	Yes	Yes

Table 19.

Extrinsic criteria

(1) The method of financing of the buffer stocks

(a) Funds to make available the purchases of commodity stock

- require participation of both importing and exporting countries;

(a) depends directly on - size of the buffer stock
- costs of storage;

(a) depens indirectly on - initial buying price
- price range.

(a) determines the capital investments to cover the costs of storage (b).

(b) capital investments to cover the costs of storage

- require participation of both importing and exporting countries;

(b) depends directly on - size of the buffer stock
- costs of storage

(b) depends indiractly on - initial buying price
- price range.

(2) The phenomenon of the degree of instability in prices

Strong price fluctuation determines the urgency of establishing of buffer stock.

Relatively not excessive price fluctuation determines the urgency of establishing of buffer stock.

(3) The phenomenon of natural products vis-à-vis syntetic substitutes

Existing financial factor (enough funds)
economic factor (price stabilization)
technical factor (quality control)

for the buffer stock provides sufficient elements that natural product can overtake in competition with synthetic substitutes.

B - APPLICATION OF THE CRITERIA TO THE BUFFER STOCKS KNOWN AT PRESENT

In this section our main objective will be to analyse the way in which theoretical criteria, which lead to the establishment of types of buffer stocks dealt with in the previous section, are applied in practice. This will make it possible to obsrve their effects in a more definite way and the conclusions will reflect their connection with reality.

Therefore, our interest here will be concentrated on the performance of two commodities, tin and cocoa, which were, and still are, the subject of the implementation of the buffer stock operations.

1. <u>The application of criteria in the case of tin buffer stock</u>

In the case of tin, the buffer stock control scheme has been in use for a long time. Accordingly, it is feasible to determine the theoretical criteria established and discussed previously. The first case to be taken into consideration is one where the importance of intrinsic criteria appears.

a) Tin intrinsic criteria

Natural qualities

Tin is a raw material because its combines are used in dying, weighting silk, fireproofing and medicine. Nearly fifty per cent of all tin is used as tinplate, as a thin coating of tin in the food-canning industry, or a thin coating on iron and steel in the electric and engineering industries. Economists give few data about the natural qualities. Our opinion is, however, that the natural qualities must be fully clarified before any primary commodity can be dealt with and classified any further.

Tin is a lustrous crystaline silver-white metallic element. Its characteristics are that it is very soft and can therefore be extended by beating, and is barely affected by humidity. Tin is scarcely affected by any external factors, except if heated in the air, and then it oxides only on the surface.

When the temperature is below 18°C, it tends to turn to grey powder. Tin is resistant to weak acids and, for that reason, is used to protect other metals, as a base mixture.

Due to its natural qualities and characteristics, it can be concluded that tin can be classified as a durable commodity. There is also the fact that tin is a natural product produced mainly in LDCs. In keeping with these characteristics, tin was, and still is, a commodity where buffer stock operations are used as a control commodity scheme. As such, it is stockable with no major difficulties concerning deterioration in quality.

Nature of production

Tin is a mining product and the volume of its production is not influenced by natural conditions (i.e. variation in weather, etc.), a factor which is of great importance when agricultural commodities are in question. Therefore, it is important to add that natural conditions have no effect on the tin production cycles.

Tin rarely occurs in a pure form in nature and, for that reason, tin metal is obtained by extracting it from tin concentrates. The trends in the world tin production and consumption are presented in a summary, in Table 20, of the world figures, and this is followed by the annual and quarterly charts, respectively A and B. Each of the given data shows clearly that production in primary tin metal and in tin-in-concentrates exceeds consumption, which shows marked fluctuations from 1973 onwards, with the lowest level of 178,100 tons in 1975 (included in the period between 1971 and 1979 as shown in Table 20).

The existing tin reserves are still abundant and, therefore, the variation in its production cycle is not a cause for worry. One reason for anxiety is that the progressive exhaustion of the existing reserves has not been covered by a discovery of new tin deposits. From these statements, it can be concluded that the whole pattern of tin internationally traded is therefore dependent on the price of tin. Thus, as tin is

Table 20.

World figures of the primary tin metal production and consumption

Annual	Production '000 tonnes	Consumption '000 tonnes
1971	185.5	189.4
1972	191.3	192.0
1973	187.3	214.2
1974	181.1	200.1
1975	178.1	173.9
1976	182.2	193.9
1977	179.7	185.2
1978	193.2	185.8
1979	204.0	188.2
1980	198.9	175.6
1981	202.	162.

Source: International Tin Council, Monthly Statistical Bulletin, June 1980, No. 6, vol. XXIV, London.

especially sensitive to the changes in consumption, its production also relies on the price obtained (14).

Stockability

Commodities from the mining sector have a larger potential of conservation than agricultural products, and this potential extends to an unlimited period of maintenance. The period,therefore, during which tin can be stored and still preserve its qualities without disproportionate deterioration can be qualified as unlimited (15).

Classified as a durable product due to its natural qualities, tin manifests a high stocking ability, and the higher the stockability, the easier the regulation of quantitative supply. The stocking ability meets the economic limits in the costs of storage, which, in the case of tin, demands less specific conditions (i.e. temperature, humidity, etc.) than for the agricultural products. The extent to which the costs of holding and maintaining stocks for tin, tin-in-concentrates and tin metal differ in temperate and tropical zones can be seen from Table 21, established on the basis of UNCTAD data.

It seems important, therefore, that a glance should suffice to show the composition of the total storage costs, as they are a complex and decisive factor in analysing the suitability of commodities for stocking.

As for the holding and maintaining of stocks, there are a certain number of problems which arise. These can be systematized as follows:

- "the method of calculation utilized in computing rental costs and rotation costs in order to construct total storage costs;

---

(14) EDWARDS, John, "The International Tin Agreement", J.W.T.L., vol. 3, No. 3, May-June 1969, pp. 237-250.

(15) In Table 21,the available data of the UNCTAD were used, which helped to show that the maximum conservation period,as well as maximum storage period,for tin-in-concentrates and tin metal, in both temperate and tropical zones, are characterized as unlimited.

WORLD TIN PRODUCTION AND CONSUMPTION

■ Production of tin-in-concentrates

☒ Production of primary tin metal

☐ Consumption of primary tin metal

CHART A: ANNUAL

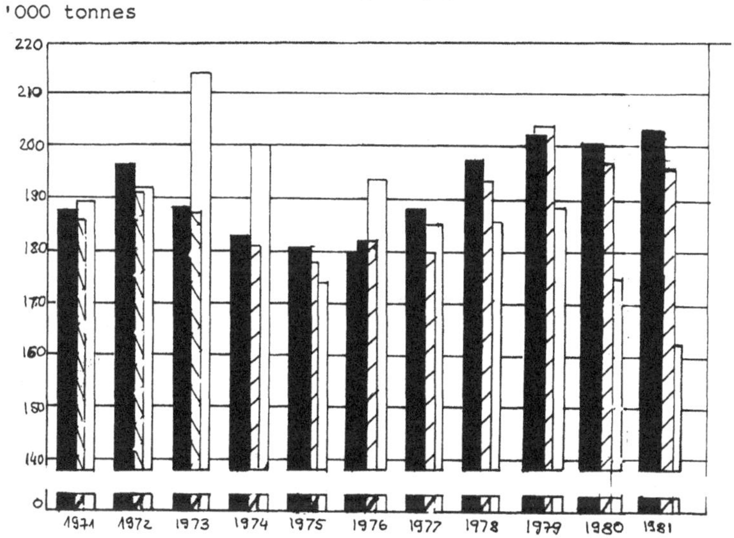

CHART B: QUARTERLY

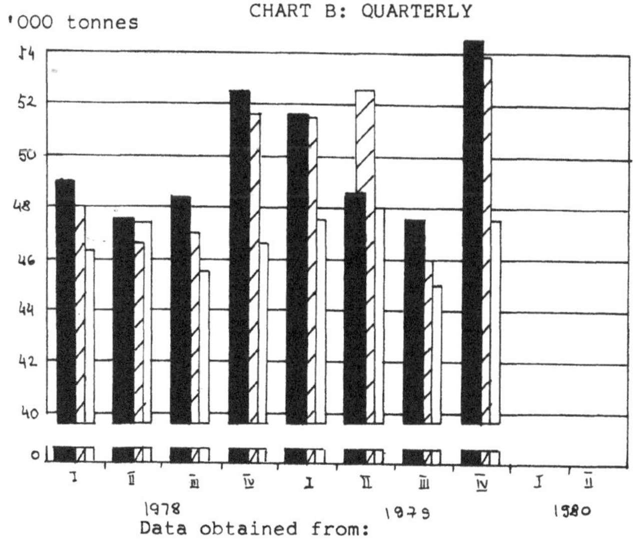

Data obtained from:

Source: International Tin Council, Mounthly Statistical Bulletin, June 1980, No.6, vol. XXIV, London.

Table 21.

Costs of holding and maintaining stocks: Tin

$/MT/Year	Temperate zone			Tropical zone		
	Low	Medium	High	Low	Medium	High
Tin concentrates:						
Rental[a]	6.00	23.40	33.60	7.50	-	-
Rotation[b]	-	-	-	-	-	-
Total	6.00[c]	23.40[d]	33.60[e]	7.50[f]		
Tin metal:						
Rental[a]	8.76	14.56	32.00	7.00	9.50	36.00
Rotation[b]	-	-	-	-	-	-
Total	8.76[g]	14.56[h]	32.00[i]	7.00[j]	9.50[k]	36.00[l]

Source: UNCTAD secretariat estimates. An
An integrated program for commodities: Second progress report on storage costs and warehous facilities, TD/B/C.1/198, 29 September 1975, Annex I, p.l.

c/ Bolivia
d/ United Kingdom
e/ Netherlands
f/ Indonesia
g/ United States
h/ Belgium
i/ Bolivia
j/ Indonesia
k/ Thailand
l/ Malaysia

- the identification of representative costs between exporting and importing countries and geographic regions;
- the problem of distinguishing between long- and short-term storage costs" (16).

Therefore, thanks to this systematization (17) in the case of tin, rental costs, associated with rotation costs, will give, as a result, the total cost for holding and maintaining the stocks. Here information should be provided with regard to rental and rotation costs.

Rental costs - represent the total of insurance costs, interest and amortization on capital costs of the facility, maintenance, management overheads, labour energy and profit margins. The cost of moving a commodity into, and out of, storage during the regular commercial transactions is also included in the rental costs (18).

Rotation costs - are those costs associated with moving a commodity into or out of storage, in order to prevent physical deterioration. These costs are calculated on a yearly basis. If, for example, a commodity needs to be rotated twice in one year, then the in-and-out costs would have to be multiplied by a factor of two (19).

In Table 10, the costs of holding and maintaining stocks for tin were calculated for three representative levels of costs - low, medium and high. From this, it can be seen that low rental costs for tin metal, combined with

---

(16) COLEBROOK, J., "The Cost of Storing Primary Commodities", J.W.T.L., vol.2, No. 4, July-August 1977, p. 370.

(17) Colebrook's systematization is based on the analysis of UNCTAD's data for the ten "core" commodities especially covered in the UNCTAD documents TD/B/C.1/198, TD/B/C.1/187 and TD/B/C.1/196.

(18) An Integrated Programme for Commodities: Second progress report on storage costs and warehouse facilities, UNCTAD, TD/B/C.1/198, 29 September 1975, Annex I, p. 1.

(19) An Integrated Programme for Commodities, ibid., Annex, p.1.

low rotation costs, result in a low total cost estimate in developing countries. For this reason, it can be conluded that tin can be stored at relatively low costs, which satisfies one of the criteria for determining its suitability for buffer stocks operations.

b) Tin extrinsic criteria

Financing of the buffer stock

In the case of tin, financing of the buffer stock has been effected mainly by the producers, all of which are developing countries (20), although certain consuming countries have made voluntary contributions (21). The fact that voluntary contribution in financing the tin buffer stock appeared only in the Fourth International Agreement shows the importing countries' refusal to accept their share in the task of market stability,

This reveals that, for a long time, there was no international financial support. The first source of financial aid appeared in 1969, when the International Monetary Fund made available the financial resources for producing countries that were members of the Agreement.These resources were granted to finance the international buffer stock operated by the International Tin Agreement. The borrowing scheme was of the short-term type and the amount in question was rather small (US $ 37 million). If the consuming countries had been willing to supply the required finances, the international tin buffer stock could have been effective even during the period of rising prices. In a situation like this, the consuming countries could have

---

(20) Annual world production of tin is about 200,000 t., 37% of which is produced by Malaysia, 19% by Bolivia, 17% by Thailand and 16% by Indonesia.

(21) Voluntary contributions were made during the Fourth International Tin Agreement only by two consuming countries, France and the Netherlands. The number of voluntary participants in the current Sixth International Tin Agreement has increased to eight consuming countries, namely Belgium, Canada, Denmark, France, Japan, the Netherlands, Norway and the United Kingdom.

saved considerably, while increasing their annual tin consumption. This would have constituted an economic gain greater than the capital costs involved. Moreover, if the financial burden had been shared, exporting countries could have been in a position to raise financial resources that could have been used for development.

These were past experiences which,however, took on a new dimension with the establishment of the Common Fund under the Integrated Programme for Commodities (22). The principle which has been accepted is the joint financing of buffer stocks by the producing and consuming member countries participating in the Sixth International Tin Agreement.

From this point of view, it can be said that the participation of both tin importing and exporting member countries underlines the need for large financial sums to satisfy the double requirement for the financing of the tin buffer stocks:

- funds necessary to make available the purchase of tin stock, and
- certain regular capital investments necessary to cover costs of storage, including the interest costs on the capital employed in the operation.

Nevertheless, taking a broad approach, it can be added that the financing of the tin buffer stock, as an extrinsic criterion,does not stand alone and should be regarded as one element which is interdependent on the other factors, where the predominant rôle is played by the size of the buffer stock and its price range.

Degree of instability
in prices

It is an indisputable fact that the criterion of the degree of instability in tin prices represents an important factor for the buffer stock typology. The nature and characteristics of tin price instability can be defined

---

(22) Agreed in March 1979,but not yet ratified.

through its

- annual average fluctuations, and
- year-to-year fluctuations.

As a mining product, and due to its intrinsic criteria, tin can be regarded as a commodity with relatively not excessive price fluctuations. This, however, does not necessarily mean that tin price fluctuations are not sufficient to justify buffer stock intervention.

It is true that the price oscillations in the market are more limited, but this is due to the international buffer stocking arrangement and the US strategic stockpile behind it. Thus, to see how the degree of instability in tin prices varies from year to year, quarterly and monthly, Table 22 may be useful. In the period extending over the last ten years, as presented in Table 22, tin prices have shown a steady increase. The significant increase in 1979 reveals a level nearly six times greater than that reached in 1971. During the ten-year period, especially 1973-1974 and 1977-1978, the increase in the price of tin was twice as large as in previous years, and in 1979, over a period of one year, it doubled once again. After the fall in the first quarter of 1978, tin prices continued to increase, although still subject to certain minor oscillations. In general terms, it can be said that these price changes are directly related to the changes in supply and/or demand for tin in the international market. Both producing and consuming countries are therefore interested in price stabilization methods. Producers wish to see such methods introduced because of the decreasing prices (this can be explained partially by the liquidation of US strategic stockpiles), and because consumer see them as a means of security.

So far the intrinsic and extrinsic criteria of the tin buffer stock have been considered. An attempt has been made to apply the theory and to see how realistic it is in practical terms.

Table 22.

World figures of the primary tin metal prices

Annual	New York US c/lb.	Quarterly	New York US c/lb.
1971	167	1978 I	542
1972	177	II	533
1973	227	III	601
1974	396	IV	684
1975	340	1979 I	672
1976	375	II	700
1977	533	III	705
1978	589	IV	752
1979	707	1980 I	811

Monthly			
1978 J	553	1979 J	640
F	557	F	677
M	521	M	697
A	503	A	692
M	533	M	696
J	562	J	710
J	567	J	715
A	600	A	691
S	635	S	712
O	691	O	734
N	709	N	749
D	650	D	776
1980 J	782		
F	810		
M	841		
A	815		
M	805		

Source: International Tin Council, Monthly Statistical Bulletin, June 1980, No.6, vol. XXIX, London.

Figure 11.

World tin metal production

1981

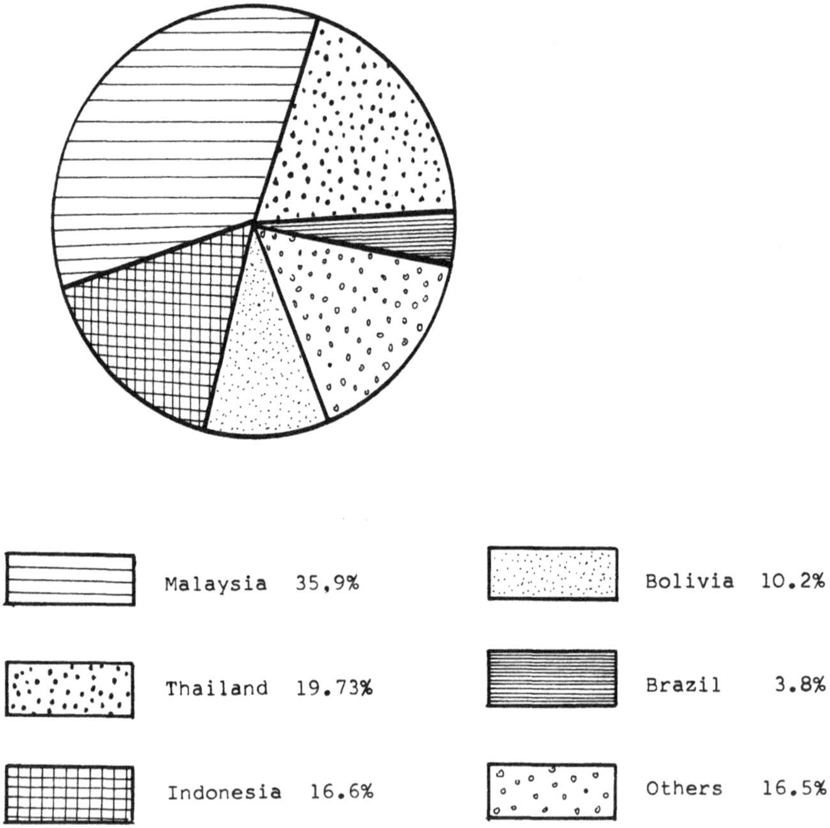

Source: The Figure is plotted on the basis of data computed from International Tin Council, 1980.

At this point, various factors may be distinguished which contribute to the fact that tin qualifies as one of the primary commodities especially suitable for the application of the buffer stock procedure as a means of price stabilization in this market.

In conclusion, it can be affirmed that tin is a durable commodity; durable in terms of the natural characteristics developed within the intrinsic criteria. Therefore, it is evident that it cannot be subject to seasonal fluctuations.

Another intrinsic criterion, storage cost, has been shown to be low in relation to its value and this is an incontestable asset as regards its stocking potential.

As far as the tin market itself is concerned, it must be pointed out that the greatest part of the tin negotiations and commercial business are carried out in three chief markets - Penang, London and New York.

Additionally, the consideration which is of major importance when an international agreement is to be concluded is that producing countries are few in number (see Figure 11). This constitutes a sound asset as regards reaching an agreement and it applies to the case of tin.

2. The application of criteria in the case of cocoa buffer stock

In the case of cocoa there is a specific commodity to be dealt with. For a long while, it was proposed that cocoa should be regulated in the international market through the buffer stock mechanism. This control scheme has been the most precisely elaborated in the case of cocoa.

Theoretically, the International Cocoa Agreement was operative, as was its buffer stock control scheme, but in practice, it proved to be exactly the opposite - inoperative

(23). Our particular aim here will be to apply to the case of cocoa both the intrinsic and extrinsic theoretical criteria already established.

a) Cocoa intrinsic criteria

Natural qualities

Cocoa is a primary commodity as it is a crop (moreover a perennial crop), i.e. grown on the land. It is a tropical American tree which bears fruit, the pods containing a sweetish pulp in which are rows of seed, so-called "cocoa-beans". These beans are used for trade. After being dried, the seeds are screened, roasted and skinned. The result are clean kernals known as cocoa nibs. They are processed into various products, e.g. edible chocolate and cocoa, and cocoa butter, they are used medicinally (for emollients, etc.) and in cosmetics (fine soaps); surplus is pounded into to cocoa powder and used for beverages and flavouring. As a brief concluding remark about the characteristic traits of cocoa, it can be said that it would be of considerable interest to expand this rough outline concerning natural qualities. They are interesting and important for the reader. As opposed to tin, which is a mineral product and hence a durable commodity, and therefore a stockable one, cocoa is an agricultural commodity with its own features, which classify it as a relatively non-perishable product. As such, it is stockable for a certain period without any appreciable deterioration in its quality.

---

(23) Briefly, to recall, the main reason for the failure of the International Cocoa Conferences was the attitude of the importing countries towards the fixing of the floor price. Although there was a basis for compromise, the importing countries (led by the United States) could not agree on a floor price.

Nature of production

Cocoa is an example of a tropical agricultural product. It is a tree crop and hence the volume of its production is highly influenced by

- natural conditions (variation in climatic conditions) and/or
- plant illness, and
- the time-lag for harvest.

The time-lag between the planting and harvesting of cocoa is eight to twelve years. In this period, harvest yields for cocoa may either increase or decrease. A decrease in cocoa yields can be avoided if the soil gets enough nourishment, which, in turn, will help the cocoa-tree to improve during its total period of productivity, which averages thirty to forty years.

The extent to which the weather can influence the cocoa yield and its quality is very difficult to estimate, although this will affect cocoa prices and, therefore, elasticity of supply. Evidence of this sort is related to the fact that, between the period when the cocoa flowers blossom and the development of the mature pods, there is a six-month time span. During this period, only a small number of flowers produce mature pods owing to different plant illnesses or flower dropping due to the changeable climatic conditions (heavy rains).

As far as the time-lag for harvest is concerned, another relevant factor must be taken into account, i.e. the current cocoa price. If the cocoa price shows an upward trend, then there is a risk that cocoa will be harvested before it is sufficiently matured. Such a process will result in a deterioration in the quality of the cocoa beans which, in turn,will lower the quality of the products manufactured from them (24). Therefore, natural conditions have an important effect on the cocoa production cycles.

The response of cocoa planting to changes in prices is rather slight as it takes eight to twelve years from the planting to the harvesting of the first crop. Therefore, cocoa supply is largely price-inelastic (25). With regard to demand, it can be said to be concentrated in a relatively small number of consumer-countries where it is used as a component part in beverages, edible chocolate, cosmetics and pharmaceutical products. All these sectors where cocoa is used as an ingredient do not represent an essential need. For this reason, price elasticity as regards demand is greater than for coffee,for example, or tea, as a greater preference is shown for these. Therefore, due to severe price fluctuations, cocoa supply and demand can hardly be matched. Such a situation in the cocoa market shows its great instability, which makes it a domain urgently needing stabilizing intervention.

The imbalance between the cocoa production cycle and consumption trends can be seen from Table 23, which presents a summary of the world production and consumption of cocoa beans. Table 23 is followed by the annual chart C. Each of the given data shows the existing imbalance between the production and consumption from the crop-year 1966-67 up to 1980-81. In the period from 1966-68, production and consumption were more or less levelled. Then,in the crop-year of 1968-69,supply movements were too low in comparison with the demand, marking the lowest production level of 1, 236,000 tons.

---

(24) C.P.Brown suggests a threefold division of factors affecting crops: long-run, medium-run and short-run. According to Brown, in the case of cocoa it could be said that long-run factors affecting cocoa crops correspond to the yield of cocoa-trees which comes only 8-12 years after planting. Medium-run factors are those which have an influence during the time which is needed for the flowers to produce mature pods, and short-run factors affecting cocoa crops are the current prices. For a more detailed discussion of these factors affecting crops see BROWN, C.P., <u>op.cit</u>., pp.6-8.

(25) The reader should keep in mind the two factors concerning the nature of production, which are: natural conditions, and elasticity of supply elaborated in section A.

Table 23.

World Figures for the Production and Consumption of Cocoa Beans

Crop Year	Production '000 tons	Consumption '000 tons
1966-7	1,336	1,367
1967-8	1,352	1,366
1968-9	1,236	1,410
1969-70	1,424	1,353
1970-1	1,493	1,357
1971-2	1,583	1,439
1972-3	1,398	1,567
1973-4	1,447	1,557
1974-5	1,550	1,478
1975-6	1,502	1,463
1976-7	1,348	1,519
1977-8	1,503	1,366
1978-9	1,499	1,367
1979-80	1,623	1,422
1980-81 1/	1,629	1,493

1/ Estimates by Secretariat of ICCO

Source: Commodity Year Book, 1980, International Cocoa Organization, vol. 7, No.2, March 1981.

WORLD COCOA BEANS PRODUCTION AND CONSUMPTION

■ Production of cocoa beans
▨ Consumption of cocoa beans

CHART C: ANNUAL (Crop Year)

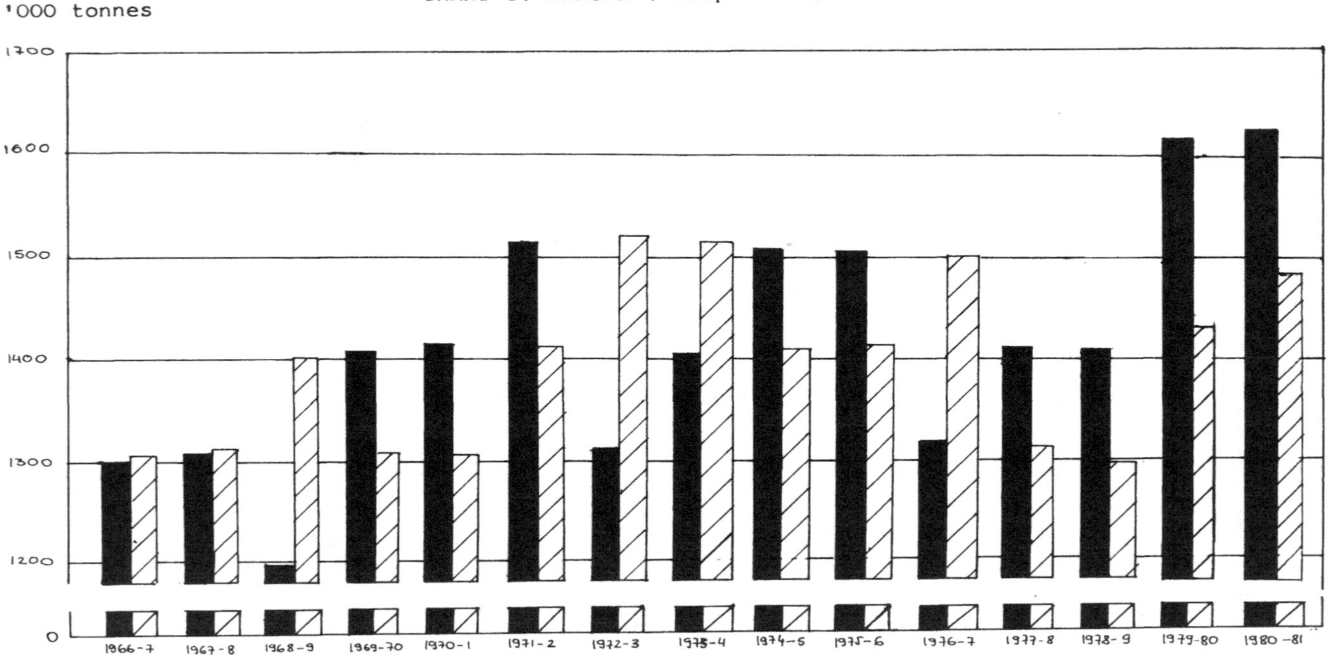

In the period 1971-72, production showed a remarkable recovery owing to the favourable crop-year, and reached a level of 1, 583,000 tons. Consumption was lower due to the price boom and rose in the two successive crop-years, from 1972 to 1974. In 1976-77 production slumped to 1, 341,000 tons due to unfavourable weather conditions. In this situation, consumption did not react accordingly as it showed quite a high level of 1, 519,000 tons. The years 1979-80 and 1980-81 reflect the increased production of 1, 607,000 and 1, 612,000 tons respectively, due to the favourable supply conditions.

As is shown by the world figures over the last 15 years, cocoa production and consumption manifest great instability due to unfavourable weather, and adverse political, conditions.

The data for production and consumption of cocoa beans can be supplemented by the figures for the world exports and imports, all of which present a real picture of the world trade in cocoa. For this reason, the last five years presented in Table 24 have been chosen to give an indication of the world figures of the annual exports and imports of cocoa beans.

The short-run behaviour of exports and imports, i.e. quarterly, can be seen from Table 25, which covers quarterly data for 1978-79 and the 1979-80 crop-year. These tables are followed by the annual and quarterly charts, D and E respectively, of the world exports and imports of cocoa beans.

According to the data available from the ICO secretariat, world exports of cocoa beans were substantially higher in the 1975-76 crop-year compared with the exports realized in 1979-80, with a visible difference of 151,000 tons. World imports of cocoa beans during 1979-80, compared with the 1975-76 crop-year, dropped by 190,000 tons. If the world imports of cocoa beans during 1979-80 at 976,000 tons are compared with the previous crop-year, it will be observed that they dropped by 6 per cent.

Table 24.

World figures for the exports and imports of cocoa beans

Crop Year	Exports '000 tonnes	Imports '000 tonnes
1975-76	1,120	1,166
1976-77	970	1,049
1977-78	981	1,007
1978-79	991	1,039
1979-80	969	976

Source: Quarterly Bulletin of Cocoa Organization, vol. VII, No.2, March 1981, International Cocoa Organization, ICCO, London.

Table 25.

World total cocoa beans exports and imports quarterly
1978/79 - 1979/80

Quarterly	Exports '000 tonnes	Imports '000 tonnes
1978/79		
Apr-Jun	188	244
Jul-Sep	162	215
1979/80		
Oct-Dec	241	210
Jan-Mar	271	249
Apr-Jun	175	266
Jul-Sep	280	250

Source: Quarterly Bulletin of Cocoa Statistics, vol.VII, No.2, March 1981, International Cocoa Organization, ICCO, London.

WORLD TOTAL COCOA BEANS EXPORTS AND IMPORTS

Exports of cocoa beans
Imports of cocoa beans

CHART D: ANNUAL (Crop Year)

'000 tonnes

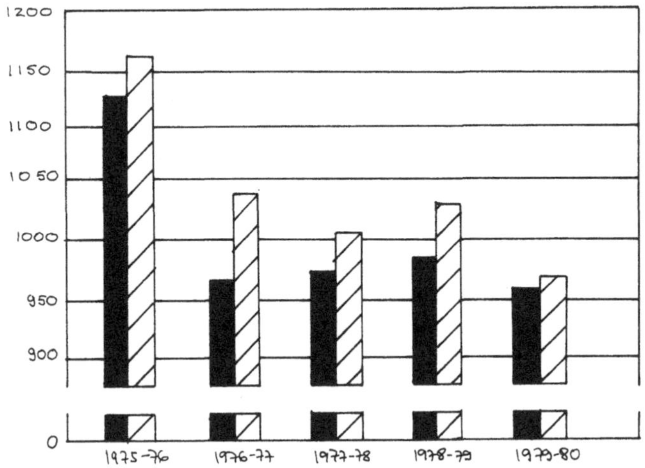

CHART E: QUARTERLY

'000 tonnes

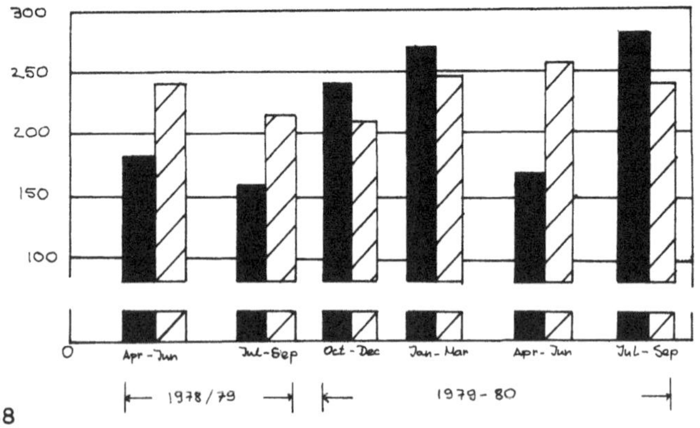

With regard to the quarterly behaviour Table 14 may be consulted. As the given data show, world exports of cocoa beans in the last quarter of 1979-80 (June-September 1980) exceeded 280,000 tons. This is substantially higher than the exports for the final quarter of 1978-79 (June-September 1979). The world quarterly imports of cocoa beans in July-Sptember 1980 amounted to 250,000 tons. This represents an increase of 16 per cent over the same quarter of the previous year.

Therefore, on the basis of the data given for world trade in cocoa in the 1979-80 crop-year, it can be said that, compared to those for 1978-79, despite higher production, world exports of cocoa beans decreased by 2 per cent. These statements are enough for us to conclude that trade in cocoa is one of the most unstable domains in the primary products that are internationally traded. An indication has been given of the tendency of cocoa where production exceeds consumption, and vice versa. This presentation underlines the major problem in the trade of less-developed countries, as cocoa exports represent a significant proportion of the export earnings of several LDCs.

Stockability

Contrary to the case of commodities from the mining sector, agricultural products have a limited duration of conservation. For this reason the time dimension, the period during which commodities are properly stored and preserved without disproportionate deterioration, is of fundamental importance for agricultural commodities, i.e. in our case of cocoa.

Due to its natural qualities and the nature of production, cocoa cannot be stored easily in the producing countries, that is to say, in tropical zones. The quality of cocoa deteriorates rapidly in the hot, humid climatic conditions in which it is grown. Therefore, it must be shipped correctly, and any agreement to stabilize prices must take this fact into account. If cocoa is stored in tropical or temperate zones, a period must be allowed for, during which, if properly stored, it can be preserved without disproporionate deterioration.

Cocoa beans, can be stored for 3-4 years given the proper temperature and humidity (26), and if that period is exceeded, the percentage of deterioration will be a 2 per cent weight loss. Opinions are divided as to the maximum length of the cocoa storage period, and some of them suggest that the storage period can be substantially longer than 3-4 years, while others argue that cocoa can be stored for up to two years in temperate zone warehouses but not more than two months in tropical zones because of the risk of fermentation.

These opinions concerning the cocoa storage period meet the economic limits in the costs of storage. In the case of cocoa, since it is an agricultural product, certain specific conditions are required (i.e. humidity, temperature, etc.). The extent to which the costs of holding and maintaining cocoa stocks differ in the temperate and tropical zones can be seen from Table 26. The conditions laid down in Table 26 represent a share of representative total storage costs (rental and rotation) (27), elaborated for eleven primary commodities (28) by UNCTAD. Data given in Table 26 provide information about low, medium and high costs of holding and maintaining cocoa stocks. From this point of view, while cocoa rental costs are low in tropical zone conditions (3.47), rotation costs are nearly seven

(26) An Integrated Programme for Commodities: Progress report on storage costs and warehouse facilities, UNCTAD, TD/B/C.1/187, 3rd June 1975, Annex I, p.3.

(27) Storage costs are calculated in U.S.$ per metric ton, per year.

(28) Copper, tin, sugar, vegetable oilseeds, hard fibres, jute, cotton, rubber, tea and cocoa (i.e. ten "core commodities" plus vegetable oilseeds as a specific case).

Table 26.

Costs of holding and maintaining stocks: Cocoa

$/MT/Year	Temperate zone			Tropical zone		
	Low	Medium	High	Low	Medium	High
Cocoa:						
Rental[a]	16.65	24.01	54.29	3.47	16.48	-
Rotation[b]	4.30	10.60	3.42	24.00	20.74	-
Total	20.95[c]	34.61[d]	57.71[e]	27.47[f]	37.60[g]	-

Source: UNCTAD estimates.
An integrated programme for commodities: Second progress report on storage costs and warehaus facilities, TD/B/C.1/198, 29 September 1975, Annex IV, p.l.

a/ Rental costs include: insurance, interest and amortization on capital cost of the facility, maintenance, management overheads, labor, energy, profit margines.

b/ Rotation costs are those costs associated with moving a commodity into or out of storage in order to prevent phisycal deteri ration. These costs have been calculated on a yearly basis. For those commodities where period rotation - movement into and out of storage - is necessary to preserve quality, in and out charges must be multiplied by the number of times rotation and internal cycling is required within a year. If, for example, a commodity is required to be rotated twice in one year, than in and out costs would have to be multiplied by a factor of two. If on the other hand, a commodity required rotation only once every two years, in and out costs would be divided by a factor of two.

c/ United Kingdom

d/ Germany, Federal Repablic of.

e/ France

f/ Ghana (Takoradi/Tema)

g/ Ivory Coast/Abidjan

times higer (24.00) because of the need for more frequent rotation. Therefore, the total low cost in tropical zones is much higher than the total low cost in temperate zones (developed countries), although here the situation is reversed, i.e. low rental costs are higher (16.65) than rotation low costs (4.30).

Such considerations point to the conclusion that, due to its natural qualities, its nature of production and its stocking ability, cocoa is a storable commodity and can be classified as relatively non-perishable. Hence, it has all the necessary qualifications for international buffer stock regulation.

b) Cocoa extrinsic criteria

Financing of the buffer stock

In the case of cocoa, financing of the buffer stock has been affected mainly by the number of cocoa-producing countries. Only nine countries produce significant amounts (29). Five of these (30) are alone responsible for 80 per cent of the total world cocoa exports. The producing countries accumulated financial resources which were deposited with the International Cocoa Council,the purpose of which was to deal with pecuniary resources and finance the buffer stock control mechanism when needed, i.e. in the periods of surplus supply of cocoa on the international market.

---

(29) Producing countries exporting 10,000 tones or more of bulk cocoa annually are Brazil, Mexico, Nigeria, Togo, and United Republic of Cameroon. International Cocoa Agreement 1980, TD/COCOA.6/EX/R.1, 17th November 1980,Geneva, Annex A.

(30) Ghana's exports, as the largest producer for 1978/79, amounted to 206,826 tons, Ivory Coast 267,990, Nigeria 124,491, Brazil 145,858, Cameroon 67,182 tons.

The new, Third International Cocoa Agreement (31), in order to improve its performance and as a reinforcement of the International Cocoa Council (ICC) in regulating the financial side of the buffer stock in periods of over-supply, under article 32, is related to the Common Fund for Commodities. The ICC"...shall have the authority to negotiate the modalities, ... with a view to making full use of the financial possibilities offered by the Fund"(32), but only when the Common Fund for commodities becomes operational (33). This statement embodies the global concept of the co-operation of producing and consuming countries. This was the cocoa producers' aim when the ICA on cocoa was established, for they had to find the means of financing stocks. Indeed, the buffer stock intervention fund of 230 Mio $ under the administration of the International Cocoa Organization is made available to the exporting countries by the new agreement with the aim of stabilizing cocoa prices.

Only the future will show the way in which the financing mechanism will operate, for the institutionalised price support effected by the manager of the buffer stock in association with the International Cocoa Organization did not take place until the beginning of the 1981/1982 crop-year.

---

(31) The Third International Cocoa Agreement was established on 19th November, 1980, after a long period of negotiations. It came into force on 1st August, 1981.Nevertheless, the Ivory Coast, today's first world cocoa producer refused, and still refuses, to ratify it, as does the USA, the world's major cocoa importer. In spite of this fact, ICA on Cocoa came into force because at least 80% of the voters from cocoa-producing countries and at least 70% from cocoa- importing countries were in favour of its being signed. Today the Ivory Coast realizes 23% of the total world exports, (which means that Ghana and Brazil have been left behind), and its active participation in the ICA on cocoa is of considerable importance.

(32) Third International Cocoa Agreement, 1980, UNCTAD, TD/COCOA.6/EX/R.1, 17th November, 1980, Art. 32, p.21.

(33) Agreed in March 1979, but not yet ratified.

The fact should be borne in mind that the attitude of the Ivory Coast in not ratifying the Agreement calls into question the real functioning of the ICA on cocoa. Whether the Ivory Coast, as the main producer, and the USA, as the main consumer, could take a more co-operative line, is still uncertain.

Nevertheless, there are a number of points in favour of the Cocoa Agreement (such as the unstable price trend), and therefore there still remains some hope that the Ivory Coast and the USA will join it and facilitate its operation, which, in turn, will facilitate, and render more realistic, the financing of the cocoa buffer stock.

Finally, it should be pointed out that the financing of the cocoa buffer stock was an unsolved problem in the previous ICA on cocoa. Buffer stock was capable of financing its own purchases from its own resources, and the factor that made it inoperative was prices which were much higher than the agreed price range.

The majority of producing and consuming countries are willing to provide the large financial resources which would satisfy the basic requirements for the functioning of the buffer stock:

- funds available to make necessary purchase of cocoa stock, and
- certain regular capital investment necessary to cover the costs of storage.

Thus it can be concluded that the financing of the buffer stock does not represent the most difficult problem to be solved in the case of cocoa as it does in the case of tin.

Degree of instability
in prices

The criterion of the degree of instability in cocoa prices represents a challenge and many attempts have been made to try to cope with it. Past experiences of price regulation of the cocoa market through the ICA s showed that it was barely capable of functioning.

For a long time, the major difficulty seems to have resided in determining the price range for intervention in selling and buying with the aim of achieving cocoa market stabilization. Indeed, cocoa bean prices, due to the nature of their production and their natural qualities, and to the interaction of the considerable inelasticity of supply and demand, were said to be "among the least stable prices of all primary commodities" (34). Therefore, the nature and general characteristics of cocoa price instability can be looked at under the headings of a two-fold phenomenon, which have been worked out theoretically:

- annual average fluctuations, and
- year-to-year fluctuations.

Cocoa, since it is an agricultural product, and owing to its intrinsic criteria, is regarded as a commodity with very strong price fluctuations which are manifested in both categories: annual average and year-to-year oscillations. In both cases, cocoa prices vary greatly. This can be seen from Figure 12, where data for cocoa bean prices have been presented, which reveal the international significance of London (35) and New York (36) spot Ghana prices.

---

(34) RASHISH, M., "A New Cocoa Agreement?", Law and Policy in International Business, 11th September, 1975, p. 17.

(35) Since 1974, the London spot Ghana price has been in bond ex store UK/North European ports, based on current market levels. Previously, it had been an estimate of Gill and Duffus for Ghana cocoa beans in bond ex store, main UK ports.

(36) The New York spot Ghana price are ex warehouse and fixed daily by the official committee.

Figure 12.

Cocoa beans price of international significance annual averages, 1960-1980

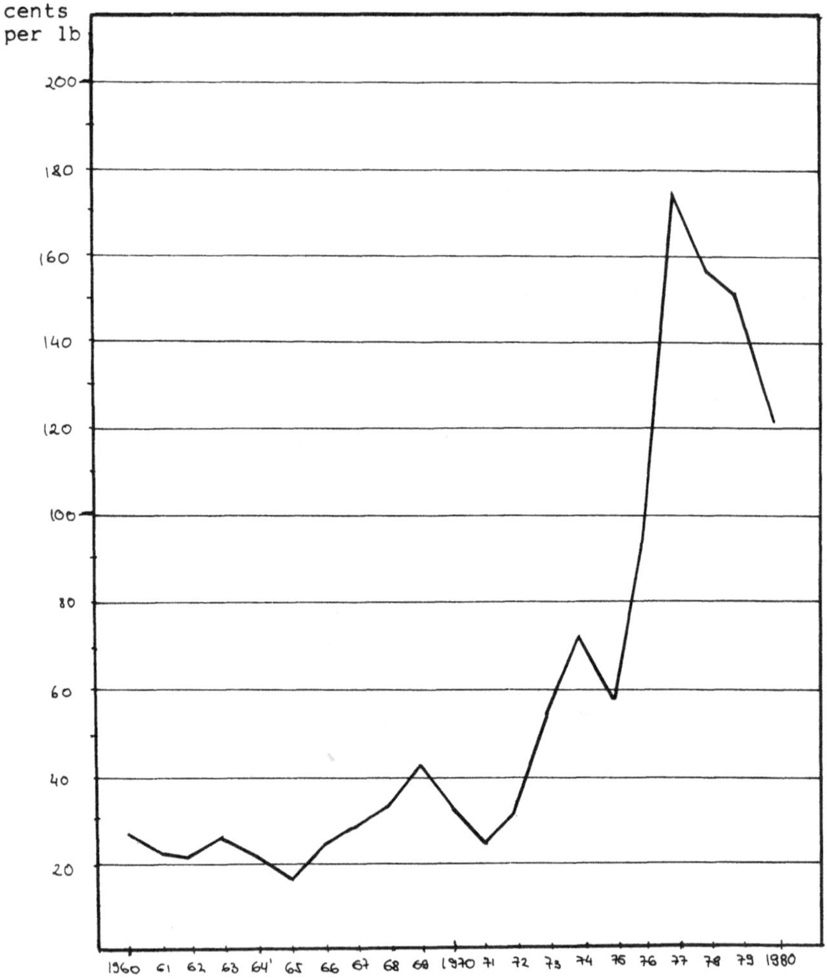

Source: Figure is plotted on the basis of data providing from: Quarterly Bulletin of Cocoa Statistics, vol.VII,no.3, June 1981.

From 1972 until 1974 cocoa prices show an upward trend which swings to and fro until 1976, when an extremely steep upward drift appeared. This lasted until 1978-79, due to tight supplies caused by the fact that world cocoa production manifested a 4% drop owing to the poor 1977-78 harvest. The calendar year 1979 was marked by a downward slope in the price trend, which moved upward at the very beginning of the 1979-80 crop-year. Because of the improved supply situation, world cocoa bean prices continued their downward trend. The downward drift in cocoa prices continued in the first quarter of 1981. From an average of 98.58 cents per pound in November 1980, according to data available from the ICO Secretariat, the daily future price (37) fell steadily to an average of 92.57 cents per pound in February 1981. This is shown in Table 27, where the monthly and annual averages of daily future prices in cocoa beans for the last ten years are shown, i.e. from 1970 up to 1981, where data are available for the first two months only.

Thus far the cocoa price trend has been examined, and, in general terms, found to reflect the corresponding situation which exsists between supply and/or demand in the international cocoa market. Therefore, the sooner the producing and consuming countries find an optimal solution, the better the general state of the cocoa business will be, i.e. as the Cocoa Agreement has come into force, only the question of the active participation of the Ivory Coast and the U.S. remains unsolved.

---

(37) "The daily futures price for cocoa beans is the average of the quotations of the nearest three active future trading months on the New York Cocoa Exchange at noon and on the London Cocoa Terminal Market at closing time. The London prices are converted to US cents per pound by using the current six months' forward rate of exchange published in London at closing time. The time for shift to the next three months' period is the fifteenth of the month immediately preceding the nearest active maturing month". Quarterly Bulletin of Cocoa Statistics, International Cocoa Organization, op.cit.,p.34.

Table 27.

Monthly and annual averages of daily futures prices of cocoa beans

January 1970-February 1981

Year	Jan	Feb	Mar	Apr	May	Jun	Jul	Aug	Sep	Oct	Nov	Dec
1970	33.86	30.67	30.38	29.80	27.30	26.68	28.91	33.46	33.85	32.06	30.38	29.48
1971	27.23	25.48	24.47	24.76	23.16	24.04	25.89	26.91	25.00	22.47	21.96	21.79
1972	24.26	24.94	26.12	26.37	27.87	28.19	29.24	31.04	32.85	33.02	32.51	33.37
1973	32.47	33.87	38.30	42.73	53.03	58.02	70.30	64.22	60.25	58.72	51.87	51.74
1974	50.89	58.38	67.39	82.60	82.71	70.28	71.67	73.48	72.35	79.18	75.59	64.36
1975	67.19	67.84	62.64	56.20	48.01	44.90	52.85	53.25	52.47	56.70	55.99	59.83
1976	63.70	65.04	64.17	74.32	80.20	87.26	88.75	96.23	108.41	111.59	132.67	134.92
1977	156.45	173.15	182.92	162.66	171.35	192.84	197.84	180.02	174.65	167.48	157.87	144.87
1978	135.08	128.14	153.35	156.10	142.19	135.68	143.47	152.43	170.09	173.57	182.77	179.03
1979	165.77	158.85	154.02	147.29	152.32	157.82	147.47	142.18	146.13	138.72	136.77	144.52
1980	143.60	146.78	140.18	131.97	117.24	113.27	111.77	104.85	108.20	104.54	98.57	95.70
1981	94.94	92.57	95.97	95.69	87.68							

Year	Average	Year	Average	Year	Average	Year	Average
1970	30.57	1973	51.29	1976	92.77	1979	149.32
1971	24.43	1974	70.74	1977	171.84	1980	118.06
1972	29.15	1975	56.49	1978	154.33		

Source: Quarterly Bulletin of Statistics, International Cocoa Organization, Vol.VII, No. 2, March 1981, ICCO, London.

The main producer, the Ivory Coast, at present under pressure due to the current market instability, obviously finds it difficult to adapt to the conditions laid down by the Agreement, linked with the price offer made by the consuming countries. Article 27 of the new ICA on cocoa indicates that "... there shall be established: a minimum price of 100 U.S. cents per pound, a maximum price of 160 U.S. cents per pound, a lower intervention price of 110 U.S. cents per pound and an upper intervention price of 150 U.S. cents per pound" (38). This is the main condition to which the Ivory Coast objects in refusing to ratify the Agreement, as it is not in accordance with the special economic circumstances of the country.

Therefore, it can be said in a few general lines, that the old problem of matching the fields of interest of the producing and consumimng countries emerges once again and remains an open question where the answer is difficult to predict. That is to say, the co-existence and co-operation of the producers and consumers must be accepted as a necessary pre-requisite for market regulation.

As noted above, the analysis has been focused on the question as to whether the theoretical intrinsic and extrinsic criteria are applicable in the case of cocoa. These considerations were given specific form as cocoa represents one of the most unstable markets on the international level.

It should be evident from this discussion that cocoa is a non-perishable commodity according to its natural characteristics, in terms of intrinsic criteria, which facilitates keeping it in stock. Nevertheless, storage costs are higher (than in the case of tin) in relationship to its value, which does not facilitate its stocking at all, as it demands, in turn, relatively high financial resources for stocking.

---

(38) International Cocoa Agreement, 1980, op.cit., Article 27, para. 1, p. 18.

Figure 13.

World cocoa bean production

1981

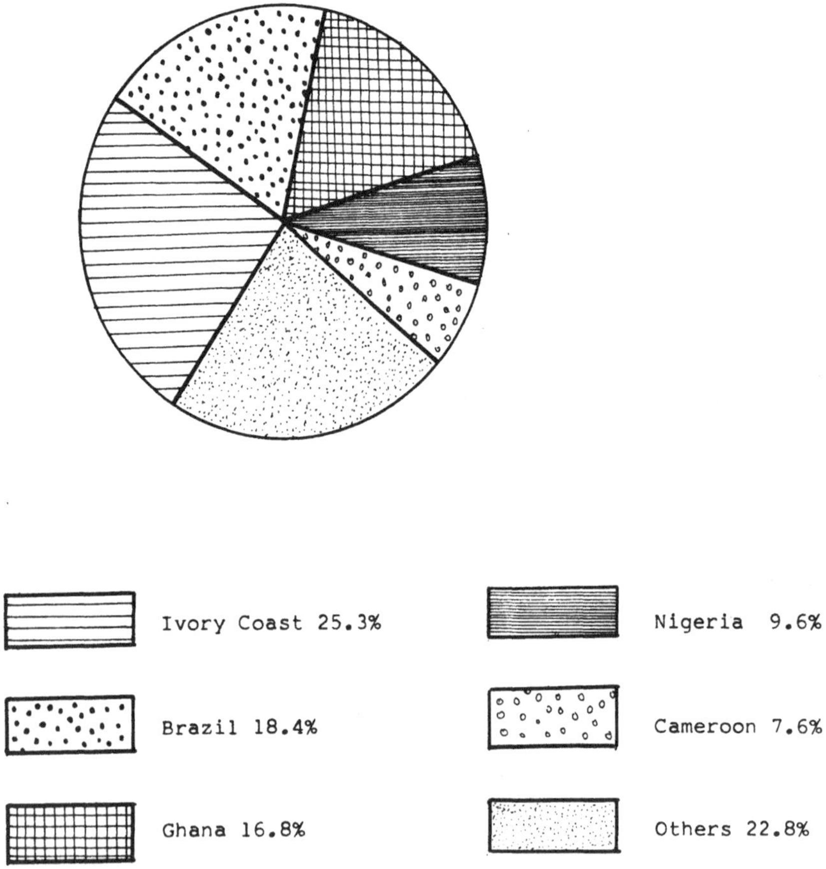

Source: The Figure is plotted on the basis of data computed from: Raport et perspectives sur les produits,FAO, 1981-82, FAO, Rome 1982, no.22.

The general situation of the cocoa market is determined mainly by the commercial situation brought about in the world's three largest markets - London, NeW York and Ghana. In addition, the fact that effective cocoa producers are few, which can be seen from Figure 13, means that it is exceptionally easy to set up an international agreement for this commodity. Such an agreement is even more suitable for application of the buffer stock control scheme, due to the great price instability of the commodity.

C - USEFULNESS OF A BUFFER STOCK TYPOLOGY IN INTERNATIONAL TRADE

The purpose of this section is to point out the findings made in the preceding pages, concerning the proposal for a buffer stock typology. Then some general comments will be made about the importance of these factors and how they are put to use in international trade.

The full significance of the conception and application of the buffer stock typology can be demonstrated by the attempts made to answer the legitimate questions which arise:

- does buffer stock typology ensure the choice of products suitable for buffer stock activities, and
- could typology dictate whether another commodity control should be used for the functioning of the buffer stock mechanism?

Proposed answers to both questions will be seen in divisions 1 and 2 which follow, respectively.

1. Does buffer stock typology ensure the choice of products suitable for buffer stock action?

This division will attempt only to outline and discuss those features which seem to be of relevant importance and of special interest to the question suggested.

a) General basic criteria for the buffer stock typology

It was pointed out earlier that our investigation concentrated on financing and delimiting criteria which could lead to the establishment of types of buffer stocks. As a basis for such an approach, a description was given of the groups of common elements which are of importance in the operational system of different buffer stocks (39). These attempts have been summarized in Table 28 in this chapter, which indicates that this approach towards the buffer stock typology can be accepted as justified, on the basis of the analysis of the three hypothetical commodities. That is to say, a picture has been formed of how intrinsic and extrinsic criteria seem to group buffer stocks into different categories. From this it can be seen that the grouping of buffer stocks into different categories can be manifested in a different way in commodities.

According to the general basic critéria, i.e. whether a commodity is suitable for storing or not, there might be a need for an appropriate mechanism of control in the form of the buffer stock. This situation has been summarized in Table 28, which indicates that each of these general criteria corresponds to a different behaviour, purpose and method of the buffer stock scheme.

b) Particular basic criteria for the buffer stock typology

From the approach presented in Table 28, it can be seen that all the important factors for the buffer stock typology can be divided into two categories, from which a group of commodities that cannot be candidates for storing, can be automatically eliminated, and are thus not truly suitable for a buffer stock control scheme.

---

(39) The aim of this was to point out the fact that typology studies and classifies different types of characters and their common characters.

The question as to which are the commodities that belong to the criteria of non-acceptance is answered in Table 29, which provides information about commodities that are not suitable for storing, i.e. commodities that are not suitable for price stabilization by means of the buffer stock mechanism.

In contrast, Table 30 shows which types of commodities are suitable for storing, what the reasons for their storing are and what the rôle and feasibility of using a buffer stock technique is.

The proposed division into two types of criteria, i.e. commodities that are unsuitable and suitable for storing, should not be applied too strictly. As an example, we can refer to the case of iron ore, which can be regarded as a storable commodity as well as non-storable commodity due to its natural features and its great bulk and low unit price, respectively. The purpose of this presentation is to show that there can be different interpretations of the relations of the proposed phenomena. It can, therefore, be said that typology draws out a particular order. This order restricts the ways in which the phenomena can be accounted for and, in the manner indicated, it can be seen that typology ensures that suitable products are chosen for buffer stock action.

2. Could typology dictate whether another commodity control should be used for the functioning of the stocks instead of the buffer stock mechanism?

In order to give a clear idea of the usefulness of the conception and application of the buffer stock typology, an attempt should be made to answer the question put forward in this heading.

There are two factors which are important in the consideration of this issue. They are

- financial resources, and
- utility.

Table 28.

General basic criteria for the buffer stock typology

Criterion	What is the intention of the buffer stock?	What arrangement should be made for storage?	What action is expected?	What sort of commodities could be re-presentative?	Commodity prototype requests, e.g.
Commodity is not suitable for storing	there is no purpose in storing	no method to be used	no performance of the buffer stock	perishable	bananas
Commodity is suitable for storing	price stabili-zation (to even out strong fluctu-ations)	adequate according to commodity's intrinsic and extrinsic criteria	performance of the buffer stock, i.e. its functioning	durable and relatively non-perishable	tin iron ore copper lead cocoa tea rubber jute and hard fibres sugar wheat cotton manganese phosphates bauxite

Table 29.

Types of commodities not suitable for storing

Type of commodity	Reasons for not storing	Commodity prototype requests, e.g.
Perishable	spoilage	bananas
Durable	great bulk and low unit price	iron ore
	multinational companies transform the raw material into the final product	bauxite, alumina, and aluminium
Not homogeneous	there is no one regulatory price	cotton
Perishable and relatively non-perishable (close substitutes)	price of natural product is largely undercut by the price of synthetic substitutes	rubber, jute and hard fibres
Perishable (those with structural problems)	secular decrease in demand	tea jute (•)

(•) Jute can appear in two categories as indicated above, due to its specific structural characteristics and competition from synthetics.

Table 30.

Types of commodities suitable for storing

Type of commodity	Reasons for storing	Rôle of the buffer stock	Commodity prototype requests, e.g.
Durable	easily storable	price stabilization	tin copper lead iron ore
Relatively non perishable	relatively difficult to store - high storage costs	price stabilization	cocoa coffee tea (39) rubber jute and hard fibres copper sugar

(39) Tea is a commodity which might be a case in point or not, in view of its structural problems.

Natural rubber is exposed to competition from synthetics. Therefore, a stabilization of strong fluctuations in natural rubber prices will encourage the use of natural rubber and will discourage the purchase of the competitive synthetic rubber. The history of price stabilization in the rubber market is a long one. The first ICA under the UNCTAD Integrated Programme for Commodities was concluded in October 1979 for natural rubber. It has been a success. Despite many obstacles, it is the first commodity under the IPC for which a buffer stock scheme has been established. The size of the stock is 550,000t. (Normal stock of 400,000t. and contingency stock of 150,000t.). The financing of the buffer stock is shared eaqually between the members. The purpose of the Natural Rubber ICA is to regulate trade in natural rubber by stabilizing prices and assuring supplies. For the major producing countries the "white gold" is of primary economic importance as a major source of foreign exchange. Percentage shares of total net exports are as follows: Malaysia 48%, Indonesia 25%, Thailand 12%, Sri Lanka 4.5% and Singapore 4.5%.

The former element represents a crucial point in determining whether another control scheme should be used instead of the buffer stock mechanism. The latter element concerns the utility of another commodity control if such a choice should be made.

a) The rôle of the financial resources

One of the major problems of general buffer stock regulation lies in its financing. It should therefore be kept in mind that specific characteristics of the commodity market play a decisive rôle in determining the amount of the resources needed to stabilize the commodity prices within the agreed price range.

The method of financing the buffer stock depends directly on its price range. The nature of its dependence on them can be seen in the cases of both tin and cocoa, discussed above, where, according to their different natures concerning price oscillations, adequate measures for the stabilization of their prices were taken through the buffer stocks.

In accordance with this, the same essential characteristics can be said to exsist for different commodities (in our case , for tin and cocoa). For this reason, the existence can be pointed out of different types of characters and their common characteristics, which, in one word, means typology. From this point of view, the realisation that there exists a possibility of discussing different types of price range, the size and the other conditions of the buffer stocks, such as price fixing or economic policy approach, for example, gives rise to the possibility that there may have been favourable circumstances in such an approach. This underlines the advantages of the conception of a buffer stock typology.

b) Utility

Could typology distinguish whether another commodity control should be used for the functioning of the stocks instead of the buffer stock mechanism? This also depends on the factor of utility. In the following statement an attempt will be made to find the answer to the question of whether the factor of utility could be crystallized through the typology. It is well known that typology helps to identify and/or investigate by setting up a restrictive relationship between observed phenomena. Some typologists go beyond the problem of order and help to show the importance of particular factors. A comparison of two examples of a single type can show the existence of differences in proportions or in rates of change, leading to additional conclusions such as the assumption of a causal relationship.

Therefore, it may be said, that if changing through control is used to conceptualize elements changing through time, (which is a principal characteristic of a typology), then the essential aspects and implications of a typology are accepted as adequate, and such a commodity control could be used for the functioning of the stocks instead of the buffer stock mechanism.

* * *

In this chapter an attempt has been made to point out the stronger side of the argument in favour of the conception and application of the buffer stock typology in international trade. In the manner indicated, the existence was established of different sorts of criteria, i.e. groups of generally common elements, which were divided theoretically into two groups:

- intrinsic criteria, and
- extrinsic criteria

and later on their existence was tested on two different products by applying them in the cases of tin and cocoa. Those groups of generally common elements, which exist in the case of tin, showed that the same criteria are applicable in the case of cocoa. The final result of the study, however, showed that each of them performs differently due to its own particular characteristics. This means that buffer stock of one commodity varies from that of another and therefore, although the mechanism has the same principle, it may be different in different commodities and, through buffer stock typology, the choice of suitable products for the buffer stock action may be ensured. To this extent, and with the above considerations in mind, it may be concluded that descriptions of typologies are acceptable to the degree where they purport to contribute solutions to the problems.

In conclusion, this chapter may be said to confirm, that typology contributes to the improvement of the buffer stock policy to a certain extent as it introduces a new point but is not sufficient to provide a definite solution for regulation in commodity markets.

CHAPTER II

THE ENUNCIATED ADVANTAGES AND THEIR REAL SIGNIFICANCE

Chapter II is devoted to the above-mentioned advantages, their real meaning and the importance of the use of the buffer stock control scheme in international markets.

Complex inquiries into theoretical, and less successful practical, effects obtained by this method of control have been well known for the past four decades. Especially in the late seventies and early eighties, buffer stock control mechanism received extended interest due to the worsening situation and tension between the producing and consuming countries.

The historical dimension, as well as a theoretical and empirical analysis of the buffer stock method of control, have already been presented in Part I of this work. Our aim is to situate the present study within the substructure which covers the direct effects of the buffer stock on the price fluctuations, and its indirect effects on export earnings. In both cases, these factors will be looked at from the point of view of the arguments which either speak in their favour and have thus contributed to its successful operation, or those which reject, or call into question, its effects and therefore represent elements which have contributed to its failure. Further on it will also be viewed as a method of quantity regulation.

A - DIRECT EFFECTS ON PRICE STABILIZATION

The nature and the problem of the price stabilization of primary commodities, internationally traded, and of instability in export earnings represent nothing new from the point of view (40) of either the DCs or the LDCs.

(40) It is true that remarkable research work has been done in this field. These attempts have been wholly praiseworthy and have been useful in so far as they cast a new light on the old problem.

As regards trading partnership, the LDCs and DCs manifest continual attempts to move towards less economic inequality (41). Therefore, one of the main issues in their multilateral action constitutes a price stabilization of primary commodities realized through the international commodity agreements (42). The means used are a stabilization mechanism preceded by the buffer stock control scheme. This issue is backed by the argument that if primary commodity prices could be stabilized, one of the biggest obstructions to the development of the LDCs' economies could be avoided.

1. The arguments of the buffer stock supporters

Before the advantages of price stabilization and the buffer stock as a method of control are considered, an attempt must be made to define what is covered by the concept of instability in commodity markets and where the necessity for stabilization comes from.

a) The necessity of fighting the instability of commodity prices

It is difficult not to say that the problem of instability in the commodity markets was, and is, the main characteristic of the trade in primary products.

Fluctuations in the prices and quantity of traded commodities indicate the instability which is revealed in the supply and demand for them. Sources of international

---

(41) For more details of the primary commodities export shares of the LDCs see Table 1 in Chapter III, Part I.

(42) According to the Integrated Programme for Commodities, the ten "core" commodities are cocoa, coffee, cotton, copper, hard fibres, jute, sugar, tea and tin. Buffer stock agreements are suggested for each of these commodities.

instability are definitely reflected not only in the variations already mentioned but also in those manifested in incomes, export earnings and profits. All together they complete the general notion of instability varying in the size and frequency of their changes, creating market conditions undesirable for both producers (LDCs), and consumers (DCs) (43).

What is generally meant by primary causes of market instability can be summarized in five major groups, as follows:

1. situation and dependence of LDCs,
2. various factors affecting supply (natural factors) resulting in an immediate price-sensitive response, which, in turn, affects the quantity demanded (price elasticities of supply and demand),
3. encouraged substitution by synthetics,
4. speculation,
5. fluctuations in prices themselves,
6. vis-major (such as wars, etc.) and politics (44).

From the above presentation it is apparent, that commodity instability can be specified in different ways. This suggests that the traditionally-regarded causes of instability, shifts in demand or in supply, involve a whole chain of different factors which interpenetrate each other's fields and, in this way, render more intense the economic and political tensions existing between the producers (LDCs) and consumers (DCs) especially in their permanent research of primary commodity market stabilization.

---

(43) BROWN, C.P., op.cit., pp. 4-5.

(44) For further details of the causes of market instability see LAW, A.D., op.cit., pp. 2-17.

Due to the facts presented, it is traditionally argued (45) that the LDCs have to face two main problems when dealing with their own trade and development:

1. that the LDCs have suffered a long-run deterioration in the terms of trade concerning their primary commodities,
2. that the great instability of commoditiy prices and export earnings has seriously affected the LDCs' development process.

As far as the first problem of the terms of trade is concerned, it is well known that it represents an area of relatively great magnitude in the negotiations between the LDCs and DCs (46). It appears wherever the distribution of benefits obtained through trade is concerned.

In other words, it is a question of whether the LDCs export earnings, realized through the exports of primary products, should meet the needs of their development programme.

One line of Prebish's argument is that the terms of trade of the LDCs concerning primary commodities are subject to a long-run deterioration due to the disproportion in international trade. This signifies that if there is a permanent decline in the prices of the LDCs' primary commodity exports relative to the prices of manufactured imports realized by the LDCs, the LDCs' export earnings will not be enough to carry through their development programme.

In the long-run, therefore, the industrial imports indispensable for the rate of growth of the LDCs will show a downward tendency.

---

(45) This argument was presented by economist Raul Prebish, first Secretary-General of UNCTAD, and was followed by Singer, Myrdal and other economists and has been adjusted over years.

(46) It is worth noting here that the terms of trade are worsening for the LDCs because of the behaviour of petrol and other primary commodity prices.

Table 31.

Terms of trade: Central and South American Coffee and Cocoa facing US Steel

Year	Coffee Columbian and Mild Arabicas US cents per lb	Cocoa annual averages of cocoa beans US cents per lb	Steel in plates export US $ per cwt f.o.b.	Terms of trade: lb of coffee in US $ per cwt of steel	Terms of trade: lb of Cocoa in US $ per cwt of steel
1960	44.89	26.72	5.75	12.80	21.51
1961	43.62	22.00	5.43	12.44	24.68
1962	40.77	20.81	5.38	13.19	26.83
1963	39.55 f/	25.05	5.44	13.75	21.71
1964	48.80	22.85	5.63	11.53	24.63
1965	48.21	16.57	5.63	6.68	33.97
1966	47.35	23.48	5.63	11.89	23.97
1967	41.61	27.13	5.63	13.53	20.75
1968	42.42	32.70	5.92	13.95	18.10
1969	44.44 f/	40.97	6.42	14.44	15.67
1970	56.60	30.57	6.89	12.10	22.53
1971	49.01	24.43	-	-	-
1972	56.70 f/	29.15	8.15	14.37	27.95
1973	72.52	51.29	8.49	11.70	16.55
1974	77.81	70.77	11.59	11.48	16.37
1975	81.31 f/	56.51	13.16	16.18	23.28
1976	157.72	92.79	13.41	8.50	14.45
1977	240.21	171.92	14.63	6.09	8.50
1978	185.20 f/	154.32	16.51	8.91	10.69
1979	183.41 f/	149.32	18.47	10.07	12.36
1980	178.82	118.06	20.57	11.50	17.42

Source: Quarterly Statistical Bulletin on Coffee, vol.4, Nos.2-3,1980, Cocoa Statistics,ICO, June 1981,vol.7,No.3.
f/ Serious frosts in Brazil

The LDCs'terms of trade (an example) are portrayed in Table 31. This was achieved through a series of annual average prices of coffee and cocoa exported as raw materials, which indicate their purchasing capacity. The latter is brought about through imports of steel, which constitutes a manufactured commodity needed for the LDCs' development programme.

There is no question, however, about the general trend of the terms of trade, which are pointed out in Table 31. From the complete series of data presented, it will be seen that, in general, the trend registers a fluctuations. In the LDCs' terms of trade which are taken into account, deterioration is persistent over a period of time. Nevertheless, several ups and downs are apparent; for cocoa it was the periods 1968, 1973-1974 and 1977-1978. As far as coffee is concerned, it was 1965, 1976-1978. These periods were of short duration and therefore seem to be insignificant when considering the overall impression. Moreover, in the period 1980-1983 (no data available) the sharp fall in primary commodity prices reflected a drastic deterioration in the overall terms of trade, which indicate a continuing decline. Therefore in reality, the LDCs' real income suffers a reduction, which, in turn, restrains their economic growth.

The second question of importance to be dealt with, is that of <u>instability in commodity prices and the LDCs' export earnings</u>. This question cannot be avoided when the subject of world markets for primary commodities is being discussed.

It is well known that most LDCs acquire their export earnings through the export of primary products to DCs. To what extent LDCs depend on the primary commodity exports can be seen in the fact that, for some of them, they represent more than 90 per cent of their total export earnings (47).

---

(47) For more details of the primary commodity export market shares of LDCs see Table 1 in Chapter C of Part I.

It is true that some LDCs' exports are large in amount and are concentrated in one or two primary products. Where the "core" commodities are concerned (48), the LDCs' exports are nearly 75 per cent of the total and over 50 per cent of each of those commodities. As a rough estimate, they account for half of world production. Therefore, their total export earnings are subject to extreme fluctuations for even the slightest change in the condition of world demand for primary commodities may result in an important rise or fall in the export income of the LDCs. In this respect, the instability of LDCs' export earnings is due to the great price fluctuations apparent in a large number of primary commodities.

The fact is that movements in commodity prices, when compared with those of industrial products, show a marked tendency to fluctuate. This is due to the short-run elasticities of demand and supply which are rather low for a number of primary commodities. In the case of agricultural primary products, weather and other natural conditions are mainly responsible for the variations in supply, which, in turn, bring about the uncontrolled movements of commodity prices. In the case of metals and minerals, supply instability is due to the fluctuations of demand in DCs, although here, supplies are not so unstable as is the case in the sector of agricultural products. The low price elasticities constitute a rather serious problem for LDCs. There are three reasons for this:

1. a small increase in supply relative to demand causes a relatively considerable decrease in price, and

(48) According to the Integrated Programme for Commodities (IPC) developed by UNCTAD, the ten "core" commodities are cocoa, coffee, cotton, copper, hard fibres, jute, rubber, sugar, tea and tin. Buffer stock agreements are suggested for each of these commodities.

2. small variations in demand cause a relatively large instability in prices.
3. low prices bring about an increase in supply (in certain circumstances).

To reinforce this argument of instability, see Table 32. The statistics given here refer to the free market prices of primary commodities exported by LDCs in the late 1970s. The combined price index can be seen to display rather changeable behaviour. Agricultural raw material price indices show a continuing upward trend, and the price index for minerals and metals reveals a steady increase after 1976. A sharp rise of 27 per cent in 1979 is due to the 45 per cent increase in copper, the 22 per cent increase in iron ore and the 9 per cent increase in tin. However, the price index for the latter commodity group rises considerably less than the indices of other commodity groups after 1972, which is taken as the base year (49).

Therefore, on the basis of the data given in Table 32, it can be concluded that the combined commodity price index has registered a decline, which indicates the importance of the changes in prices for most of the LDCs' economies.

The instability of commodity prices and the LDCs' export earnings will be reflected in the development of the LDCs' economies. From this can be inferred that commodity price stabilization in markets for primary commodity products is more than desirable.

A correlation exists between these two problems. This is manifested in the same basis from which both issues stem, i. e. the LDCs' great dependence on export earnings realized through the exports of a few primary commodities. Therefore, as long as instability is predominant in export earnings, the LDCs' development growth rate will be greatly influenced.

---

(49) UNCTAD, General Review of the World Commodity Situation, The World Commodity Situation and Outlook, Report by the UNCTAD Secretariat, TD/B/C.1/207/Add.1, 26th August 1980.

Table 32.

Free market prices of primary commodities exported by developed countries, 1975-1979

Index numbers (1972 = 100)

Commodity	Year				
	1975	1976	1977	1978	1979
A. Nominal prices					
Food and beverages	195	210	292	237	257
Agricultural raw materials	165	197	210	232	286
Minerals and metals	170	167	176	187	238
Combined index a/	182	195	244	226	262
B. Real prices					
Food and beverages	121	130	165	119	116
Agricultural raw materials	102	122	119	117	130
Minerals and metals	106	103	99	94	108
Combined index a/	113	120	138	114	119

a/ Excluding fuels; weighted according to the relative importance of each group in the value, in terms of US dollars, of exports from developing countries in 1972-1975.

Nominal prices are in current dollars.
Real prices are nominal prices divided by the UN index of unit values of manufactured goods exported by developed market-economy countries. For 1979, the average value of first three-quarters was used for this deflator.

Source: UNCTAD, General Review of the World Commodity Situation, The World Commodity Situation and Outlook, Report by the UNCTAD Secretariat. Addendum, TD/B/C.1/207/Add.1, 26 th August 1980, p.5.

For that reason, efforts made to control and to stabilize commodity markets would seem to be more than desirable. It must be added, though, that it is not only a matter of the finance required for growth which is of decisive importance to the LDCs' development programme. The inclusion of their political situation, which in turn determines their position in commodity trading, is equally as important as the fact previously mentioned.

Another argument to which DCs often refer whenever demands are made to fight instability in commodity prices, is that of the increasing inflation rate, which becomes apparent in their economies as a result of price increase. The basic assumption drawn from this complicated argument is that the wage/price spiral is flexible upwards and not downwards. This is known as a "ratchet effect". This means that, during inflation when there are periods of price increases, the prices of final products and wages will tend to increase due to the costs of production. It therefore creates the cost-push inflation. On the other hand, in periods when there is a decrease in commodity prices, it should in principle, produce the opposite effect. However, this is not the case because, when export earnings and the aggregate level of demand tend to fall, prices and wages do not fall as they are rigidly fixed by economic and social factors (e.g. oligopolies, syndicates,etc.),who have difficulty in deciding on measures to reduce and adjust prices.

The manner in which rates of inflation, due to the effect of primary commodity fluctuations, should be carried into the opposite direction, depends largely on the "central government macro-economic policies", as was indicated in the evaluation of the ratchet effect made by the American economist, J. Behrman (50).

---

(50) BEHRMAN, Jere J., International Commodity Agreements, Washington: Overseas Development Council, 1977, p.46.

Various careful analyses have shown that the ratchet effect can hardly be regarded as an important element in establishing commodity agreements. One of these analyses, elaborated by D. McNicol, points out that, in 1975, GNP in the United States was $ 1, 516,3 billion. Imports realized from the LDCs, with the exception of petroleum-exporting countries, was $ 178 billion, which represents only 1.2 per cent of GNP (51). From this example, it can be seen that the direct effect of the prices of imported commodities on those of the final product has hardly any impact in initiating the inflatory effect. This can be even better seen from the ratchet effect analysis carried out by M. Finger and D. De Rosa (52). They arrived at the conclusion that "... the ratchet effect argument, like the stultifying effect on economic growth of export instability, fails to provide a valid economic justification for commodity-price stabilization". This concerns the direct connection between the prices of the final product and the prices of commodity input. The causes of inflation are much more important and do not arise from one source only. It is more probable that the sources of the ratchet effect are due to the effects which instability in the prices of primary products has on terms of trade and the balance-of-payments of the countries concerned.

Whatever the case may be, the instability itself must somehow be reduced. A number of stabilization schemes in the form of commodity agreements have been proposed to combat the temporary fluctuations of supply and demand in primary commodity markets. These have been carried out over

---

(51) McNICOL, David L., op.cit., p. 22.

(52) FINGER, Michael and DeROSA, Dean, "Commodity Price Stabilization and the Ratchet Effect", The World Economy, London, vol. 1, No.2, January 1978, pp. 195-204.

the years, but they have been of little use. Theoretically, their objectives were settled on the way so as to take into account the interests of both participating members, exporting and importing countries respectively. These objectives were formulated in the following manner:

1. to moderate unstable short-term price movements,
2. to stabilize the prices and ensure a steady long-term growth of prices or incomes. This brings about transfer of resources from consumers (DCs) to producers (LDCs), (in addition to point two, we may mention the fact that western countries have always opposed this concept), and
3. to combat the instability of the commodity prices and export earnings of the LDCs (53).

It is well known that instability can be fought by using different control mechanisms. There are three basic forms regarding the mechanisms of price control for the operation of commodity agreements:

- multilateral contracts,
- quota agreements, and
- buffer stocks schemes.

Besides these measures, there also exist a price-compensation scheme, the indexation of prices and "long-term contracts" (as put forward in Resolution 93 (IV)). In the following discussion our attention will be focused upon the three basic methods of price control employed in a number of international commodity agreements.

These schemes can be presented alone or as a combination of one ,or sometimes two of them according to what is needed for the operation of an international commodity agreement on the price stabilization. In brief, their principles are as follows:

---

(53) BLAU, Dr. Gerda, "International Commodity Agreements", in Problems in Economic Development, Proceedings of a Conference held by the International Economic Association. Vienna 1962, ed., by ROBINSON, E.A.G., London, MacMillan & Co., Ltd., 1965, pp. 553-573, and McNICOL, David, L., op.cit., p. 24.

Multilateral contracts

The method of multilateral contract agreement is based on the mutual obligation established between the exporting and the importing countries. The exporting countries undertake to supply, and the importing countries to buy, certain specified, guaranteed quantities of primary products. These guarantees have to be put into effect at prices which may oscillate within a price range where the maximum and minimum prices are agreed in advance to last for the duration of the agreement. To function effectively, the price range established for multilateral contract agreements should not be too wide, and nearly two-thirds of the total trade should be covered by the participating members. This kind of agreement can be realized only in a highly-organized market. This method of control is used under the International Wheat Agreement.

Export quota agreements

The principle of the quota agreement is based on a regulation of the quantity of primary products which may be exported. This is attained through the use of an export quota system allocated to each country, and where changes in price indicate the adequate adjustments, i.e. when prices tend to rise above a certain level, exports are increased and quota restrictions are imposed on exports. On the other hand, when prices show a tendency to fall below a certain level, exports are reduced by means of considerable quota restrictions. The export quota system functioning should help to ensure longer term adjustment to demand trends and thus discourage movements towards over-production.

The effectivness of the quota agreement depends on several elements:

- participation of all producers, actual and potential, so that the sources of exports can be brought under control,

- the importance of the commodity traded, and
- the availability of the substitutes (54) (this element is also of importance for another system of control).

The main problem lies in the re-distribution of basic quotas among the participating members. In principle, this point very often causes sharp conflicts amongst the exporters. The agreement generally decides on the quotas according to past production or the volume exported by the participants. It tries to safeguard coherence of action amongst producers. This is rather difficult to achieve due to their different stages of development. In addition, there is always the possibility that a single producer might break away from the export-quota control scheme, attracted by the possibility of selling larger quantities at higher prices. Further difficulties may arise from the fact that this type of agreement is rather rigid, thus making it difficult for low-cost exporters to increase their supply at the expense of high-cost producers.

Although this type of agreement has a number of disadvantages, its further development and its use in combination with other methods of market regulation may improve its positive features. This type of control mechanism, where the main aspect is the adjustment in supply, was used in the agreements on sugar (in the case of this commodity, the internationally co-ordinated national stocks were also of importance) and coffee.

The third form of the mechanisms used to combat instability is concerned with the buffer stock scheme and its stabilization effects. An attempt will be made to discuss these in the following paragraph.

---

(54) BLAU, Dr. Gerda, Ibid., p. 559.

b) Stabilization through the buffer stock as a means of control

To achieve greater economic stability through the stabilization of international commodity prices, another type of agreement is used which the reader is already familiar with - the international buffer stock agency.

The facts noted earlier on in the first Part about this method of control, can be summarized in a single phrase - buffer stock operations are based on the simple buying and selling mechanism. In other words, the buffer stock manager or agency buys a commodity for a stock when prices are low and its supply high, and sells the commodity from the stock when prices are high and supply low.

It is obvious that the successful functioning of such a simplified mechanism could easily be realised if future price oscillations could be predicted with certainty. In practice, it is difficult, if not impossible, to suggest any solution stated in these terms. Therefore, uncertainty of price behaviour represents a matter of considerable importance which should be taken into consideration whenever the buffer stock scheme is brought up in discussion (55).

Specific interest in the buffer stock scheme as a mechanism of control used in price stabilization has not just recently been developed. For a long time, its obvious merits have been taken into account and viewed as a favourable short-term stabilization measure and as more concrete and, thus, superior to other measures. This was pointed out in the early 1940s at the Hot Springs Conference on Food and Agriculture (1943), where interest in this control technique first started to develop. It was suggested that the buffer

---

(55) This uncertainty represents an essential element in assessing the profitability of buffer stock operations. This can be seen from the illustrative Monte Carlo simulation analysis done by GOREUX, Louis, M., in his article "The use of the Buffer Stocks", <u>Finance and Development</u>, December 1978, vol. 15, No. 4, pp. 23-27.

stock aim should be viewed as "combining a short-period stabilization of prices with a long-period price policy which balances supply and demand and allows a steady rate of expansion to the most efficient producers" (56). Buffer stock was viewed even more as a measure "preferable to one based on export or production quotas" (57).

It is evident that those were optimistic opinions expressed in favour of this control scheme before it could be improved in practice by a commodity agreement. Over the years, the advantages of the buffer stock principle have been seen through its performance in the International Tin Agreement. Nevertheless no attempt will be made here to follow its evolution process, and the following will be confined to summarizing its merits. In brief, the characteristic advantages of the buffer stock are as follows:

- it does not automatically need the participation of all exporting and importing countries (as long as the bulk of world imports and exports is represented in the ICA);
- it does not restrict production in producing countries;
- it provides a defence against sudden price fluctuations, as its buying/selling mechanism exercises a short-term price stabilization.

The way in which its buying/selling mechanism will function and therefore bring into effect its short-term price stabilization depends largely on the fixing of an adequate price range. This means that the buffer stock can eliminate the short-term price fluctuations, and the price range fixed around the desired price trend can be neither too wide nor too narrow. Bearing in mind the broad scope of the price range, the main purpose of the buffer stock remains, however, to reduce the price variations around the desired price trend, without increasing the general price level.

---

(56) Report on "Economic Stability in the Post-War World", League of Nations, Official No.: C.1.M. 1945.II.A., Geneva, 1945, p. 315.

(57) Ibid., p. 315.

All these arguments indicate that the characteristics of a buffer stock scheme need to be adjusted according to the particular type of commodity market where it is expected to play a stabilizing rôle.

As a concluding remark about its advantages, it can be said that practice has shown that buffer stock operates through the market, thereby improving the market. Therefore, it is seen as a useful and effective tool for combating instability.

2. The arguments which call into question or reject the direct effects of buffer stocks.

It can be said at once that the above explanation of the arguments favouring the buffer stock has been accepted but, nevertheless, sharp controversies have continued to persist regarding its performance when put into practice. We shall, therefore, proceed, at this point, in the opposite direction and consider those arguments which claim to state its disadvantages.

a) The problem of the long-run equilibrium price

Like all the other control schemes which are used as stabilization policies through the ICAs, buffer stock involves a number of problems and difficulties, despite all its merits. One of these problems has a direct link with the notion of the long-run price trend.

The reader may recall that to establish a price trend is already a problem in itself. The principle is as follows: the establishment of a trend is based on the result obtained over a period of several successive years. However, if market conditions change, the trend will gradually adopt a new shape in order to adapt to the new conditions. This is what will happen if there is no buffer stock scheme or other stabilization measure. If the buffer stock exists (or some other method of control), then, although the market conditions change, and the trend gradually adopts a new position which is different from the unregulated market equilibrium, stabilization will be maintained. Therefore, the short-run stabilization of prices could be attained.

As far as the long-run stabilization is concerned, the principal difficulty of the buffer stock scheme is to predict the long-run equilibrium price. The buffer stock manager or agency, therefore, runs the risk of setting the price either too high or too low. With regard to the first case, the stocks would become larger and would continue to increase, thus creating a new situation whereby the stocks would either have to be stored at an increasing loss, or destroyed. In the latter case, the stocks would be sold out at a loss, as the price could not be kept down for a long time. These could be the possible effects, if the forecasts of price and the long-run price trend are not attained.

For such reasons, the fact cannot be disputed that the buffer stock scheme becomes inoperative because of the difficulty involved in predicting the long-run equilibrium price. At this point, the following question may arise: is it possible actually to forecast a long-run equilibrium? In theory, the general concept of equilibrium is one where the market situation is characterized by a set of interacting forces, where everything remains unchanged until the optimum situation is attained. In practice it is difficult, if not impossible to assume that everything remains unchanged, especially in the commodity market. Past experience may be viewed as a useful indicator for the future, but great uncertainty remains, nevertheless, as to the causes of market instability (for example, inelasticity of supply and demand, progress in technology, and others).

The assumption, therefore, that, in the long-run, primary commodity prices will remain stable and will ensure ideal free market conditions, could only be discussed theoretically as a hypothetical case. Consequently, it would be better to leave the problem concerning the long-run price trend alone. In this way, the functioning of the stock would become free of pressure, thereby bringing about a shift in terms of trade in favour of the producers. Instead, it would be more effective and useful to concentrate on the way in which the initial price range (which requires the price revision when requested) could be fixed, thereby avoiding accumulation of surplus stocks, or the situation where the available funds start to run low.

b) Capital and storage costs of operating the stock

When this problem is considered, the size of the stock should also be borne in mind. This can be explained briefly as follows: the cost of maintaining the buffer stocks will depend directly on how large the buffer stocks have to be. Therefore, as far as the size of the buffer stock is considered, it should be large enough to counterbalance an average fall in supply or to absorb average surpluses, and it should be large enough to prevent excessive price fluctuations. Consequently, maintenance of the adequate buffer stock for a specified commodity will introduce a set of costs necessary for its operation. For some storable commodities, on one hand, this set of costs can run high, thereby making the buffer stock costly to operate. However, on the other hand, for some commodities, the buffer stock scheme would not work at all.

Whenever the costs of storing primary commodities are concerned, the costs included in transport and storage, the costs of physical operations, and the interest costs on the capital employed must also be taken into consideration.

In order to determine all of these, the size of the buffer stock must first of all be decided on. This should be done by means of an analysis of the short-term changeable market conditions, and the price stability that may be required.

In the contents of the IPC, UNCTAD has made an illustrative estimate of the financial requirements for establishing and determining the buffer stocks for ten "core" commodities. Table 33 provides information illustrating the importance of stock requirements and capital requirements for those commodities. The buffer stocks required are computed in such a way as to maintain prices within a range of ± 10 per cent of the target price within a "95 per cent confidence limit" (58), over a period of 5 years, 1979-1983. (The information presented in Table 33 was formulated seven years ago. It was a forecast for the period 1979-83 and can serve as an illustrative example of the discrepancy between the forecasted estimates and the present situation in 1983).

To maintain prices within the given range of ± 10 per cent of the target price, it is important to have the adequate maximum size of buffer stock. This is illustrated in the first column of estimated figures in Table 33, which are stock requirements. These figures depict the quantitative amount of each of the given commodities that needs to be purchased for the stock. The second column, the value of stock required at the lower limit of the price range, shows capital requirements - the exact sum of money needed to purchase all the commodity stock if the price reaches floor level, thereby preventing it from falling any lower.

Furthermore, it can be seen that the estimates of UNCTAD's model, facilitate an understanding of the relationship existing between stock requirements and capital requirements.

---

(58) "95 per cent confidence limit" means that the probability of success of a buffer stock of a certain size would be 95 per cent. See UNCTAD, Consideration of issues relating to the establishment and operation of a Common Fund, Common Fund: financial requirements, Note by the UNCTAD Secretariat, TD/B/IPC/CF/L.2, 29th December 1976, p. 10.

Table 33.

Buffer stocks required to maintain prices within a range of ± 10 per cent of the target price, 1979-83

Commodity	Stock requirements 95% CL a/	Value of required stock (1976 $ million) 95% CL b/
Cocoa	459	768
Coffee	680	1256
Tea	111	143
Sugar	4734	1934
Cotton	495	672
Jute	420	174
Sisal(fibre)	149	86
Rubber	753	586
Copper	854	1365
Tin	37	267
Total assuming agreements financed separately		7251

Notes: a/ '000 tons

b/ "95 per cent confidence limit".

Source: UNCTAD, Consideration of Issues relating to the Establishment and Operation of a Common Fund, "Common Fund: Financial Requirements", Note by the UNCTAD Secretariat, TD/B/IPC/CF/L.2, December 29, 1976, pp. 13-14.

It might be interesting to note here that a change in one of these does not in itself cause a change in the other. Therefore, the figures given in Table 33 clearly illustrate that the carrying-out of buffer stock operations is dependent not only on the physical existence of stocks but also the availability of sufficient financial funds to cover the set of costs required for its operation (administrative costs, costs of physical operations and interest costs on the capital employed). Moreover, if these costs run high, it is obvious that the functioning of the buffer stock control mechanism can no longer be achieved.

Thus, the calculation of the costs for maintaining commodities in stock, represents one of the principal conceptual difficulties. It is highly dependent on a number of factors, amongst which the nature of the product and the funds available for the stocking operation are most important. Therefore, in order to run a buffer stock efficiently, a very carefully-formulated commitment is demanded from both producing and consuming countries to avoid its obvious difficulties and problems and exploit its advantages.

B - INDIRECT EFFECTS ON EXPORT EARNINGS

In addition to what has been considered with regard to the functioning of the buffer stock and its direct effects on price fluctuations, this section will now try to summarize the effects of price stabilization on the size of the export earnings of producing countries brought about by the use of the buffer stock mechanism.

1. Arguments in favour of indirect effects

When a reference is made to the effects brought about through the process of stabilization, it is of particular importance to recall to mind the fact that stabilizing prices does not automatically stabilize the export earnings of producing countries, if supply changes. It is important to recall that this fact was ascertained by the British economist, Alasdair MacBean. In his econometric research work concerning the price fluctuations of primary commodities, he showed that the changes in the output, which are difficult to control, are the elementary cause of the fluctuations in the export earnings of producing countries, and not the price fluctuations themselves (59).

a) Demand

It is generally accepted that stabilization of prices and the stabilization of the export earnings of producing countries are two different targets. Nevertheless, in certain circumstances, the former might provide an appropriate approach to the stabilization of export earnings. Therefore, to estimate how the buffer stock will perform and what the effects will be on the variability and the size of the export earnings of producing countries, our summary will proceed by making a distinction between its operations in the demand shift market and those executed in the supply shift market. Reference will be made here to the same simplified assumptions made for the process of price stabilization exercised through the buffer stock mechanism as described in Part one. These constitute the linear form of functions, their parallelism, etc. and these, in turn, imply that the consequences of the simplified forms of intervention should be considered.

---

(59) See Mac BEAN, Alasdair, Export Instability and Economic Development, London, Allen & Unwin Ltd. 1966.

According to theoretical analysis (60), the demand shift market should be considered first. Here supply schedule stays unchanged, and the demand schedule performs parallel changes being price inelastic, as is shown in Figure 14. Form this figure the way which price stabilization influences revenue stabilization can be observed. Here, there is a price inelastic demand. Therefore, price stabilization may bring about revenue stabilization. Since $\mathcal{E}_d < 1$, the $(OP_oR_2^*Q_2^*) < (OP_2R_2Q_2)$ and the $(OP_oR_2^*Q_1^*) > (OP_1R_1Q_1)$, then the average of two eaqual periods shows that, at the price $P_o = \frac{OP_2+OP_1}{2}$, price stabilization will bring about revenue stabilization because

$$\frac{(OP_oR_2^*Q_2^*)}{(OP_oR_1^*Q_1^*)} < \frac{(OP_2R_2Q_2)}{(OP_1R_1Q_1)}$$

However, this is not necessarily the case, as can be seen from Figure 15 where the effect is just the opposite. This means that a price stabilization will bring about a revenue de-stabilization due to the elasticity of the demand schedule. This time it is a case of a price elastic demand, Where $\mathcal{E}_d > 1$, and $(OP_oR_2^*Q_2^*) > (OP_2R_2Q_2)$, and $(OP_oR_1^*Q_1^*) < (OP_1R_1Q_1)$. Therefore, price stabilization at price $P_o = \frac{OP_2+OP_1}{2}$ will bring about revenue de-stabilization because

(60) In the field of literature, the analysis of such a market situstion received great attention and was a subject of a number of works (R.H.Snape and B.S.Yamey, H.G. Grubel, and others). Here, nevertheless, more interest was deveoted to the situation in the demand shift market than to the supply shift market.

The following suggestion which will receive attention here was offered in a prior extensive analysis of price stabilization for certain primary commodities, which would benefit most LDCs. In the following pages, an attempt has been made to compress the elaborated ideas. The analysis was done by BROOK,E., GRILLI,E., and WALEBROECK,J.,"Commodity Price Stabilization and the Developing Countries: The Problem of Choice", I.B.R.D., July 1977, Bank Staff Working Paper No. 262.

Figure 14.

Demand shift market with price inelastic demand

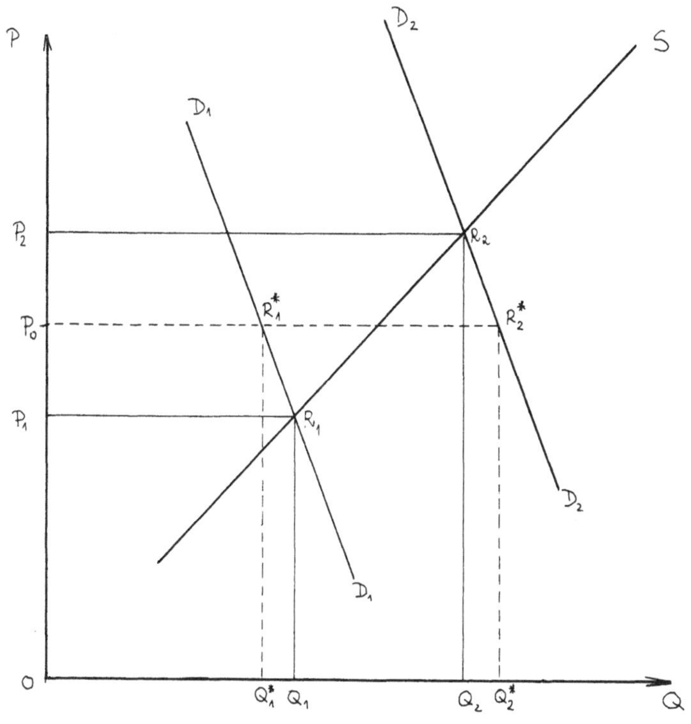

Figure 15.

Demand shift market with price elastic demand

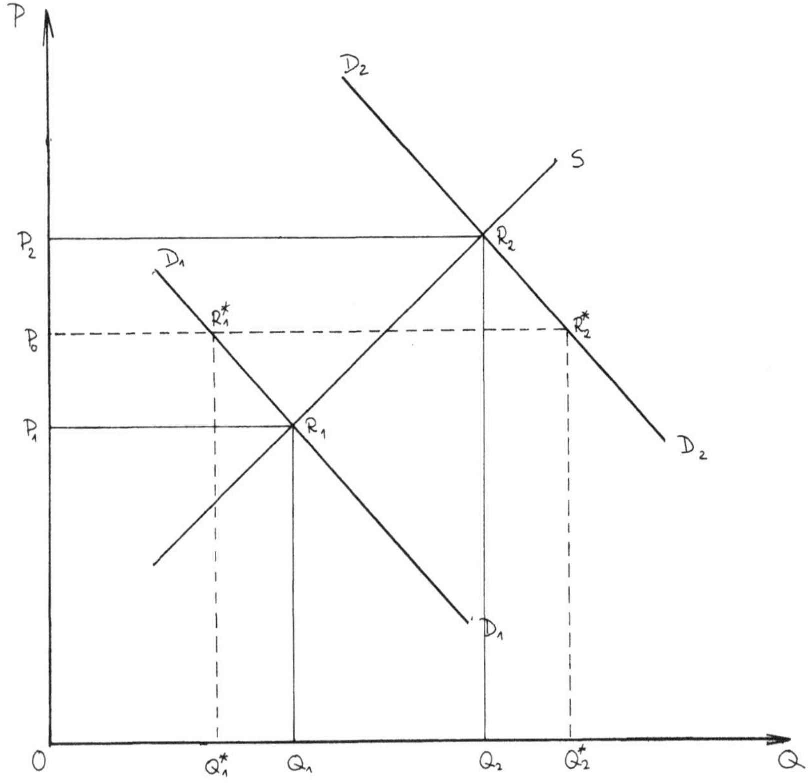

$$\frac{(OP_oR_2^*Q_2^*)}{(OP_oR_1^*Q_1^*)} > \frac{(OP_2R_2Q_2)}{(OP_1R_1Q_1)} \quad (61).$$

Where the total export earnings of producing countries and the impact of price stabilization on these earnings are considered, in the case of variable demand, it has been proved that they will have decreased. This is achieved through the buffer stock control scheme. In works written on this subject (62) it is always presented by a simplified model of a variable demand case. Under the assumptions already made, a model has been depicted in Figure 16. It shows that the total revenue over two periods is given by the sum of $(OP_1R_1Q_1)+(OP_2R_2Q_2)$. Here the prices will be seen to be variable and there is no buffer stock intervention. The revenue obtained over the two-period cycle is higher than the revenue attained through the use of the buffer stock control scheme over the same period: $2(OP_oR_oQ_o)$. It can be said, therefore, that the price stabilization at the price $P_o = \frac{OP_2+OP_1}{2}$ decreases export revenue as

$$(OP_1R_1Q_1) + (OP_2R_2Q_2) > 2(OP_oR_oQ_o).$$

Or, as H.G. Grubel indicates: "under the given assumptions the increase of revenue in one period fails to compensate for the decrease during the second period so that the

---

(61) This approach and what follows is partly derived from the comprehensive and profound analysis of commodity price stabilization and the income and welfare effects done by BROOK, E., GRILLI, E., and WALEBROECK,J., "Commodity Price Stabilization and the Developing Countries". Banca Nacionale del Lavoro, Quarterly Review, No. 124, March 1978, pp.79-99.

(62) The model, which examines the effect of the price stabilization on export revenue through the use of the buffer stock, is likely either to increase or decrease in the demand shift market, as was presented by H.G.Grubel. See GRUBEL, H.G., "Foreign Earnings and Price Stabilization Scheme", The American Economic Review, vol., LIV June 1964, No. 4, Part I, pp. 378-385.

Figure 16.

Impact of the price stabilization on the export earnings of producing countries by a buffer stock: case of a parallel shift in demand only

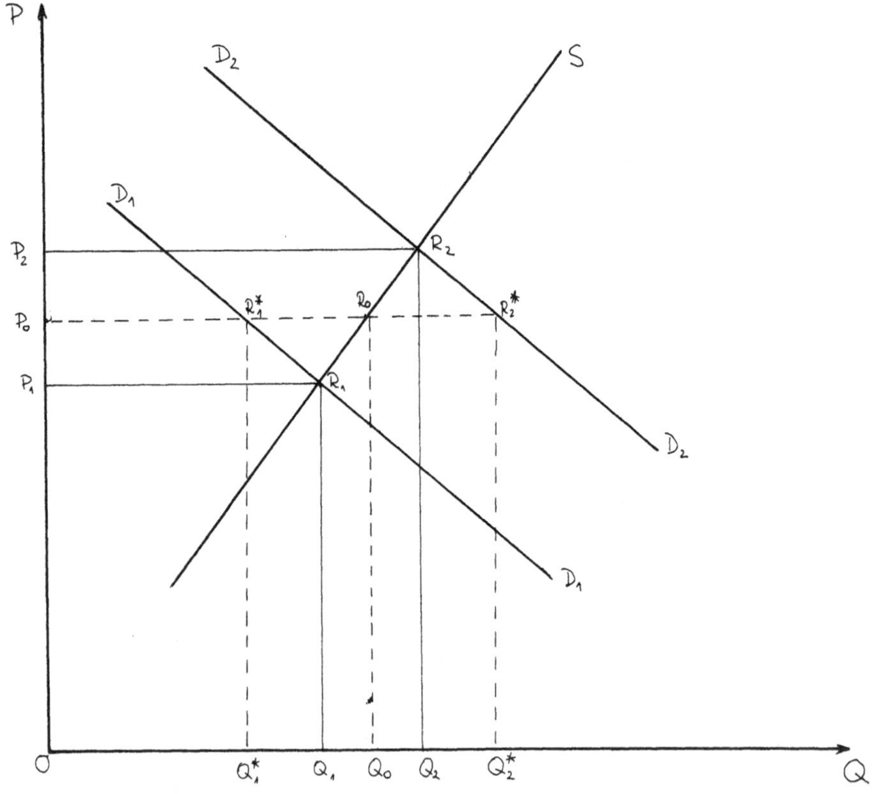

buffer stock always reduces foreign exchange earnings below what they would be if the unrestricted market were allowed to function" (63).

The situation in the tin market could be said to bear a resemblance to the case developed above. The supply of tin is always stable, which is the case for most metals, but the demand for imports will be variable as it will fluctuate according to the operation of the economy in the developed countries.

This is a well-known fact, and it has already been pointed out that fluctuations in the export revenue of developing countries have an important impact on their economic and industrial development. Therefore, their balance-of-payments will be greatly influenced by the fluctuations in export revenue from commodity exports. This means that a measure of stabilization has to be undertaken. Here the following question may be asked: is it necessary to use the costly method of a buffer stock control scheme to achieve the required stabilization in export earnings through price stabilization, or does there exist a less expensive way of attaining the stabilization objective? The answer may be given, as follows: if the export earnings were the countries' only objective, then stabilization could be attained through the compensation financing of the shortfalls in export revenue. However, as was discussed earlier, price stabilization of the primary commodities represents a complex and important problem in itself, which may contribute to export revenue stabilization.

For the LDCs, abrupt changes in their export revenue will bring about large-scale repercussions in their balance-of-payments in the form of deficit or excess. Several data from the major tin-exporting country, Malaysia, may provide some supplementary information about it.

---

(63) GRUBEL, H.G., Ibid., p. 380.

Table 34 shows the correlation between Malaysia's trade balance and the primary tin metal prices on the Penang market. According to the standard statistics, the correlation coefficient for the given period 1969-1979, is 0.84. From this, the narrow significant positive correlation and dependence between these two magnitudes becomes evident.

Therefore, it is in the interest of the LDCs to use the buffer stock control scheme for commodity price stabilization. This, in turn, will affect the size of the export earnings of the producing countries. It must be borne in mind, however, that these two objectives are neither symmetrical nor alternative (64).

b) Supply

The approaches stated above are considered with regard to the conditions in the variable demand market. In a subsequent analysis, an attempt will be made to show the effects of price stabilization, exercised by the buffer stock mechanism, on the export earnings of producing countries, in a market where demand remains stable and changes occur on the supply side.

In the works written on this subject, more attention was paid to the demand changes than to those which might appear in the case of a supply shift market. The latter case was analysed mathematically by Professor H. Johnson (65).

---

(64) STAKHOVITCH, A.,"A European View of Commodity Problems: Stabilization of Prices and Stabilization of Receipts", op.cit., pp. 235-240.

(65) JOHNSON, Harry G., "Commodities: Less Developed Countries' Demands and Developed Countries' Responses", op.cit., pp. 240-253.

Table 34.

Correlation between Malaysia's Trade Balance and Primary Tin Metal Prices of the Penang Market

Year	Trade balance (in million of U.S. dollars)	Penang tin prices M $ per picul
1969-72	257	637.34
1973	546	686.28
1974	98	1136.63
1975	277	963.79
1976	1467	1146.56
1977	1455	1588.03
1978	1496	1743.19
1979	3378	1960.65
Correlation coefficient[a/]	r= 0,84	

a/ Own computation

Source: Data provided from the Handbook of International Trade and Development Statistics, UNCTAD, 1980, and Tin International Statistical Supplement , August 1981.

The geometrical approach concerning effects on the revenue of shift in supply alone, with and without price stabilization obtained through buffer stock, has already been depicted in Part one of this work (66). This was considered according to arguments developed by Professor J. Behrman in his work concerning the implications of price stabilization on variability and level of revenue (67).

Here two cases were considered :the first one was concerned with the situation in a supply shift market, where there is a price elastic demand,and the second where there are inelastic supply and demand curves. As regards the former case, price stabilization has been seen to bring about revenue de-stabilization and in the latter case, price stabilization gives rise to revenue stabilization.

From the assumptions already made, the possible consequences of price stabilization through the use of buffer stock on the total export earnings of developing countries will be depicted when demand remains stable and supply alone changes, and both are relatively elastic. The effects are outlined in Figure 17. As can be seen from Figure 17, the total export revenue obtained in two periods without the intervention of the buffer stock method of control is represented by $(OP_1R_1Q_1 + OP_2R_2Q_2)$. This magnitude is less than the total export revenue obtained with the intervention of the buffer stock mechanism in the two periods represented by $2(OP_oR_oQ_o)$ or

$$(OP_1R_1Q_1) + (OP_2R_2Q_2) < 2(OP_oR_oQ_o)$$

This means that price stabilization carried out at the stabilized market price $P_o = \frac{OP_2+OP_1}{2}$ increased the total export revenue in the supply shift case.

---

(66) See Part one, Chapter II, Section C, paragraph c) on the effects on the revenue of shifts in supply curves from the price stabilization policy by means of a buffer stock.

(67) BEHRMAN, Jere R., International Commodity Agreements, op.cit., pp. 10-13.

Figure 17.

Impact of the price stabilization on the export earnings of producing countries with the use of a buffer stock: case of a parallel shift in supply only

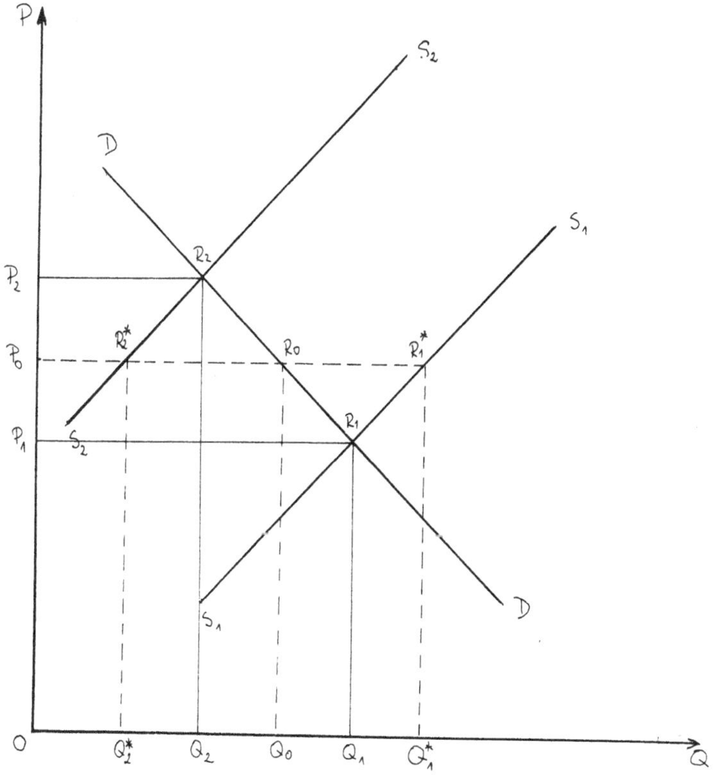

In conclusion, it could be said that if price stabilization could be obtained through the use of an adequate and sufficient buffer stock mechanism in the case of the commodity in question, then it would have a positive effect on the export earnings of producing countries and stabilization could be attained.

This situation, where demand for imports remains stable and the supply is subject to fluctuations, can be found in the case of cocoa, coffee and some other commodities belonging to the group of foodstuffs and beverages. If cocoa is taken as an example, it can be seen that it is an export commodity for West Africa. In Equatorial Guinea it accounts for 70 per cent of the total export earnings; in Ghana it accounts for 62 per cent; in Togo for 35 per cent; in Cameroon for 27 per cent; in Ivory Coast for 21 per cent, and for Western Samoa for 24 per cent. It is therefore one of their key sources of export earnings. This, in turn, implies that stabilization is of vital importance in their economic development.

In fact, it can be concluded that the assumptions made to achieve a simplified market model helped to develop the analysis in a way that provided information about the theoretical possibilities involved in certain cases. Nevertheless, it should not be forgotten that this simplification does not correspond to the real world situation and might, therefore, remain, and be accepted as, only a hypothetical case.

2. Arguments calling into question or rejecting the indirect effects

A look will now be taken at the arguments which call into question the effects of commodity price stabilization on the export earnings of producing countries through the buffer stock mechanism.

a) Does buffer stock create more advantages for producing countries?

All the distribution problems of gains and price stabilization are generally known and have been analysed in a number of works. Nevertheless, it might be useful, at this point to call to mind several points which H.G. Grubel discussed in his 1964 study.

In his discussion of non-parallel shifts in demand, he underlined the importance of relative price elasticities of supply and demand curves (their steepness) and their influence on price stabilization and on the total export earnings of producing countries during the "boom period" (68). His conclusion was that "the introduction of world primary commodity stabilization schemes does not necessarily increase total foreign earnings accurring to the producing countries" (69).

Using the same means of theoretical analysis, an attempt might be made to see what the situation will be if the change occurs as a parallel shift in demand curves. From Figure 18 it can be seen that there is a net loss in producing countries, which is clearly shown by the shaded area, representing a loss in export earnings.

This confirms and, in a way answers,the question asked in the heading of this paragraph, i. e. that the buffer stock scheme does not favour producing countries in the case where the change occurs in demand function.

---

(68) "..if demand is typically less elastic during periods of high demand than it is during periods of depression, buffer stock schemes are likely to decrease foreign exchange earnings below what they would have been in the absence of such schemes because stable prices over the cycle forego the opportunity to exploit the inelasticity of demand during boom periods. Under these circumstances buffer stock schemes therefore lead to a conflict between the stabilization and earnings -maximisation objectives pursued by government agencies". GRUBEL,H.G., "Foreign Exchange Earnings...", op.cit., p.384.

(69) Ibid., p. 384.

Figure 18.

Possible loss of producing countries in a demand shift market

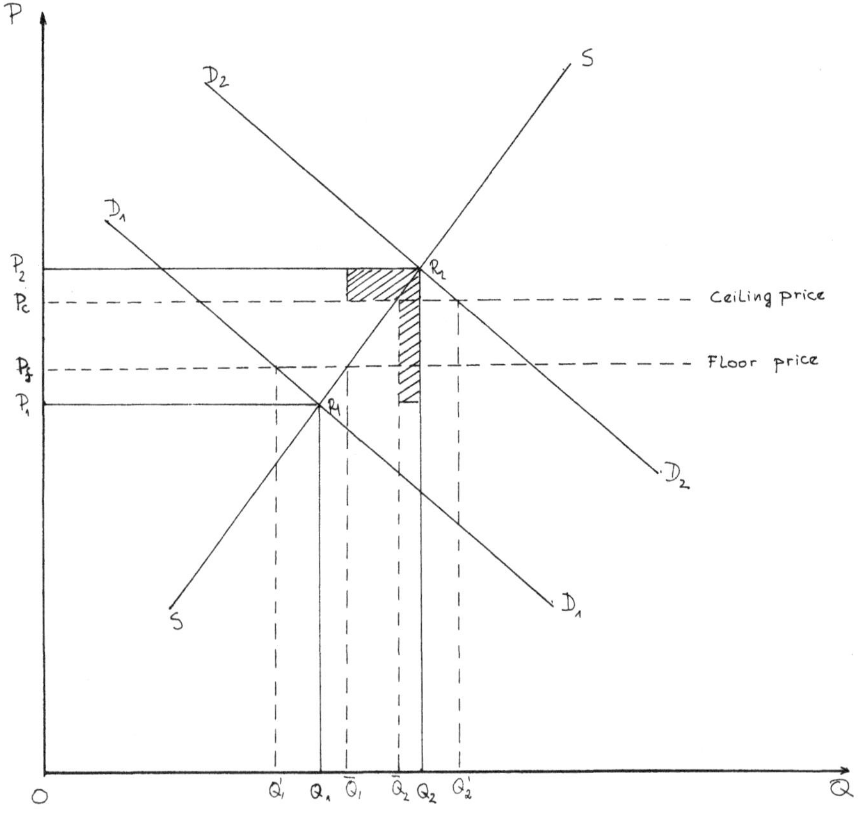

To support this argument in practice, the case of tin metal should be considered, where the loss in export earnings would be rather small, due to its insignificant price elasticity of supply.

b) Inconvenience of commodity price stabilization brought about by buffer stock due to the surplus risk

There is another important fact which should be considered when commodity price stabilization by the buffer stock is put into practice, for it would, in turn, influence the export earnings of the producing countries. This is related to the possible effects of an over-estimation of the price trend.

The problems of trend forecast are already known and always involve negotiations between both producing and consuming countries, where the purpose is to achieve the price stabilization around the trend. These difficulties are closely related to the agreement made by both sides regarding the use of the buffer stock scheme as a control mechanism. This is due to the fact that if the trend forecast does not correspond to the real situation, which is often the case, commodity agreements based on the buffer stock method of control could disrupt the market conditions.

The situation that would result in the case of an overestimation of the price trend can be seen from Figure 19 (70). The commodity agreement is established. During the period OA the trend forecast corresponds approximately to the real trend and the buffer stock of the ICA function according to its routine principle. Nevertheless, the situation changes considerably between A and B. The real trend does not follow the path of the one forecasted. The latter stays far above the former in the period of the

(70) Figure 19 and what follows is partly deduced from BROWN, C.P., Primary Commodity Control, op.cit., pp. 147-149.

Figure 19.

Possible effects of an over-estimation of the price trend

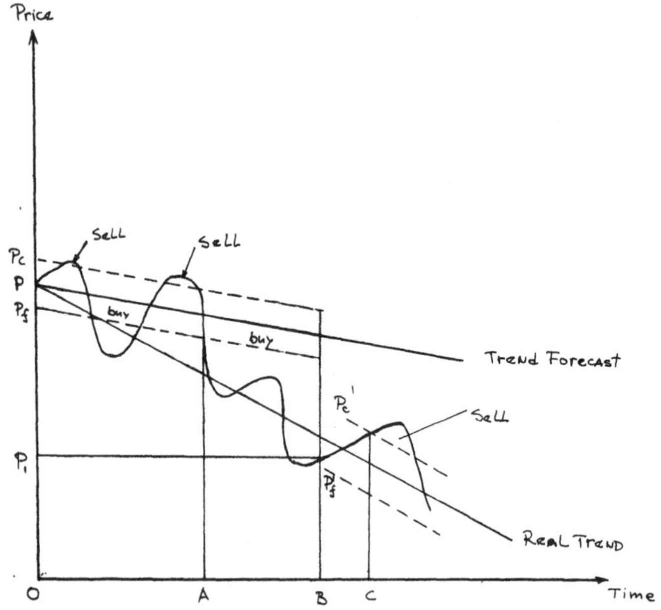

agreement duration. In practice, this situation was met with in the Third Cocoa ICA. From A to B there is a securing period where the buffer stock financial resources would be exhausted. After B, therefore, due to the insufficiency of resources, the agreement would be interrupted and the new situation would demand the fixing of a new price range, p'_c and p'_f around the new decreased price P_1. Due to the discrepancy in overestimation between the real and the forecasted trend, the period A to B would be characterized by the accumulation of stocks which would create the risk of surplus. Surplus could be sold after the estimation of a new price range at C, but would be sold at a loss.

It goes without saying that, in a situation where there is an over-estimation of the price trend, producing countries would be put into the difficult position of facing the risk of surplus and loss of valuable financial resources.

Here the question may be asked as to whether or not such buffer stock operations would have the impact of price stabilization on the total export earnings of producing countries. As shown in Figure 19, due to the over-estimation of the price trend, price stabilization could be brought about by the buffer stock method due to a lack of sufficient resources necessary for its functioning (buying/selling of the commodity concerned). This, in turn, might have an impact on the export earnings of the producing countries and would bring about their de-stabilization due to the changes which would occur on the demand side. At this point, therefore, the importance of the fact that stabilization of prices does not automatically imply stabilization of export earnings should be borne in mind. In fact they represent two different goals but a combination of the two might appear, which would depend on the structure of the demand and supply of the commodity concerned, which was shown in the previous analysis developed in this section.

In the approach presented in this section, it was our aim to contemplate not only the desirable effects, but also others that might appear through the mechanism of the buffer stock regulation, with the purpose of increasing, if possible, the welfare of the LDCs. In this case, the LDCs'demand for

- higher prices for their raw materials intended for export,
- stabilization in export earnings and
- greater stability of the investments in LDCs,

could be met.

C - ANALYSIS OF REGISTERED PROBLEMS

Two aspects of the buffer stock method of control will be considered in this section. The first will cover the problems of building up the buffer stocks, and the second will deal with the problems which occur when this method of control is put into operation. Later on, in order to consider its problems in a general way, it will be observed in combination with another method of control.

It may be found important to discuss these problems with the purpose that, if they can be avoided, then buffer stocks will bring about an important contribution in evening out the instability in the economic sector of the LDCs where the primary products are to be found. If this could be achieved, it would have a beneficial influence on the LDCs' whole economy and, in turn, their economic development.

1. Technical problems of the buffer stock scheme

Before an agreement based on the buffer stock method of control is established and brought into operation, both producing and consuming countries have to agree on its technical and practical procedures. Basically there are five issues which should be taken into consideration when the establishment of a buffer stock scheme is being discussed. These are

- the stockability of some selected primary commodities,
- the price range and the size of the buffer stock,
- the cost of storing, and
- the financing of the buffer stock.

The importance of these issues is reflected in the capacity of the buffer stock to provide adequate defence when unexpected price stabilization occurs. For the moment, our attention should be concentrated on the size of the buffer stock and its price range, as the other issues mentioned above were covered at the beginning of Part II. The basic characteristics of these two features, both of great importance in governing the operation of the buffer stock scheme will therefore be recalled briefly.

a) The size of the buffer stock

One of the factors necessary for the effective operation of a buffer stock control scheme may be found in its size. The way in which a buffer stock should be determined depends firstly on the nature of the commodity traded and the degree of instability that the commodity concerned is subject to.

Further on, the following question might be asked: what amount of quantitative resources of the commodity concerned is needed for the correct establishment and financing of the buffer stock scheme? Here, theoretical and practical analysis clearly shows, that various factors are of preponderant importance in determining the capacity of the buffer stock. At this point, several parameters should be taken into consideration when the size of the buffer stock is to be discussed.

One of these is related to the price elasticity of demand and supply of the commodity concerned. Here, it would be ideal if the estimates could reveal some stability in the elasticity of demand for the commodity concerned. The same applies to supply conditions. Nevertheless, it is preferable to take great care where the estimates are concerned because, if there is an overestimation or underestimation of the conditions of demand or supply, then there is a risk that the size of the buffer stock will not be of adequate capacity to meet the fluctuations which might appear on both the demand and supply side, respectively.

Furthermore, the parameter which is correlated to the previous one represents the extent to which surplus or shortages in following years influence supply and demand for the commodity concerned. The greater they are, the larger the demand for quantitative resources will be. Here, another factor appears to be of importance. This concerns the reactions of production and consumption to causal changes, such as weather conditions or an economic crisis; and the influence and consequences they have on the world commodity markets. In addition to this, not only should the level of the buying prices be taken into consideration but also the level of the selling prices, i.e. the limits of the defined price range (71).

Taking these points into consideration, UNCTAD compiled an estimate of what the quantitative requirements should be, i.e. the size of the buffer stock for a certain number of commodities traded internationally. Table 35 traces UNCTAD's procedure in estimating the stock requirements for the period 1979-1983 with the objective of maintaining prices within a range of ± 10 per cent around the target price. Table 35 refers to the maximum size of the stock necessary for successful functioning of the buffer stock for the commodities concerned. The physical quantities of each commodity are estimated to be necessary to enable the probability of success of the given size of the buffer stock

(71) An Integrated Programme for Commodities: The rôle of the international commodity stocks, UNCTAD, TD/B/C.1/166/Supp.1, December 1974, p. 20, para 44.

Table 35.

Estimates[a/] for the requirements to maintain prices within a range of ± 10 per cent around the target price, 1979-1983.

Commodity	Target price(a) $ per ton	Stock requirements			
		Confidence(b) limit (CL)		As percentage of projected exports	
		80%	90%	80%CL	95% CL
Cocoa	1858	378	459	31	38
Coffee	2053	558	680	16	20
Tea	1429	92	111	13	15
Sugar	454	3878	4734	19	23
Cotton	1508	397	495	10	13
Jute fibre	363	396	420	28	30
Sisal	644	144	149	26	27
Rubber	864	613	755	19	23
Copper	1776	720	854	14	17
Tin	8018	29	37	15	19

a/ Using 1971-1975 average prices in 1976 dollars. Prices for 1976 and beyond are forecasts made by UNCTAD Secretariat.

b/ Defined as the maximum level of accumulated purchases (or sales) of a commodity which would ensure, with the indicated probability that in no year in the period the commodity's price fell outside the range indicated arround the target price. Values are in '000 tons.

Source: Considerations of issues relating to the establishment and operation of a Common Fund: Common fund financial requirements, UNCTAD, TD/B/IPC/CF/L.2, 29 Dec. 1976, pp.13-14.

to be 95 per cent, which is the upper limit, and 80 per cent which is the lower limit. These values are indentified as the "95 per cent confidence limit" and "80 per cent confidence limit", respectively. The estimate for the stock requirements for each commodity is rather high. For the normal functioning of the buffer stock, i.e. to keep prices of commodities within the established range, a sufficient amount of capital must exist. When the commodity price falls to the floor price of the established price range, the money makes it possible for the quantity needed to prevent the breaking of the floor limit to be bought, and in turn, this will call into question the further functioning of the buffer stock scheme. Therefore, evidently the greater the size of the buffer stock, the greater the costs would be.

Here the evolution of the size of the buffer stocks for tin and cocoa might be taken into consideration. In the case of tin, it may be noted from past experience that in the main, they were planned rather high. This fact was shown in Part I of this work.

The buffer stock holdings from the year 1970 can be seen from the following table, where they are presented for the quarters of successive years.

Table 36.

Buffer stock holdings of tin metal (end quarter, metric tons)

	1970	1971	1972	1973	1974	1975	1976
March	3,870	2,692	8,099	10,475	142	2,893	19,631
June	955	2,692	8,119	10,069	142	11,830	2,822
Sept.	955	3,477	10,131	4,740	122	11,942	1,898
Dec.	1,232	6,637	12,479	1,001	142	20,071	806

Source: International Tin Council, Tin Statistics, 1977.

Recent experience shows that the buffer stock established in the Fifth International Agreement amounted to the equivalent of 20,000 metric tons of tin metal. During the agreement, provision was also made for a voluntary contribution of a further 20,000 tons from the consuming member countries. The holdings of the buffer stock were exhausted on 13th January, 1977 and, as an aid, a donation of 1,500 tons from the US was accepted in October 1980.

According to the Sixth International Tin Agreement, which came into force on 1st July, 1982 (72) it was envisaged that the buffer stock would amount 30,000 tons of tin metal (73), financed for the first time by both producers and consumers equally. To this, further stock of 20,000 tons of tin metal would be added, financed by warrants and government guarantees. This would be the size of the new tin buffer stock, the purpose of which would be to attain the objectives of the agreement.

In the case of cocoa, buffer stocks represent an important instrument in achieving stabilization and in the 1973 Cocoa Agreement, were planned to be of a capacity which equalled 250,000 tons. The price range of the buffer stock was set too low, and this stock never came into use, due to the fact that cocoa prices stayed above the ceiling price for the entire duration of the agreement. The new Cocoa Agreement established on 18th November, 1980 envisaged that the capacity of the buffer stock would be 250,000 tons of cocoa beans, although, during the long period of discussions, estimates were around 350,000 tons, (normal stocks of 250,000 tons and contingency stocks of 100,000 tons). The manner in which the new established cocoa buffer stock will function, depends on the price behaviour during the life of the new Cocoa Agreement.

Here, it might be pointed out that estimates elaborated by UNCTAD and presented in Table 35 should be regarded only

---

(72) The Sixth International Tin Agreement, UNCTAD, TD/TIN.6/14, p. 46, art. 55, para. 1.

(73) Ibid., p. 20, art. 21.

as suggestive as they run the risk of being either over-estimated or underestimated. This is due to the offsetting effects, which do not take into account the evidence of national or privately-held stocks, the too narrow price range and the fact that the target prices are determined at a too high level. Therefore, the estimates should be taken more as an illustrative example to show how difficult it is to determine, a priori, the correct size of the buffer stock for any commodity.

b) The price range of the buffer stock

It has been shown that the functioning of a well-designed and properly-regulated buffer stock control scheme depends directly on its size. Furthermore, it is necessary to determine its price range. The purpose of the well-defined price range is in its ability to decrease the short-term oscillations in supply and demand. These two values, the size and the price range of the buffer stock are highly correlated. It could even be said that the appropriate size of the buffer stock influences its operation and is determined by its well-defined price range.

One question remains: how should a price range be fixed? The answer to this question is that a price range definitely depends on

- fixing the floor and ceiling prices, and
- determining the most realistic price trend.

A component of crucial importance in the functioning of the buffer stock scheme is the determining of the floor price. The following question might be raised: why is it so important to set the right floor price? The answer is that the objectives of the buffer stock scheme are

- to ensure the stabilization of prices at levels which provide producers with an adequate return over the process of a full business cycle, and therefore prevent supply shortages, and

- to ensure adequate supplies of primary commodities to consumers and outlets to producers (74).

In order to be able to attain these objectives, the floor price should be determined on the basis of the market prices, taking into account the inflationary progression. Once the limits are established, the control mechanism of the buffer stock has to keep the market price between the floor and ceiling. To effect this, the buffer stock manager has to sell from the stock,or has to buy for the stock, sufficient amounts of the commodity concerned.

The dimension of the price range, therefore, would determine the nature of control. In practice, the two cases which might occur are that the price range might be set too narrow, or, on the other hand, it might be too wide. This is depicted in Figures 20 and 21, respectively.

In the former case,it would be more difficult to guarantee price control. As a result,the buffer stock manager would require great quantitative and financial resources to keep the control scheme in operation. Thus, the demand for a large amount of resources by a buffer stock manger is justified by the fact that he has to buy a great quantity of the commodity concerned at the floor price, which should, in fact, be bought at a rather higher price. If these large resources can be made available, which is very costly, such a narrow price range would assume greater stability.

Conversely, in the case where the price range is too large, it would seem, at first sight, to be easier to control the price oscillations. This is due to the fact that the bigger the price range, the less quantitative and financial requirements are needed for the operation of the control scheme. The buffer stock manager would be in a position to buy smaller quantities of the commodity concerned at floor price and would be able to purchase them at a relatively low price. Although this situation seems more

(74) International Commodity Stocks: Capital requirements and financing possibilities, UNCTAD,TD/B/C.1/186,1975, p. 5.

Figure 20.

Narrow price range: hard to control - greater stability

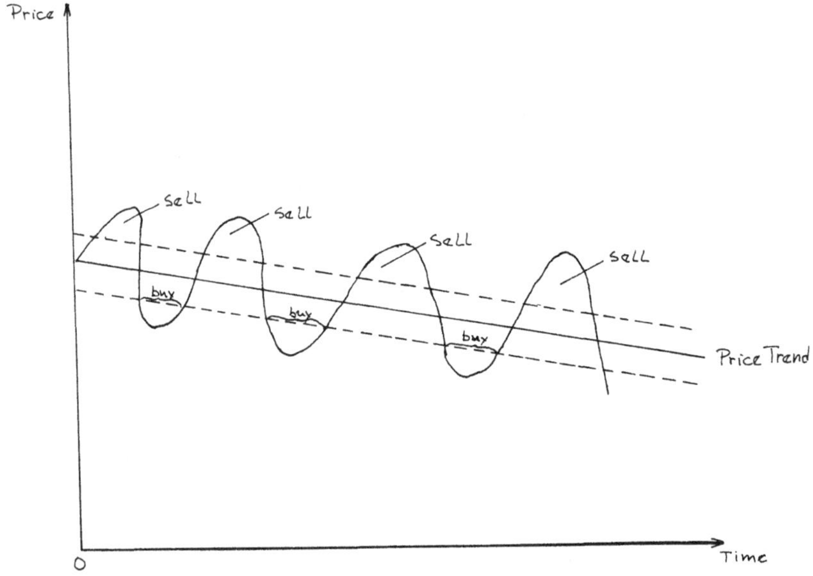

Figure 21.

Large price range: easy to control - greater instability

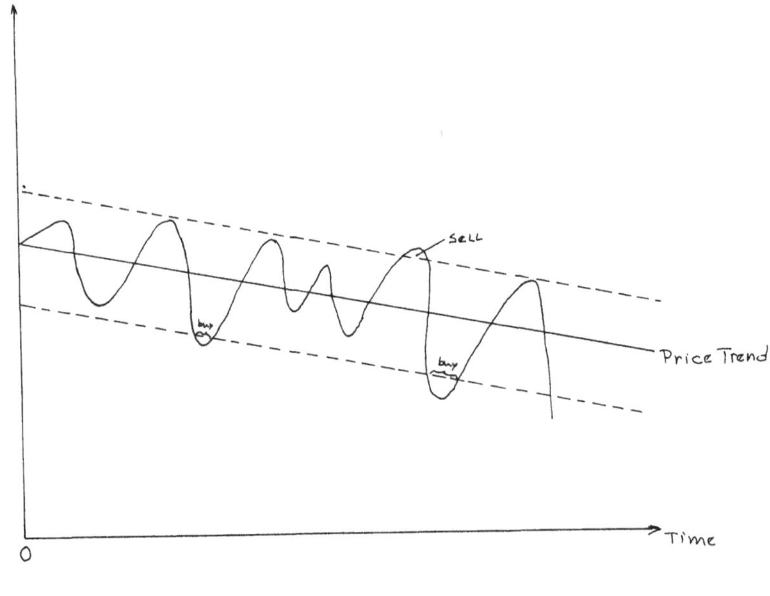

favourable than the previous one, it is not a solution, for the buffer stock manager's intervention would not seriously affect the price oscillations and instability would remain.

The difficulty involved in setting a price range can be seen from the case of the International Cocoa Agreement (75) established on 19th November 1980. In the context of the agreement, negotiations concerning setting of the price range were prolonged for nearly a year due to a difference of opinion among the participating members. The final decision was made that the floor (minimum) price was to be 100 U.S. cents per pound, and the ceiling (maximum) price 160 U.S. cents per pound. The floor intervention price was to be 110 U.S. cents per pound and the ceiling intervention price was to be 150 U.S. cents per pound. The floor intervention price would be decreased only when the intervention of the buffer stock manager had been without success or also after the purchase of 100,000 tons.

Therefore, when an adequate price range is to be fixed, the participating countries have to take care that it is neither too wide nor too narrow, but sufficient to eliminate the sharp price fluctuations which might occur around the defined price trend. To achieve this objective, i.e. to set the right price range, the participating members are advised to take into account the important market conditions and, therefore, to consider

- a frequent revision of the basic price, and
- frequent re-negotiations of the price range.

These two interventions, if effected in time and in an appropriate way, can prevent the harmful accumulation of stocks, which cannot be sold when the prices tend to reach the ceiling price and vice versa, thus bringing about the short-term oscillations in prices.

---

(75) International Cocoa Agreement, 1980 ,TD/COCOA.6/EX/R.1, 17th November 1980, Art. 27, para.1, p. 18.

2. Operational problems of the buffer stock scheme

The operational problems of the buffer stock are wide in scope and they are due to the specific characteristics of the commodity traded and the particular circumstances created by its production and consumption.

Here attention is drawn to one of the operational problems of the buffer stock agency in commodity stabilization: the element of speculation. The importance of this factor, which is negative in nature, must not be overlooked as it may be regarded as one of the basic problems of the buffer stock scheme.

a) Private speculative intervention vis-à-vis the buffer stock operations

The well-known principle of buffer stock operation is to buy the commodity for the stock when prices tend to fall, and to sell the commodity from the stock when prices tend to rise and therefore, to facilitate maximum reduction of the short-term price fluctuations.

A similar principle can be found with regard to the private speculators. They also follow the buying and selling activity according to the price movements in the market. This would be ideal if private speculators could follow the activities of the buffer stock agency. However, in reality, their speculative stock holdings can influence market supply and, therefore, in turn, have stabilizing or destabilizing effects on prices.

Stabilization effects on prices can be brought about by speculators, on one hand, if they buy the commodity concerned when prices tend to fall. In doing this, they reduce market supply. On the other hand, the opposite effect, i.e. increase in the market supply, may be obtained through the selling of the commodity concerned. These effects will come about only if the expectations of the speculators concerning the expected price are correct. If not, the wrong expectations will bring about de-stabilization of prices. As MacBean points out if "the speculator suspects that the agency's stock is too small to allow it to hold the price of the commodity at the ceiling, he will buy as much of the commodity as he can obtain at the ceiling price"(76). In this case, speculators expect prices to increase furher as they wait for the buffer stock operator to stop selling due to an insufficiency of the commodity in the stock. The effect obtained will be, on one hand that there will be no more stocks in the buffer stock agency, which creates operational difficulties for the buffer stock operator, and, on the other hand, favourable conditions for speculators to sell their stocks as prices tend to rise. This, in turn, would de-stabilize the market price, but would bring the speculators large profits. Therefore, their principal aim of maximisation of profits would be attained.

For this reason, speculators have to foresee, with a high degree of accuracy, whether or not the stocks are going to be small enough to realize their profit. If their prediction proves to be wrong, they will not realize a profit but suffer a loss. In the case of falling prices where the buffer stock operator cannot buy any more commodity for the stock due to the lack of financial resources, the operation of the buffer stock scheme will be called into question. During this period of declining prices, speculators would sell their stocks of commodities because they would estimate that prices were not going to recover. They would choose to sell to avoid the high storage costs of accumulated commodities. Therefore, the final result would be that prices would decline further.

This suggests that the intervention of private speculators does not directly affect market prices. Instead, if there is an increase or reduction in speculative stocks, this will, in effect, drive market prices to higher or lower levels, respectively, thus creating stabilizing or de-stabilizing effects.

---

(76) MacBEAN, A., Export Instability, op.cit., p. 271.

Therefore, the level of stocks held and operated by speculators can be said to depend considerably on the relationship which exists between the market price and the expected price, which, in turn, determines and influences the relationship between the private speculators and the buffer stock operations. This means that the functioning of the buffer stock scheme may be greatly influenced by the size and changes manifested in the speculative stock holdings.

b) Elements of the buffer stock operation which bring about a reduction in private speculative intervention

As has already been mentioned, buffer stock operations and private stock interventions are characterized by two different goals. The former has, as its goal, a maximum reduction in price oscillation, and the aim of the latter is to achieve maximum profit. Whether private speculators succeed in achieving their goal, depends largely on the operations of a buffer stock agency, which, in turn, will influence

- the expected profitability, and
- the risks of speculative stock holdings

for the private speculators. This is due to the fact that the buffer stock agency requires more capital funds for its operation and a larger quantity of the commodity stored than the private speculator. Therefore, once the price range of the buffer stock is set, its adjustment to the long-term price trend will appear to be rather rigid and thus more difficult to adapt to the new situation than is the case for speculators. In other words, private speculators can regulate their activity much more easily than the buffer stock agency can. They will try to predict the expected price on the basis of the present existing market price, and this will involve the risk of holding stocks for the speculative intervention which has the purpose of attaining the expected profit.

In view of this, the buffer stock scheme should be planned in such a way as to be able to reduce, as much as possible, the effects of private speculative intervention. If a certain degree of reduction in the private speculators' activities is not achieved and if their stock holdings are of great importance, their activities could create confusion for the buffer stock operator, which, in turn, will affect the direction of the equilibrium price, which has to be adjusted over a period of time.

The preventive measures, therefore, should aim at smoothing out the reciprocal effects which might appear between the buffer stock agency and private speculators. For instance, on one hand, stocks privately held might bring the buffer stock operation to a halt. On the other hand, buffer stocks, if adequately designed, could exert an important influence on the private speculators, which, in turn, will bring about the reduction of their speculative stocks.

Therefore, when the buffer stock is put into operation, it is more than desirable that it should offer a certain number of elements which would bring about a reduction in the activities of private speculators and thus assure a positive climate in the market conditions. These elements which are designed to reduce the risk for speculators should be as follows:

1. The buffer stock must have at its disposal sufficient financial resources. This factor would ensure the correct functioning of the buffer stock scheme and the maintenance of prices within the agreed price range.
2. The pure buffer stock scheme, in the case of excess supply, would not be sufficient to maintain and stabilize prices, as it would exhaust the resources necessary for its functioning. Therefore, a system of export quotas is desirable to maintain and stabilize prices at level higher than the price trend forecasted.

3. If the buffer stock manager could predict the market situation and therefore the price itself, and, combining this with his successful activity, succeed in keeping the price between the limits of the price range, this, in turn, would bring about the reduction of risks for the speculators.

4. If the buffer stock agency supplies better information on present and future situations in demand and supply, but not speculative ones, then it can bring about the exclusion of the private speculative risks (77).

In practice an example can be found in the commodity market, in the case of tin, where buffer stock operations are shown to be of use, as its stocking activity had remarkable success in suppressing private speculative interventions.

It can, therefore, be considered that the intervention of the private speculators and the risk they run with their activity, depend largely on the nature and operation of the buffer stock agency in the market for the commodity concerned.

3. Problems of coordination with the other methods of control

This heading brings us to the application of the buffer stocks when they are combined with the other methods of control. It has already been shown in Part one, that pure buffer stock is feasible from the theoretical point of view. It proved to be a rather difficult mechanism to operate when used in practice in its pure form, due to the fact that the supply of a large number of commodities is very hard to control.

---

(77) Those elements predestined to bring about a reduction in speculative risks are brought into discussion as "the desirable characteristics of a buffer stock agency" by HALLWOOD, Paul, Stabilization of International Commodity Markets, JAI Press inc., Greenwich, Connecticut, 1979, pp. 128-130.

In this section, an attempt will be made to show what sort of difficulties might arise when the functioning of the buffer stock is combined with another method of control.

a) Problems of buffer stocks in combination with the export quotas scheme

In general terms it can be said that, when a control scheme is decided on for operation in a commodity agreement based on the combination of a buffer stock scheme and export quota measures, it is important to consider how each of them should perform and what their best combination is to achieve the same aim, i.e. market stabilization.

Although the main features of the sole functioning of the buffer stock scheme and of export quotas have already been mentioned in Section B of this chapter, it is advisable to recall them here in order to show the contrast between this and their combined operating functions. So as not to repeat what has already been said about these measures of control, a reference might be made here, for the sake of the reader ,to MacBean's explanation.

Whenever buffer stock is concerned, a scheme has to be dealt with which "involves fixing a price range within which commodity prices are left free to vary but which is maintained by the stock agency's purchases and sales. When the price falls to the lower limit, the (buffer) agency stands ready to buy the excess supplies at the floor price. Provided the agency has sufficient funds, the price can be held at the lower limit by purchases for stock. If the price rises above the upper limit, the agency sells the commodity from the stocks at the ceiling price, and so long as its stocks last, the price can be held at, or below, the ceiling. The effectiveness of the scheme ... depends on the size of the gap between the ceiling and the foor price and the ability of the agency to defend these. This latter, in turn, depends on the resources of the scheme in the form of cash as well as stocks of the commodity in the desired grades" (78).

It can be seen that, if the price range of the pure buffer stock is set in the appropriate way (including the revision clause of prices - due to the inflatory effect), and if it has at its disposal adequate financial and quantitative resources, it will be able to defend the floor and ceiling prices. Therefore, the pure buffer stock control scheme will operate in a symmetrical way, evening out the extreme peaks of the price oscillation through the buying and selling processes in the market. Its main feature is that it operates without quantitative restrictions.

Where export quotas are concerned in this measure of control, there is "regulation of export quantities by adoption of quota forms", which is " another method of moderating fluctuations in commodity prices. The overall permitted quantity of exports is determined at a level which satisfies current and expected demand at prices approximating to informed estimates of long-run equilibrium price. Individual country quotas are usually determined on the basis of historical market shares. Ideally, however, they should take into account differences in cost structures in the exporting countries and should allow frequent adaptation to alterations in productivity - increasing the quotas of the more efficient, and decreasing those of the less efficient. Adaptable quota schemes could achieve the same aims as international buffer stock without the initial capital outlay, the risks of financial loss or the storage problems" (79).

It could be argued that from the total experience gained with both schemes, the fact emerges that the export quota scheme is not as costly as the buffer stock, although it achieves nearly the same aims as regards market stabilization.

---

(78) MacBEAN, A., supra note (76) at p. 269.

(79) MacBEAN, A., Ibid., p. 273.

Here the question arises: if this is the case, when everything speaks in favour of export quotas, is there any point in discussing the buffer stock schemes, which are so costly to operate and rather difficult to establish for both producing and consuming countries? The answer is that neither scheme is perfect. Each scheme has its own advantages and disadvantages, if used separately, and these differ from case to case. On the other hand, their use in combination with each other can bring about the removal of some disadvantages, which makes the combined measures much more flexible in their operations.

From the theoretical point of view, the functioning of the buffer stock is based on the following principle: it limits the commodity in stock when the price falls and reaches the lower limit of the established price range, or it releases the commodity from the stock when the price rises and reaches the upper limit. As far as the export quota is concerned, the principle is as follows: when prices tend to fall, quantitative restrictions of exports are sharpened, and when prices tend to rise, quantitative restrictions of exports are slackened.

In practice, the reactions of the buffer stock scheme to the unexpected price fluctuations are direct and prompt as it has adequate financial resources at its disposal. As far as export quotas are concerned, their reaction to unexpected price fluctuations is more vigorous due to the fact that there is no limit to financial resources. Quotas are fixed in such a way as to "freeze the status quo" for a short period, a season or a year, as envisaged by the commodity agreement. Here lies another characteristic that distinguishes this method from buffer stock intervention. Since it is fixed for a given period, there is no place for immediate adjustments when unexpected price fluctuations appear. Meanwhile, the nature of the buffer stock operation leaves a large number of possibilities open for the buffer stock manager to act, and, therefore, to be able to adjust to the new situations which can very often appear in the course of the market intervention.

Furthermore, in the period of abundant supply and low prices, export quotas imposed on the producers will create a new situation for producing countries. That is to say, although difficulties will arise, due to the fact that the export quota reaction to the market changes is lagged, by restricting supply, the latter will bring about a stabilization in prices. If the restrictions in supply are at a level below market demand, then the long-term prices can be raised. The application of the quota system reduces, to a large extent, the necessity for the initial capital expensses and storage problems, that are of importance for the buffer stock operation. This is not the case with a buffer stock control, which is created in such a way as to have adequate financial resources as well as sufficient stocks to intervene in the market.

It is well known, from the historical point of view, that an export quotas restriction scheme was largely used in commodity agreements. Whether they were successful or not depended largely on their quota system. Most of them were not successful, which means that the restriction system of export quotas was not useful enough. As far as the buffer stock system was concerned, the only commodity agreement that worked with this scheme was a tin agreement. It is worth recalling,however, that it was not a pure buffer stock agreement, but one supported by export quotas. Export quotas were regarded as a second tool for intervention in these agreements. The First Cocoa Agreement had provision for a buffer stock and was organized as a combination with the export quotas system but it never came into operation. The Tin,Cocoa, Coffee and Sugar Agreements currently in operation, are based on a combination of these symmetrical tools. This approach is due to past experiences with the Tin Agreement, where the buffer stock scheme was supported by the export quota system of control. The export quota restrictions proved to be successful when they were used to defend the floor price.The way in which export control is determined for the Sixth International Tin Agreement can be seen from the following: "the Council may,from time to time, determine the quantities of tin which may be exported from producing countries and may declare a control period and shall, by the same decision, fix a total premissible export tonnage for that control period" (80). The control periods with total permissible export tonnages will be declared by the Council only when the buffer stock contains 80 per cent or more of its assets in tin metal. This control measure will be undertaken in order to defend the floor price.

Furthermore, the direct and indirect effects of a pure buffer stock, and one combined with the export quotas, can be seen from the following explanation. When a pure buffer stock control scheme is used in the commodity agreement, its objectives are to have a direct effect on prices, and to reduce the price fluctuations. Its indirect effects should be viewed as a reduction of the fluctuations in export earnings. Where the buffer stock is supported by an export quotas scheme, the direct effects should be a reduction of price fluctuations and maintenance of the price above the long-run competitive level. The effects on export earnings of the combined scheme would occur as a reduction of fluctuations in export earnings with the possibility of an increase in average export earnings (81).

It can be seen, therefore, that an export quota restrictive scheme would be used to prevent the price from falling below the floor price established by the buffer stock scheme. Nevertheless, its restrictive objective will have no influence on the large increases in price. In this case, the buffer stock has to intervene and defend the ceiling price by selling from the commodity stock.

---

(80) The Sixth International Tin Agreement, UNCTAD, TD/TIN.6/14 1981, art. 32, p. 31.

(81) Explanations derived from Table 2-5 in Mc NICOL, D., Commodity Agreements, op.cit., p. 30.

It should be clear from this survey that the rôle of the export quotas scheme is to support the price. As far as the buffer stock is concerned, its rôle is to keep the price between the limits of the price range, i.e. floor and ceiling price, agreed by the producing and consuming countrise and set in the relevant commodity agreement.

The main problem which may appear is that of the use of the combined method: the buffer stock and export control scheme might twist the primary objective of the buffer stock to achieve the effect of the price-support control. This is not necessarily always the case. McNicol reports that it might happen if the "target price is set too high and the resulting excess supply, instead of being allowed to force the price down, is choked off with export quotas and/or production controls. The buffer stock then ceases to be a device for limiting price fluctuations and instead, becomes a way of supporting price above the long-run competitive level"(82). To avoid such a development in the market, McNicol proposes two safeguards, as follows:

1. "Controls on exports or production should not be triggered automatically when price falls below the floor price.
2. Any export quotas or production controls that are imposed should automatically lapse after a relatively brief period" (83).

These two protective approaches do not exclude the use of export quotas, but they indicate more precisely that their effectiveness should lie in supporting the floor price as a key element.

---

(82) McNICOL, David L., "Political Economy of an Integrated Programme" in ed., ADAMS,Gerard F. and KLEIN,Sonia A., Stabilizing World Commodity Markets, Lexington Books, 1978, pp. 208-209.

(83) Ibid., p. 209.

To conclude, it has been seen that these considerations confirm that the buffer stock scheme and export quota restriction scheme are two measures which complement each other.

b) Problems of the buffer stock in combination with the multilateral contract scheme

In addition to the considerations dealt with in the previous paragraph, it is interesting to contemplate the problems which might appear when buffer stocks are combined with another method of control. At this point, the combination of buffer stocks and multilateral contracts might be taken into consideration.

This control measure specifies a contract between producing and consuming countries. The import of the contract is that producing countries have to supply a specified, guaranteed quantity of the commodity concerned to consuming countries. The obligation of the consuming countries, according to the contract, is to buy the supplied quantity for a specified period of time. The prices at which selling and buying would go on may oscillate within the agreed price range. Therefore, a maximum price should be that at which the producing countries have to sell the concentrated quantities, and a minimum price should be that at which consuming countries have to buy the contracted quantities. The way in which this will operate depends on the provisions available.

This form of commodity agreement was used very little at an international level, and it came into operation in the International Wheat Agreement, with the prime objective of ensuring market stability for exporting countries and adequate supplies of wheat to importing countries (84), which, in turn, would bring about price stabilization for the commodity concerned.

---

(84) An Integrated Programme for Commodities: The rôle of multilateral commitments in international commodity trade, Report prepared by Professor C.A.BLYTH, UNCTAD, TD/B/C.1/186, 20th June, 1975, p. iii.

From these observations the fact emerges that the multilateral contract agreement, compared with buffer stocks or export quotas, is not so strictly defined and can therefore vary from case to case, i.e. from one commodity to another. This can be seen from Table 37, which shows that the buffer stock alone, or in combination with export quotas, demands the existence of a price range, which represents a vital element in its operation, contrary to the multilateral contract scheme which may maintain the price without the foregone price range. Furthermore, the former scheme could be introduced only in a period of low prices, when the buffer stock buys the commodity for the stock or where an export quota supports the floor price. This contrasts with the latter scheme, the nature of which allows it to be introduced at any time. These facts reinforce the above statement that the multilateral contract scheme will be different for each commodity and, according to it, each agreement will have its own specific characteristics. Therefore, it may be noted that this attitude embodied in the multilateral contracts makes them rather difficult to observe and analyse.

The framework of the operating problems is briefly presented by Loumiet as follows: "... under multilateral contract agreement importer nations agree to purchase all, or a stated portion, of their imports from exporter members, and the exporters agree to supply the quantities agreed upon within a stated price range. Thus, in term of shortages the exporter may not raise prices above the maximum stipulated in the agreement and in a time of surplus, importers must purchase the predetermined amount at a price not less than the minimum written into the scheme. As long as world prices fluctuate within the established range, however, the price mechanism of the agreement does not come into play and sale and purchase are at market prices"(85).

---

(85) LOUMIET, Carlos, "Towards an International Commodity Agreement on Petroleum", Journal of International Law and Policy, 1975, p. 496.

Table 37.

Buffer stocks and export quotas contrasted with multilateral contracts

Control measure	Specification of the control measure	Introduction of the control measure	Participating members
Buffer stocks and export quotas	necessary for a foregone price range to maintain the price	introduced in periods of low prices	in principle, can be operated by exporting countries only
Multilateral contracts	no necessity for a foregone price range to maintain the price	introduced at any time	both exporting and importing countries

Therefore, the extent to which an operation of this type of agreement can be successful depends, on one hand, on setting the agreed price to be able to procure the same effects to producing and consuming countries, and on the other hand, on the capacity of the exporting countries to maintain stocks when periods of supply arrive, and to release them when periods of shortages appears.

An attempt has been made in this section to provide adequate information and explanations as to the technical operational and co-ordination problems of the buffer stock scheme. Their use in practice has often been referred to, and it has been seen that past and contemporary investigations are characterized by unusual complexity and difficulties. To reduce these, the best way is to analyse and counter them in the buffer stock setting.

* * *

In conclusion of this Part, it can be said that the results of our general examination of the advantages and the real significance of different conditions have proved the value of this procedure in so far as it has provided us with an evaluation of the buffer stock system. The method employed has enabled us to develop theoretical criteria of typology and to apply them to the currently-known buffer stock agreements. Furthermore, examination of the direct and indirect effects has given an insight into the specific characteristics of the buffer stock scheme which are directly dependent on its dimensional and operational problems. Therefore, the main objective of this Part was to test them in practice. The result of our inquiry has shown that we have been dealing with a well-known phenomenon which definitely depends,on and is largely influenced by, the resources needed for establishing and maintaining a commodity buffer stock scheme.

PART III

PROPOSALS FOR AN IMPROVEMENT IN THE BUFFER STOCK POLICY

This Part presents hypothetical proposals designed to improve the buffer stock policy. Chapter I describes particular circumstances resulting from the multiple-commodity stocks approach, and the essential elements of a complementary stabilization system. Chapter II surveys the structure and financing system of the Common Fund and attempts to provide some answers to the questions concerning its improvements.

Part III discusses the development of methods and possibilities for future progress.

CHAPTER III

THE MULTIPLE-COMMODITY STOCKS APPROACH IN THE IPC

This chapter will be devoted to a brief consideration of the principal characteristics of the Integrated Programme for Commodities (IPC), developed and presented by the UNCTAD, concentrating on two points:

- the implications of the multiple-commodity buffer stock approach, and
- the way in which UNCTAD incorporates the above approach into the existing programme.

It would be useful to recall the fact that the International Commodity Agreements (1) concluded, with the purpose of stabilizing prices between the producing and consuming countries in the period up to 1976 on the commodity--by-commodity approach, proved relatively unsuccessful in that they were too slow to react and acted rather fruitlessly. This only bore out Keynes's statement (made in 1942) that such an approach would not be of much use, and he suggested aiming at some kind of multiple-commodity access. It took a further 34 years of more or less negative experiments in the "case-by-case" approach to primary commodities to arrive at the conclusion that a radical change in this domain was more than necessary. Finally, in 1976, at its 4th session, the UNCTAD main item was the criterion of the IPC. At that session, the main objectives and characteristics of this vast programme were worked out and settled.

1. Characteristics influencing commodity coverage

The general world situation at the time of UNCTAD IV in Nairobi more than ever required adequate intervention in the commodity markets. After the 1973 imbalance in commodity

(1) ICAs were concluded on coffee, sugar, wheat, tin, cocoa, and olive oil for different periods of time; see Part I for details.

supply and demand, which were aggravated by the oil crisis, greater price stability was urgently required. It was hoped that such price stability would assure better supplies and trade co-operation between the producing and consuming countries.

There was a lack of primary commodity reserves. Only 36 were internationally traded. These commodities represented a fundamental part of the exports of developing countries (75%) and an important part of the imports of developed countries (45%). Therefore, it was surprising that the key problem was to set up an IPC that would tackle the old problem of commodity trade, but on a new, international level.

1. The choice of the commodity set

In Part II, our investigation concentrated on a systematic discussion of the typology, which was presented in several steps. By now returning to the subject we do not intend to repeat the points already examined. Our interest lies mainly in the choice of the commodity set since it constitutes an important indicator for all that follows.

a) Commodities that can be stored alone

One may wonder what relevance the typology has. It may be recalled that, the established typology criteria (intrinsic and extrinsic), facilitated a discussion of the essential theoretical aspects and implications of commodities. It was noted that, by reason of the principal characteristics inherent in, and common to, primary commodities, intrinsic criteria will determine (in addition to natural qualities and the nature of production) whether a primary commodity is suitable or unsuitable for stocking. The determination of types of commodities unsuitable for storing made it possible to eliminate certain groups of commodities to which the buffer stock control scheme was inapplicable. There turned out to be many reasons for not storing (2).

It should also be recollected that the basic criteria for the buffer stock typology likewise pointed to commodities which could be stored, thus showing that it was feasible to apply the buffer stock scheme to them. In short, commodities can be categorized in two groups:

- non-stockable, and
- stockable.

We shall leave aside the non-stockable commodities and concentrate on the group of products qualified as stockable. A question may be asked here: within this general breakdown, can different combinations be found which would help us to choose the best alternative? It may be noted that, in general terms, two major groups can be distinguished according to the specific characteristics and conditions of stocking:

- primary products that can be stored alone, and
- primary products that can be stored along with others.

Which commodities belong to each group? To some extent, the answer depends on their natural and technical characteristics but another vital factor of an economic nature, namely, the nature of price fluctuations, also has to be taken into account. This factor alone can determine whether commodities are stored alone or withe other products.

The first group, where the commodities can only be stored alone, might include a natural product of key importance for both LDCs and DCs, to which not much attention has been paid so far - fuel. In view of its particular nature and extraordinary complexity, it is worth stressing its important features in the scope of this approach, and particularly the recent evolution and present state of the fuel trade. Amongst the different kinds of fuel, crude petroleum and petroleum derivatives are of special interest due to the fact that they occupy such an important place in world trade. For this reason these two fuels will be concentrated on.

---

(2) See Part II, Section C, Table 18, for more details such as spoilage, secular decrease in demand, great bulk and low unit prices, etc.

Historically, the trade in fuels can be divided into two main periods: one up to 1973, when petroleum prices rose sharply, and the post-1973 period. 1973 was a turning point, marked by the well-known quadrupling of crude petrol import prices within the space of a year.

During the first period (up to 1973), world exports of fuels represented about 10 per cent (in millions of $) of world trade as against 25 per cent in 1980 (3). In the first period, the petroleum price trend was generally downward in comparison with the price trends of the other internationally-traded primary commodities (4).

The general outlook of trade policy and the new pattern of world demand after the energy crisis inverted its price trend. The price situation after 1973 can be seen from Table 38, where the prices of crude petroleum are compared with the prices of all primary commodities traded in the last decade.

It emerges that, after 1973, there was a general decline in the total prices of primary commodities compared with crude petroleum prices, indicating a radically different situation to that prior to 1973. However, the situation has changed again and there is now an upward trend which can be seen from the data relating to the first two quarters of 1981.

As far as the export prices of crude petroleum are concerned, Table 38 shows a constant, but uneven, increase in the price trend. Taking into account the last two years, it can be seen that in 1979 the annual average increase was nearly 45 per cent, as against 74 per cent in 1980. In the first quarter of 1980, the increase was nearly 20 per cent, followed by increases of 13.5 per cent in each of the other quarters. Ther was a further increase at the very beginning of 1981. Comparing the first quarter of 1981 with that of

(3) International Trade 1980/81, GATT, Geneva, 1981, p.65.

(4) Ibid., p. 65.

Table 38.

Export Prices of Crude Petroleum Compared With All Primary Products

(Index 1975 = 100)

Year		Crude [a/] petroleum	All primary commodities
1972		22	42
1973		30	62
1974		100	105
1975		100	100
1976		116	116
1977		117	117
1978		117	119
1979		170	152
1980		295	217
Correlation Coeficient [b/]		r = 0,99	
1979	Q_4	216	117
	Q_1	293	215
1980	Q_2	293	215
	Q_3	301	222
	Q_4	306	224
1981	Q_1	326	326
	Q_2	228	225

Note: The indices are computed in US dollars.

a/ UN crude petroleum price index deflated by the UN unit value index of exports of manufacturers of developed countries.

b/ Correlation coeficient calculated on the basis of the given data - own computation.

Source: International Trade 1980/81, GATT, Geneva, 1981, Appendix Table A4.

1980, the price rose by 17 per cent (5). The steady increase in crude petroleum prices is a measure of the continuing and undeniable success of the OPEC cartel.

In order to show a degree of linear dependence between the export prices of crude petroleum and the export prices of all primary commodities, the criterion of the correlation coefficient was applied. This revealed a very close relationship and a high degree of linear dependence between the phenomena in question since they are significantly and positively correlated.

Several outlines concerning the nature of petroleum price movements have been presented in an attempt to see whether petroleum can qualify as being suitable for buffer stock action. Suitability for buffer stock action may be viewed as a possible criterion in the case of petroleum. There are, in fact, several factors which could make petroleum particulary eligible and suitable for stocking procedures. Nevertheless, its special natural characteristics make it difficult, if not impossible, to envisage it being stored in combination with any other commodity (6). From this it can be deduced that petroleum is a durable commodity, marked by wide and even excessive fluctuations in price. Furthermore, it is not subject to seasonal fluctuations, a characteristic that could arouse the interest of producers and consumers in the buffer stock scheme as a price stabilization measure.

---

(5) Ibid., p. 71.

(6) This is certainly not the only reason. There is no doubt that, with regard to supply and demand in the long term, the situation of petroleum would not be the same as for tin. Despite economic investigations, it is evident that long-term forecasts primarily represent a political problem which will be hard to overcome.

In the case of crude petroleum stored alone, a buffer stock could have the following advantages:

- security of supplies,
- short-term price stabilization,
- influence on the price level,
- influence on the price trend,
- it does not fix the price.

With the buffer stock mechanism, in the case of crude petroleum ,which is a highly-priced commodity, instability might be less unsatisfactory than appears at first sight. With the help of a buffer stock some satisfactory results might well be obtained.

b) Could one commodity be stored along with another?

Concerning the nature of the price fluctuations, we may consider the second group, that of primary commodities that can be stored together.

Specifically, it can be said that it is unlikely that the prices of the set of commodities chosen for stock will fluctuate simultaneously. In view of this, it would be useful to determine which commodities could be combined on the basis of the nature of their price movements. Some commodities fetch high prices with the result that supplies are limited, while for others ,both prices and demand are low. In order to follow the movement of prices, Table 39 shows the real price fluctuations of ten primary commodities from 1974 to the first quarter of 1980. It brings out sharp irregularities in the prices of sugar, cocoa, and coffee and, among the commodities shown, less irregularity in the prices of copper and tin. In order to see how the prices of these commodities interrelate,the correlation matrix presented in Table 40 can be used. With the assistance of statistical measurment using the correlation method, the degree of elementary linear interdependence of two variables can be evaluated. However, this does not provide evidence of periodic price movements.

Table 39.

Real price fluctuations of 10 primary products

indices of price variations are deflated

(base 100=average level prices, from 1974 to 1st September 1980)

Commodities	1974	1975	1976	1977	1978	1979	1980 (1st.Q)
Sugar	231	145	81	52	46	47	98
Cocoa	77	57	92	156	127	102	76
Coffee	61	60	115	171	105	96	82
Tea	92	83	91	145	108	89	80
Wheat	153	117	102	73	82	85	74
Rubber	109	76	97	98	104	111	110
Cotton	115	86	123	104	95	85	84
Jute	122	120	93	93	105	85	65
Copper	158	88	98	84	79	96	95
Tin	93	75	83	108	118	117	111

Source: RAMSES 1981, ed., BRESSAND, Albert, 1981, Editions Economica, p. 256.

Table 40.

Matrix of correlation: real price fluctuations of 10 primary commodities

	Sugar	Cocoa	Coffee	Tea	Wheat	Rubber	Cotton	Jute	Copper	Tin
Sugar	1.00									
Cocoa	-0.58	1.00								
Coffee	-0.69	0.89	1.00							
Tea	-0.70	0.90	0.93	1.00						
Wheat	0.97	-0.76	-0.77	-0.23	1.00					
Rubber	-0.11	0.33	0.20	0.20	-0.68	1.00				
Cotton	0.30	0.04	0.19	-0.07	0.34	0.21	1.00			
Jute	0.59	-0.20	-0.69	-0.33	0.80	-0.38	0.03	1.00		
Copper	0.58	0.11	-0.51	-0.51	0.86	0.56	0.56	0.49	1.00	
Tin	-0.59	0.73	0.48	0.46	-0.09	0.23	-0.32	-0.53	-0.24	1.00

Table 40 shows that a very high, and thus significant, positive correlation appears in the relationship between coffee, cocoa and tea. Rubber tends to show a low positive correlation which is not very significant. Cotton and jute also tend towards positive, but again insignificant, correlation. Copper and tin are positively correlated. Table 40 provides the following correlation coefficients:

20 cases of negative correlation	
6 cases of non-significant correlation	$r<0.30$
7 cases of positive correlation	$0.30<r<0.50$
3 cases of significant correlation	$0.50<r<0.70$
6 cases of close correlation	$0.70<r<0.90$
3 cases of very close correlation	$0.90<r<1$

This shows that commodities which are not intrinsically related can be highly correlated.

To answer the question asked in the heading: whether price fluctuations were to be taken as the only factor and the principal criterion for the choice of commodities suitable for storing together, the possibilities are rather limited, though it could be said that the information provided by the matrix in Table 40 suggests a certain potential in this respect. Nevertheless, it is advisable be cautious, for, in order to arrive at a definite answer, all the predominant factors in the estimation of price fluctuations have to be carefully analysed.

2. UNCTAD's view of commodity coverage

Let us now recall several facts concerning the IPC's commodity coverage. It was originally intended that a wide range of commodities should be covered by the IPC. The provisional list of commodities to be included in the programme was followed by the suggestion that it should cover a "comprehensive range of commodities of export interest to developing countries"(7). The task was not easy. It was

(7) An Over-All Integrated Programme for Commodities, Note by the Secretary-General of UNCTAD, TD/B/498, 8th August, 1974, p. 13.

necessary, in a special investigation, to choose from the wide range of internationally-traded commodities those which are prima facie suitable for international stocking at reasonably low cost. The commodities of international marketing importance to be taken into account were coffee, cocoa, citrus fruits, pepper, rice, sugar, tea, wheat (agricultural food); cotton, jute, tobacco, rubber, sisal, wood, wool (agricultural materials); coal, gas, petroleum, uranium (fuel minerals); aluminium, bauxite, copper, iron ore, lead, manganese, mica, nickel, phosphate, shellac, tin, tungsten, zinc (non-fuel minerals); meat, oilseeds, oils and fats and oilseed cake, wine.

However, it became apparent that such a vast list of commodities, although of primary importance to the economies of developing countries, could not be covered in full. A series of criteria was therefore established in order to select those commodities which needed the most assistance. Selection was made according to the following elements:

- the importance of the commodity in question in world trade,
- the importance of the origin of the commodity concerned for the export earnings of the LDC s, and
- special natural, technical and economic features of commodities which made them suitable for stocking.

The list of commodities was thus reduced to eighteen (8), bananas, bauxite, cocoa, coffee, copper, cotton and cotton yarns, hard fibres and products, iron ore, jute and products, manganese, meat, phosphates, rubber, sugar, tea, tropical timber, tin and vegetable oils, including olive oil, and oil-seeds, from amongst which preference was given to the ten most important (in view of political and other factors) and most most suitable for storing. They are well-known as the ten "core" commodities, for which agreements are to be concluded:

(8) Resolution Adopted by the Conference 93(IV). Integrated Programme for Commodities, UNCTAD, TD/RES/93(IV), 10th June 1976, p. 4.

cotton, cocoa, coffee, copper, hard fibres, tea, rubber, sugar, jute and tin. For each of these it was suggested that international agreements should be initially based on the buffer stock control mechanism supported by supply management measures, except for cotton and tea. These agreements are to be drawn up for individual commodities, but the approach would differ from the traditional one in that it would employ a set of principles, objectives, techniques and guidelines to give them more unity and thus facilitate the negotiations.

Resolution 93(IV) indicated that the total of 18 commodities taken into account did not exclude other products which could be included in the future.

a) Mutual price dependence of the UNCTAD commodity set

The question formulated in very general terms in the previous sub-section, concerning the price interdependence of the commodities concerned will now be discussed again but this time different aspects of the UNCTAD approach will be concentrated on.

Although, as it has been seen, great importance was, and still is, attached to the price stabilization policy through the multiple-commodity buffer stock approach, it may be noted that IPC does not give any information on the mutual dependence of the prices of those commodities covered by the programme.

This point was first raised by W.C.Labys and Y.Perrin (9). They worked out and discussed the empirical results of a multivariate analysis of the prices of 31 primary commodities which are internationally traded; among them are UNCTAD's ten "core" commodities.

The analysis reveals that, in the case of the buffer stock of common commodities, "as the number of commodities

(9) LABYS, Walter C., and PERRIN, Yves, "Multivariate Analysis of Price Aspects of Commodity Stabilization", Weltwirtschaftliches Archiv, 1976, pp. 556-564.

included is increased, the capital savings potential may tend to increase, but the size of the potential savings depends on the inter-relationship between the price movements of the commodities concluded" (10). Using the illustrative model of market conditions for two different commodities, X and Y, the advantages of the pooling system were explained (11).

The purpose of the analysis was to show, by means of an intercommodity covariance analysis, that the interdependence of the prices of the commodities concerned is of considerable importance in safeguarding potentially adequate financial resources for financing the multiple-commodity buffer stock programme.

Although the analysis introduces a new point into the multiple-commodity buffer stock approach which was not covered by UNCTAD's IPC, it does not, in fact, include all the elements that influence price fluctuations (12). This weakness is due to the fact that such a complex argument itself raises questions. However, in our opinion and with hindsight, this article underlines the fact that the interdependence of the prices of the commodity set covered by the IPC is of great and undeniable significance.

In consequence, the interdependence of prices could be used as a guide to future inquiry, which might produce additional and much more positive ,information on whether two or several commodities could be stored together as a compromise and, if so, how. There is no reason why this possibility should not be looked into.

b) Obstacles to commodity coverage

In general terms, several elements proved to be of importance in the UNCTAD debate on commodity coverage.

---

(10) Ibid., p. 558.

(11) The new method of pooling will duly be explained in the chapter on the Common Fund.

(12) This was recognized by the authors themselves. Supra note (9).

In 1976, years after it had been realised that something had to be done to achieve some progress in the field of primary commodities, UNCTAD passed the IPC resolution in Nairobi. However, the proposal and objectives concerning the principal issue - that of commodities and the Common Fund - were formulated in too challenging a way to be attained.

This situation was not new for UNCTAD - it could even be called routine. Goals which are set too high arouse undesirable suspicion and the fear of disappointment from not achieving them. This was borne out by the fact that, until UNCTAD V in 1979 in Manila, the slow start to negotiations gave little hope of quicker progress. Nevertheless, March 1979 was marked by noteworthy success and fruitful negotiations concerning the Common Fund, which was finally adopted in June 1980. Unfortunately, it has not yet been ratified.

Although the IPC forms an excellent basis for developing the framework of the approach of the multiple-commodity international commodity agreements programme, obstacles remained. The traditional and fundamental conflicts between producers and consumers of the commodities covered by the IPC took the form of inflexibility and a reluctance to conclude ICAs.

However, the positive attitude to the buffer stock method proved it to be of greater importance than the method of export restrictions. It was favourably received because this system serves as a buffer between supply and demand, and because it takes into consideration the negative effects of price fluctuations.

With regard to the IPC itself, the Programme, from our point of view, could be qualified as:

- too ambitious, but
- capable of improvement.

Why? To start with, its proposals seem too ambitious in seeking to conclude eighteen commodity agreements, when it is evident that very few agreements have been negotiated in the past and only one has achieved some kind of permanence. In other words, one of its major drawbacks lies in its overambitious aims concerning commodity coverage. Although it sounds highly feasible as a concept, it can, in our opinion, achieve at best, only 50 per cent of its total task.

Although eighteen primary commodities are identified under the IPC, it appears that buffer stock commodity agreements could be concluded for only half of them, i.e. for cocoa, rubber, tin, sugar, coffee, wheat, copper, jute, tea and cotton. However, it goes without saying that, although these agreements are attainable, the principal obstacle still remains. This lies not only in the purely economic relations between the LDCs and DCs but also, and perhaps more so, in the merging of their economic and political strategies.

B - THE EX POST COMPLEMENTARY STABILIZATION SYSTEM OF EXPORT RECEIPTS

This section attempts to analyse the ex post complementary stabilization system of export earnings.

We intend to examine the relationship between the integrated programme for the ex ante stabilization of primary product prices and the efforts to stabilize ex post export receipts. This will give us a better grasp of their general interactions and the possible advantages for the LDCs and world trade in general.

1. A solution of the STABEX type

The importance of this observation is not that it offers a categoric answer and definite proposal for the best solution but that it gives an insight into the existing possibility where the IPC includes a solution of the STABEX type.

It may be safe to say that the experience gained from STABEX points to some of the advantages that LDCs are expected to obtain through implementation of the Programme.

a) STABEX - Export earnings stabilization in the Lomé Convention

It might be useful to recall the observations made concerning the expected objectives for the LDCs of the export earnings stabilization scheme as set down in the Lomé Convention.

A comprehensive discussion of the Lomé Convention will not be gone into here but attention will be focused on the crucial aspects of the STABEX scheme. This subject, it is as well to recognize, has already received considerable attention from both the practical and theoretical point of view. We shall therefore confine ourselves to examining the elements which throw light on the relative advantages for the LDCs.

The full text of the appropriate part of the Lomé Convention shows clearly that the world commodity trade, and especially the LDCs, expected to be able to bring about an equilibrium between supply and demand.

One may wonder why the Lomé Convention provokes so much interest. For a more comprehensive answer we must go back to the first Lomé Convention, concluded and signed at Lomé on 28th February, 1975.

The Convention, (also known as the ACP/EEC Convention) was comcluded between the European Economic Community and its associated African, Caribbean and Pacific developing countries and was intended, where its participants were concerned, to "establish a new model for relations between developed and developing states, compatible with the aspirations of the international community towards a more just and more balanced economic order" (13). This "new model" for a better relationship and regulation of the export trade of the participating LDCs took the form of an export earnings stabilization scheme - STABEX. This scheme represents a new approach on the principle of compensatory financing to alleviating shortfalls in the export earnings of the participating LDCs.

---

(13) "ACP/EEC Convention Lomé", reprinted in "Lomé Dossier", The Courier, No. 31, special issue, March 1975.

During its first four years in operation, while the Lomé Agreement was signed between the nine EEC states and 46 ACP developing countries, STABEX was used to cover the revenue from 33 products, classified into 12 product groups. Its operation has attracted international attention, which increased with the signing of the Second ACP/EEC Lomé Convention on 31st October, 1979, which now included 57 ACP countries, with 44 products covered by STABEX.

Renewal of the agreement did not bring an end to severe criticism. As J.Galtung observed,"the Convention is economistic, even classical, not only in its formulation but also in its consequences, by emphasizing production, processing and marketing trading without keeping in mind the purpose of all that..."(14). This raises the question of whether we are now in a position to judge the fairness of this statement. As a full discussion is not within the scope of this work, an attempt will be made to counterbalance the severity of this observation and defend the agreement by revealing the substantial contribution made by the operation of the STABEX scheme to closer co-operation between the LDCs and DCs. This contribution is undeniable and worth examination.

The principle of the STABEX is to compensate financial deficits in the export receipts of the LDCs signing the Lomé Convention, these deficits being due to shortfalls in earnings from the products exported to the EEC or to natural disasters in the countries concerned. The financial compensation is paid from a special fund. The way the transfer works can be illustrated by the following case:

- cocoa exports from the Ivory Coast during the period 1975-1979, were represented as averaging 100 cents per pound. During the 1980 crop year, the Ivory Coast did not export more than 70 cents per pound, the deficit of 30 cents per pound being financially compensated by the EEC out of the special fund (15).

---

(14) GALTUNG, Johan, "The Lomé Convention and Neo Capitalism", The African Review, vol.6, 1976, p. 39.

(15) VIGNAL, Renaud, "Fond commun et stabilization des prix des matières premières" in ed., MOUTON, Claude and CHALMIN, Philippe, Commerce international et matières premières, Economica, Paris 1981, pp. 171-180.

On the basis of this principle, one might ask what the main features of the STABEX scheme are. There are in fact two, which may be defined as follows:

- first, it does not intervene in the market, and therefore has less influence on the relationship of supply and demand, and
- second, the fact that its stabilization effects are ex post of export receipts means that it has no direct influence on market prices (15a).

These features are of enormous importance since compensatory financing of the STABEX type gives balance of payments support without influencing the market mechanism. This is in the interest of DCs (such as the Federal Republic of Germany, Great Britain, the United States or Japan). It should be noted that the principle and facilities of the STABEX scheme have been applied only to ACP countries and a selected group of commodities. Application of the STABEX scheme has provided stable earnings for 12 product groups, eleven agricultural commodities and one mineral. The products are groundnuts (nuts, oil and cake), cocoa(beans, paste and butter), coffee (raw, roasted, extracts, etc.) raw cotton, coconut products, palm products (oil nut, kernel oil); hides, skins and leather; timber, fresh bananas, tea, raw sisal and iron ore. Here the following question arises: why only one mineral product? The answer may be found in the appropriate part of the Lomé Convention, which states that it is included "only for the sake of not jeopardising the achievement of the overall agreement, for it remains firmly opposed to the extension of the system to mineral products (16). Once the products have

---

(15a) For further analysis on the features of STABEX see:PERSAUD, B.,"Export Earnings Stabilization in the Lomé Convention" in ALTING von GEUSAU, A.M., ed., The Lomé Convention and a New International Economic Order, John Kennedy Centre for International Relations, The Hague, 1977.

(16) The Lomé Convention - Stabilization of Export Earnings, Commision of the European Communities, Information Directorate General Information-Development and Cooperation 94/75, Brussels.

been determined, what qualifies the country to benefit from the STABEX scheme? The criteria whereby an ACP country is eligible for application of the STABEX scheme are

- "threshold of significance", and
- "threshold of sensitivity".

The first characteristic -"threshold of significance"- means that the export earnings of the ACP country from a particular product must be 7.5 per cent or more in value of the country's total exports. There are two exceptions: the "threshold of significance" for sisal is 5 per cent for all countries, and it is 2.5 per cent for all products where the least developed, landlocked and island countries are concerned. The second characteristic - "threshold of sensitivity", i.e. a country's eligibility to receive a transfer for a product, is set at 7.5 per cent. The transfer can be effected if export earnings from the product concerned exceed 7.5 per cent of the country's total export earnings in the calendar year prior to the one in which the transfer is required. The rôle of STABEX is to compensate rapidly for the deficit of the exporting country.

To meet obligations, the STABEX fund has at its disposal only $ 490 million, to be disbursed over five years, i.e.$ 93 million per year.

The main point to make is that, in spite of its conceptual simplicity, the STABEX scheme has evident shortcomings. In brief they are

- the small size of the fund,
- the limited number of products covered,
- the conditions that arise from the problem of the terms of trade (17).

(17) This is seen as an important defect of the STABEX scheme. As B.Persaud remarks, the "scheme is concerned with the stabilization of nominal earnings rather than real earnings and export earnings could, therefore, be stabilized at inadequate levels". PERSAUD, Bishodat, "Export Earnings Stabilization in the ACP/EEC Convention" in The Political Economy of EEC Relations with African, Caribbean and Pacific States, Contributions to the understanding of the Lomé Convention on North-South relations, ed. by LONG, Frank, Queen Elizateth House, Oxford, 1980.

In spite of these obvious weaknesses, the mechanism has undeniable and highly significant advantages since the stabilization of export earnings offers the LDCs benefits that are vital for their economic growth and development, and mitigates some of the adverse effects of instability.

It is undoubtedly important in procuring financial aid for the poorest developing countries of the Third World; but, although it is seen as a mechanism of limited scope and regional character, it does not hinder the application of its advantages on a large scale.

In this connection, it should be remembered that STABEX was seen as a possible model for a scheme which might be applicable at the world level. This idea was advanced by Sweden and supported by some EEc countries at the Conference on International Economic Cooperation (CIEC) held at the Seventh Special Session of the UN General Assembly. The new global scheme had one essential difference from STABEX: it was to compensate shortfalls in aggregate earnings from all commodities, excluding fuels. This feature had occasioned some misguided criticism to the effect that it could not be experimentally confirmed and the idea proved unacceptable to the 19 participating developing countries.

The rejection of STABEX as the model for a global scheme in an international framework does not mean that there are no other ways in which the STABEX idea could exercise its export earnings stabilization principle. For instance, as it has proved possible to operate STABEX as a regional scheme in that it has already produced concrete results, the possibility could be considered of applying STABEX on a world-wide basis - but regionalized. It seems interesting, however, to point out that the regionalization might turn out to have certain negative aspects since it will favour certain countries. The principle would remain the same, and the regions could be envisaged as follows:

Present model: the EEC is responsible for ensuring the stabilization of export earnings of the ACP countries.

Future
possibility I: the United States could do the same thing for the Latin American countries.

Future
possibility II: Japan could provide for the needs of the Asian Thirld World countries (18).

These are proposals which might work. However, it is, perhaps, too early to make positive statements in this field. All speculation on this topic has to be treated with caution as there is no point in looking for a direct relationship between these potentialities,which is needed in a system to co-ordinate them at the world level. Only then could the question be answered of whether STABEX, which is, after all, a small model of limited scope, could serve as the pattern for a regionalized approach to commodity financing thoroughout the world.

b) The STABEX system in comparison with the IMF compensatory financing facility and the processes within the IPC

The second current scheme for the direct stabilization of the export earnings of countries is the compensatory financing scheme of the International Monetary Fund (IMF).

In contrast to STABEX's regional character, the scope of the IMF Compensatory Financing Facility is global and it has a world-wide programme. Before STABEX came into existence, this scheme (19) was the only one with aims which included the stabilization of export earnings.

The principal characteristics and objectives of these two schemes and their relevance are contrasted in Table 41, which seeks to show the reasons behind our selection of different aspects of the two methods of compensatory financing. It is evident that they have a number of features in common which, although they shade off into each other, are essentially different in their approach.

---

(18) VIGNAL, Renaud, Op.cit., p. 176.

(19) The IMF compensatory financing facility was set up in 1963.

Table 41.

Comparative relationship of the STABEX and IMF Compensatory Financing Schemes

Characteristics of the scheme	IMF	STABEX
magnitude of operation (first year of operation)	$ 3.25 billion	$ 89 million
capacity of consideration	global balance of payments consideration	commodity-by-commodity consideration
applicable to	all exports	only exports to the EEC(few exceptions allowed)
Attitude of the scheme towards participating countries	not discriminatory: loans available to LDCs as well to DCs (exc. Australia)	discriminatory: poorest LDCs of the Third World are favoured
method of calculating shortfalls	five-year moving averages.For centre taken the current year and forecasts are only for the two further years	four year period of reference to past earnings and levels
availability of loans and grants	loans: bear interest (although of modest rate and limited to the quota system of the IMF)	loans: more liberal, and interest-free grants:given in many cases

Source: General informations about the IMF and STABEX are obtained from: Compensatory financing issues and proposals for further action, UNCTAD V, TD/229/Supp.1, Manila 1979, pp.4-16 and 17-19; and ed., Frans A.M. ALTING-GENSAN, The Lomé Convention and a New International Economic Order, A.W. Sijthoff-Leyden, 1977, pp. 81-90, and STAKHOVITCH, Alexander, "A European view of commodity problems: Stabilization of prices and stabilization of receipts",in KLEIN, S. Op.cit., pp. 235-240.

Although each of these approaches has its undeniably positive side, it is obvious that neither of them is perfect. Criticism shows both as being inadequate in several respects, as has already been mentioned, for the operation of compensatory financing scheme is very complex. The general problem is one of co-ordination or, to put it more precisely, the fact which has already emerged is that some states are able to benefit from the financial facilities of both schemes at the same time. Eight states managed to take advantage of this situation in 1975 (20). Some way will have to be found to prevent this from happening again as it stimulates the uneven growth of export earnings (and therefore the economic development requirements) of some developing countries without closing the discriminatory gap with the other LDCs whose needs are as great or even greater.

The necessity for, and aims of, the compensatory financing schemes can now be seen. They are expected to moderate and mitigate the problems arising from the unstable nature of export earnings. This is achieved by offering loans and grants to the poorest countries with temporary export earnings problems. This implies that the long-term problems which derive from fluctuations in export earnings come within their scope. A solution to their long-term decline could be expected through, and by processes within, the IPC.

The problem can be considered from another point of view. Could the system of straightforward buffer stocks, as incorporated in the IPC, be regarded not only as a way of directly reducing the fluctuations in the prices of primary commodities and indirectly limiting fluctuations in the LDCs' export earnings, but, in additition, as a possible means of achieving a considerable impact on the growth and development of LDCs - which is, in fact, the main purpose of these two compensatory financing facilities?

The implications of this should be examined carefully. Parts I and II of this study have provided enough information to show that price stabilization and export earnings

---

(20) GOREUX, Louis, "Use of compensatory financing", Finance and development, 14, No.3, 1977, p. 21.

stabilization through buffer stocks have had a real impact on economic growth and development. However, it is apparent from what has been said that this impact is not enormous. They could not, therefore, be regarded as the sole instruments for the development of the LDCs but one could imagine them being united with other appropriate measures.There is thus reason to think that these new relationships could become, on the whole, more advantageous to LDCs. However, it is clear that the buffer stock schemes, used alone or in combination with some other measure, should not be regarded as a means of transferring income to the LDCs, or mistaken for an instrument to promote trade, aid and international co-operation in development.

However, care must be taken here. The preceding discussion amounts to the assumption that the pre-eminent question concerns the processes within the IPC. Which stabilization system should be chosen as an appropriate tool for dealing with the problems arising from the decline in the export earnings of the LDCs? On one hand, it is evident that compensatory financing could be adequate for certain commodities and under special circumstances (as has been seen in our explanation of the STABEX system).On the other hand, buffer stocks may be preferable where other commodities are concerned (e.g. minerals (20a), largely absent in the STABEX approach, are included). At this point, the importance of the situation in which buffer stocks take on great significance should be taken into account.

Here, the interest of LDCs in an appropriate use of the commodity agreements based on the buffer stock control scheme as an instrument of income transfer for their own benefit is undeniable. It could lead to price increases and high prices in the long run. Nevertheless, great care should be taken not to regard the buffer stocks as a principal instrument

(20a) SYSMIN - mechanism of price stabilization in certain mineral products. Consider: copper, cobalt, phosphates, bauxite, aluminium, manganese, tin and iron. SYSMIN scheme is a part of the Second Lomé Convention concluded in 1979, and came into force on 1st January 1981.

for transfer to the LDCs or as the best approach to international co-operation in development. If they are judged by this criterion, they should be considered the second best solution.

A summary can now be made of the major conclusions concerning the ex post complementary stabilization system of export receipts and the ex ante stabilization of the prices of primary products. As has been seen,

- each system is independent of the other,
- they are based on the same principles,
- they do not have to follow on from each other,
- each undoubtedly has very attractive features for LDCs and DCs,
- they are not opposed to each other, and
- they can be interrelated, although this would create obvious complications.

It can be concluded from these basic elements that there is nothing that rules out the fact of the combination of the price stabilization system with the solution of the STABEX type (IPC includes the compensatory financing),and that it would be worth investigating the question further.

2. A solution of the PANCAFE type

Here the experience of the Bogota group of Latin American coffee exporters will be examined to see if their approach could be combined with the Integrated Programme for the ex ante stabilization of primary product prices as a complementary ex post stabilization system of export earnings.

a) PANCAFE - the experience of the Bogota Group

Since 1973 when OPEC (Organization of Petroleum Exporting Countries) introduced the oil embargo and succeeded so well in forcing several successive increases in oil prices, the possibility and advantage of using the same method of cartelization for other primary products became an extremely important issue. A certain number of primary commodities registered substantial increases in price and the governments concerned were ready to examine how OPEC's success could be repeated in the case of their own primary commodities. The possibility of setting up "two, three ... many OPECs" (21) was given serious consideration. The point was that, although the producers' associations wanted defensive measures or stabilization, it was also important for them to raise the real level of prices and earnings. These were the aims of the producers' associations. Besides the OPEC experience (22), which showed how a commodity cartel could increase the export earnings of its members, there has been much analysis of this topic.

Each group had its own way of looking at things. Here the interventions of the coffee producers in the futures market will be considered. This will explain why the efforts of the Bogota Group aroused so much international interest.

The coffee producers' association, which has eight members (23) and is known as the Bogota Group, was established in 1978. In that year,Columbia disposed of large quantities of coffee; intervention became necessary and the Bogota Group undertook to support the coffee price. To be able to intervene in the market, the Bogota Group of producing countries set up an international marketing company, PANCAFE S.A., with a fund of $ 150 million (24) at its disposal.

---

(21) BERGSTEN, Fred C., "The Threat from the Third World". Foreign Policy, 11, 1973, pp. 102-124.

(22) The striking success of OPEC will be hard to repeat; it was, and is, the only case where all exporters were united in their action. Such unity is rather improbable in any other primary commodity.

(23) The member countries of the Bogota Group are Brazil, Columbia, Costa-Rica, Guatemala, Honduras, Mexico, El Salvador and Venezuela.

(24) The financial capacity in 1978 was $ 150 million; the amount was gradually increased until the fund had $ 500 million at its disposal for its activities. PANCAFE stopped intervening in the autum of 1980.

The PANCAFE marketing company was able to intervene in the coffee futures market on a large scale. It placed $ 100 million in the futures market for direct intervention on the New York and London spots. The result was that coffee prices were held at a higher level than they would have been without the intervention.

At this point, let us look at the intervention mechanism of the Bogota Group. It has been summarized instructively by Y. Simon. Experience had shown that "généralement sur un marché à terme, moin de 1% des contrats sont exécutés sous form de livraison (annulation) de l'opération initiale. Si, à l'échéance, le groupe de Bogota avait revendu les contrats préalablement achetés, ces ventes auraient pu faire baisser les prix pour éviter cette chute, le groupe de Bogota n'a pas cherché à dénouer les contrats de café qu'il détenait. Les vendeurs ne pouvaient dès lors honorer leurs engagements qu'en rachetant les contrats à un cours supérieur à celui auquel ils avaient précédement vendue. A défaut, il leur restait à se procurer du physique pour exécuter les obligations des contrats qu'ils avaient vendus, ce qui ne pouvait qu'élever le prix du café vert. Dans les deux cas, les producteurs étaient gagnants" (25).

The immediate results for the producing countries of the Bogota Group were more than satisfactory: their success was encouraging not only for them but for the producers of other primary products, too. This evidently encouraged them to prefer transactions on the futures market to the possibility of negotiating international commodity agreements.

But was it really the best solution for the producing countries? Was this the closest collaboration that producing countries could achieve? The answer can be found in subsequent events.

---

(25) SIMON, Yves, "Les interventions des pays producteurs sur le marché à terme de marchandise: l'example du groupe de Bogota" in ed., MOUTON, Claude et CHALMIN, Phillipe Commerce international et matières premières, Economica, 1981, pp. 131-132.

In 1980 weak demand owning to high prices and competition between Brazil and Columbia for market shares caused prices to fall. Natural conditions were favourable (no frost) and prices declined by about 35 per cent between May and September 1980. PANCAFE, in spite of having considerable funds at its disposal, was unable, with its intervention, to stop the downward trend. This was an evident setback for the PANCAFE marketing company and the producers in general, who found themselves incapable of influencing changes in the market arising from the interplay of demand and supply. In addition, the activities of PANCAFE were seriously objected to by some major importing countries. The result was severe: PANCAFE ceased operation and was supposed to liquidate its holdings. It was now in the immediate international interest to develop better understanding and co-operation between the coffee producing and consuming countries, with the common objective of reducing wide price fluctuations. One solution to the dilemma appears in the ICA proposal under the UNCTAD Integrated Programme. A solution will certainly be found since market developments will be largely determined by the degree of successful co-operation between producing and consuming countries. But when?

The above has shown that the direct impact on prices of the activities of the Bogota Group was more than satisfactory, but this was not all. It was, in particular, pointed out that their action was dynamic and their influence on the international coffee market incontestable. It should, however, be clear from this discussion that cartelization in the coffee market is hard to achieve for several reasons:

- there are a great many coffee producers,
- they are too far away from each other,
- there are great differences between the incomes of producing countries,
- the majority of these countries are LDCs, and some are among the poorest of them,
- there are different types and qualities of coffee,

- there is the danger of substitutes, and
- the price of coffee is relatively elastic.

The Bogota Group's cartelization of the coffee market was a test of the cartel concept and principles. However, the important success of PANCAFE should not be exaggerated. Its life was too short, and experience has shown that a producers' cartel in the coffee market has very little chance of survival. The fraudulent price-fixing arrangement between LDC producers alone had no success at all.

b) Acceptability of the PANCAFE solution

The question of whether a solution of the PANCAFE type can be regarded as complementary to the ex post stabilization of export earnings should be looked into a little more closely.

From this point of view, the following observations can be made concerning PANCAFE:

- In the futures market there is no question of producers being able to gain an advantage by means of their intervention alone. There are no obstacles to the participation of consumers.
- The intervention measures of the Bogota Group should not be considered a producers' policy to be used alone in the futures market, but rather as one component of a policy needed for the futures market (26).
- The rôle of intervention by the producers in the futures market through the international marketing company PANCAFE cannot be examined without taking into account the importance of speculation in international trade. Here it should be stressed that the PANCAFE solution was regarded and developed more as an instrument for managing the market than as a means of pure speculation.

---

(26) Op.cit., p. 136.

Finally, it should be emphasised that both theoretical and practical studies have shown that a cartel can increase the export earnings of the member countries by restricting exports only in special circumstances (i.e. when demand for the product is inelastic) (27).

Do these features qualify PANCAFE for possible combination with the UNCTAD Integrated Programme?

From the above investigation, it can be deduced that PANCAFE provides no more than the minimum required to ensure the ex post stabilization of export earnings. Put more succinctly, it is a solution of the cartel type which covers only producers and leaves consumers out of the price-fixing mechanism.

In the previous section it was pointed out that STABEX is seen as a possible solution in combination with the IPC. That these two schemes are contrasted can be observed from their different characteristics, as depicted in Table 42. These notions have proved particularly useful in highlighting the fundamental differences between them.

The comparison reveals little evidence of coherent and comprehensive compatibility between the potential characteristics of these schemes, but there is enough to show that although the price stabilization in combination with a STABEX type approach is feasible, combination with a solution of the PANCAFE type is clearly out of the question.

*

In conclusion of our inquiry in this section, it may be noted that the ex post complementary stabilization of export earnings and the Integrated Programme for the ex ante stabilization of the prices of primary products are, on the whole, not necessarily antagonistic. Their combination is feasible - but to what extent? To find the ideal balance,

---

(27) Mathematical findings concerning this remark are given by VAN DUYNE, Carel, "Commodity Cartels and the Theory of Derived Demand", KYKLOS, vol. 28, 1975.

Table 42.

The PANCAFE colution in comparative relationship to the STABEX type scheme

Peculiarity	PANCAFE	STABEX
advantages	- to raise prices - commodity-by-commodity consideration	- to compensate the shortfalls in the export earnings - commodity by-commodity consideration
risks	- difficult to maintain the artificially-elevate price-level - in the case of the current price-fall, a buyer in the futures market has to be able to produce the important financial facilities	- due to its limited capacity might not be able to cover all needed shortfalls in the export earnings
inconveniences	- in protecting the risks in the current price-fall there is a deprivation ipso facto of the increase in the current price	- method of calculating shortfalls in export earnings is based on the historical period
consequences	- co-operation between the producing and consuming countries was reduced - due to the threat of the substitutes, purpose of the intervention was more to stabilize prices than to increase them	- co-operation between LDCs and DCs is favoured - availability of loans and grants

Source: General information about the PANCAFE is provided in the article by SIMON, Yves, Supra., note (24) and for STABEX in Table 31 of this Section.

it is worth devoting some thought to whether or not a given proposal can be derived from the elements which form a network consisting of

- internal links, and/or
- the motivation needed to produce enough support for the search for an adequate solution.

To what extent this can be brought about, clearly depends on the sufficient elaboration of an substantial compromise between those elements.

CHAPTER II

IMPROVEMENTS TO THE FINANCING SYSTEM OF THE COMMON FUND

The general objectives of the Integrated Programme for Commodities have already been presented and discussed. In this chapter an attempt will be made to set forth and test the objectives and advantages of the Common Fund as a key component of the UNCTAD IPC. The technique used should also reveal possible improvements to the financing system of the Common Fund and cast light on immediate or future and, at present, unforeseeable changes that are important for further development.

In our approach to this problem, the basic characteristics of the Common Fund will be described as laid down in the final agreement concerning the IPC at UNCTAD IV, which was held from 5th to 27th June, 1980 in Geneva.

The fact that this new financial institution, is of great importance in the relations between the producing and consuming countries, better known as the North-South Dialogue (28), deserves to be emphasized.

A - THE FINANCING SYSTEM

Neither the need for, nor design of, the financing system which appeared in its final form as the Common Fund was new. In fact, Lord J.M.Keynes had, as early as 1942, advanced the very constructive idea of creating an international economic system for financing commodity stabilization. In brief, this was proposed by the "International Clearing Union" (which later became the IMF) and supervised by the "General Council for Commodities Control". These ideas were elaborated in the course of time. Efforts to bring it about spread over sixteen long years of discussion and negotiations between producing and consuming countries from the first

(28) The Conference on International Economic Co-operation (CIEC) better known as the "North-South Dialogue" was held in Paris in May 1977.

UNCTAD in Geneva in 1964, when the existence of a financial institution of this kind became crucial for the functioning of international commodity agreements. Two years before the Nairobi conference, UNCTAD considered that "if stock management was planned as a key element in an integrated international policy of commodity stabilization "(29), then "the negotiations of commitments on international commodity trade, including agreements for stocks, would be greatly assisted ... if there was a financial authority ready to support operational arrangements of an appropriate kind" (30). It was seen that "... the common fund and international stocking policies are the core of the programme. A common fund for stock financing is essential if impetus is to be given to the building up of international stocks of major storable commodities. The possibility of reaching agreement and operating stocking schemes as the principal new features of a comprehensive range of commodity arrangements is unlikely to be realized rapidly and effectively unless such a fund is created" (31).

As presented by UNCTAD, the establishment of the Common Fund was a key feature of the Integrated Programme. This was officially stated in the Nairobi Resolution 93(IV) of 1976, which indicated that it was the best means of reaching multi-commodity agreements and, indeed, the only way of satisfying the specific economic interests of the LDCs.

The deadline for implementation was set for February 1978. Although the climate of the negotiations became strained, agreement was finally reached on the Common Fund in March 1979, and it was formally adopted in June 1980, although

(29) An Integrated Programme for Commodities: A Common Fund for Financing of Commodity Stocks, Report by Secretary General of UNCTAD, TD/B/C.L/166/Supp.2, 12th December, 1974, p.2.

(30) Ibid., p.2.

(31) An Integrated Programme for Commodities: Specific proposals for decision and action by governments, TD/B/C.1/193, 28th October, 1975, p. 5.

it still had not been ratified (32) by the participating members.

The complexity of the problem, which owes much to the relations between LDCs and DCs against the background of the New International Order, constitutes an important aspect of the present international economic situation. The hopes were, and are, great that, once established, the new financing system would give a fresh impetus and provide an additional instrument for the conclusion of new international commodity agreements, This was deemed the most acceptable approach to the stabilization of the market in primary products. It was considered preferable to set up the Common Fund as a central financing system for the commodity approach, rather than to set up several costly individual funds. One of the very first proposals was that the overall financial needs of the Common Fund should be about $ 6 billion (33) for it to achieve its aim on account of its great borrowing power, and on the assumption that the physical size of the buffer stock for each commodity should be one-eighth of the annual consumption of that commodity. On the basis of detailed investigations, the amount proposed was reduced first to $ 10 billion and, in a further step, to $ 6 billion which was estimated as sufficient to support the storage requirements of 10 core commodities instead of eighteen (34).

---

(32) When this work was written,it had still not been ratified. Ninety participating countries, which, financially, represent two-thirds of the capital needed, i.e. more than $ 400 million, were to sign and ratify the constitutive agreement on the Common Fund by 31st March 1982. The situation was less encouraging: by this date, 82 countries had signed the agreement but only 22 had ratified it. The participating countries have indicated that the necessary ratification will probably take another year.

(33) In the earlier reports on the financial requirements for the Common Fund ,UNCTAD indicated an initial contribution of $ 1 billion and borrowings of $ 2 billion, which could be followed by an additional contribution of $ 1 billion and additional borrowing of $ 2 billion, for the possible total capital requirements of $ 6 billion. Consideration Of Issues Relating to the Establishment and Operation of a Common Fund, UNCTAD, TD/B/IPC/CF/2, November 10,1976, pp. 7-8, and TD/B/IPC/CF/L.2, 29th December, 1976, pp. 3/4 and 7.

(34) NUSBAUMER, Jacques, L'enjeu du Dialogue Nord-Sud: partage des richesses ou guerre économique, Economica 1981, Paris, 87.

The Common Fund was seen as an urgent necessity for the IPC but what were its chances of success? In answer to this extremely complex question,no attempt will be made to present a full description of its experimental stage or evaluate its merits in terms of whatever economic and political factors may apply. Our attention will be focused on the principal characteristics of its financial structure.

1. Significance of the Fund

Although our analysis has shown the need to create the Common Fund, it has not explained its significance. In our opinion, this lies in the general objectives of the Integrated Programme, which must be attained and then improved through the conclusion of multiple commodity agreements for primary products based on the system of buffer stock control, a point of crucial importance for some LDCs.

This should be achieved through a central source of finance - the Common Fund. The Common Fund is thus seen, and expected to perform, as the common denominator in international co-operation between the LDCs and DCs and as an essential instrument for the economic development of the LDCs. To live up to these hopes, the Common Fund is expected to combat a threefold problem:

- the financing of buffer stock activities,
- the financing of activities other than buffer stock, i.e. diversification and marketing that will promote the economic development of the LDCs, and
- to trade, to a certain extent, on its own behalf in the international market.

a) Purpose of the Fund

The chief purpose of the Common Fund as a dynamic financial institution is to meet major objectives of recognized importance in the international markets of the world and to be the instrument of the Integrated Programme for Commodities. In particular, it emerged that "the very existence of the Common Fund would help to focus international attention on commodities on a continuing basis" (35) and the fund would prove to be indispensable by providing financial backing for the stabilization of international trade in commodities.

This special source of finance is seen as a unique instrument,the operation of which has been ensured by the joint mandatory participation of producing and consuming countries.

The negotiations advanced step by step for four years and were eventually crowned with success in the establishment of a Common Fund which was expected to meet the Programme's objectives, This financial institution could make financial resources available in order to finance the buffer stocks, which serve as a mechanism for the stabilization of commodity prices. This factor should be seen as the principle reason for creating the Common Fund. It follows that the main target of the fund is to have sufficient financial resources at its disposal in order to support the conclusion of commodity agreements for primary commodities under the IPC. In contrast to the individual commodity approach of the past (although there have, in fact, been only a few commodity resources),the Common Fund is regarded as a less expensive way of backing several different agreements at once. This is due to the fact that the negotiations and conclusions of the commodity agreements could be more easily brought about in view of the fact that the Common Fund retains its obligation to lend financial resources to associated ICOs.

It is,therefore, possible to argue that the preference for a Common Fund as an instrument to deal with general financing requirements is justified by

- the integrated structure of the IPC, and
- the need to increase the credits available for each buffer stock.

---

(35) Articles of Agreement of Common Fund adopted, UNCTAD, TAD/INF/1185, 30th June 1980, p. 1.

Thus the evidence derived from the basic goals of the Common Fund allows us to conclude that both the LDCs and DCs expect potential benefits from the price stabilization provided. The previous analysis showed how LDC economies largely depend, directly or indirectly, on the behaviour of prices in the international market. If the stabilization hoped for is achieved, this, in turn, would affect the relationship that exists between the buying capacity of the LDCs and their growing requirements for manufactured goods. This point finds support in the argument advanced by K. Laidlaw and R. Laishley, who remarked, in their study on the Common Fund, that "a loss of third world purchasing power caused by a dramatic fall in the prices of commodities can lead to loss of export orders and increased unemployment for industrial countries" (36). The truth of this can be seen from the fact that the price fluctuations in the 13 primary products have caused nearly "$ 15 billion in lost output through their effects on employment and productivity during 1963-73" (37).

b) The Common Fund in operation

Here, in particular, it was necessary to find, and develop, methods and facilities to provide the necessary conditions for the Common Fund to function.

The very existence of the Common Fund, and hence the methods developed to set it up, provided "powerful proof of the capacity of the entire international community, acting through the United Nations, to negotiate concrete and complex matters" (38). To get 82 states to agree upon

---

(36) LAIDLAW, Ken and LAISHLEY, Roy, Fund for the future, UNCTAD's Common Fund for Commodities, Prepared by the Development Press services in collaboration with the UNCTAD Information Unit, 1980, p. 8.

(37) Ibid., p. 8. This conclusion is based on an analysis of the study carried out by the University of Pennsylvania.

(38) Statement of the Secretary-General of UNCTAD, Gamani COREA, to the final plenary session.

its adoption, in other words to go through the long and difficult process of preliminary discussions and negotiations, to reach a common accord on its fundamental elements and to steer all this towards ratification, not only represents an undoubted success for North-South relations, but also marks the beginning of fundamental economic and political changes and a big step towards a more orderly situation in the complex field of international relations. Its creation provides a clear guarantee for the producing and consuming countries, especially after the extreme confusion in the world markets during the early 1970s.

To obtain the requisite degree of clarity as to how the Common Fund functions, there has been a great deal of analysis of separate components. One remarkable element is the voting structure. However, the following question may be asked: why should the voting structure be considered so important when the financial structure has already been established? The fact is that both the distribution of votes and the management structure of the Fund emphasize the importance of the decision-making process, which is fundamental to its effective operation (Table 43). The interest of the producing and consuming countries are protected from possible abuses arising from the different policies that could be pursued by each group of countries. This applies especially to the LDCs as they laid claim to the majority of votes. The control over decisions is therefore the basis for the voting procedure, which, in turn, depends on the financial contributions. All these elements have emphasized the principle of equality between the participating countries. On the basis of information concerning the countries' voting rights obtained from the Agreement establishing the Common Fund for Commodities (39), the diagram presented in Figure 22 was plotted, which shows the distribution of votes amongst the participating countries.

---

(39) Agreement Establishing the Common Fund for Commodities, UNCTAD, TD/IPC/CF/CONF/24, 29th July 1980, Schedule D, Annex.

Table 43.

Countries' financial and voting contribution

Countries groups[a/]	Financial contribution in m.of $	%	Voting contribution	%
Group B	241.6	51.4	42 000	40.2
Group 77	151.0	32.1	47 000	45.0
Group D	46.0	9.8	8 000	7.7
China	16.0	3.4	3 000	2.9
Other countries[b/]	15.4	3.3	4 400	4.2

a/ Group B - 24 western industrial countries (including Japan)

Group 77 - developing countries (now consisting of 128 developing countries)

Group D - 7 socialist countries of Eastern Europe central market (COMECON)

China - China forms a separate group of its own.

b/ These consist of the Holy See, Liechtenstein, Monaco, San Marino, Israel, South Africa, Mongolia, Byelorussian USSR, Ukrainian USSR, Zimbabwe, St.Vincent and the Grenadines, and Nauru.

Source: The Table has been established on the basis of data provided from the Agreement Establishing the Common Fund for Commodities, UNCTAD, TD/IPC/CF/CONF/24, 29th July 1980.

Figure 22.

Countries' financial and voting contribution

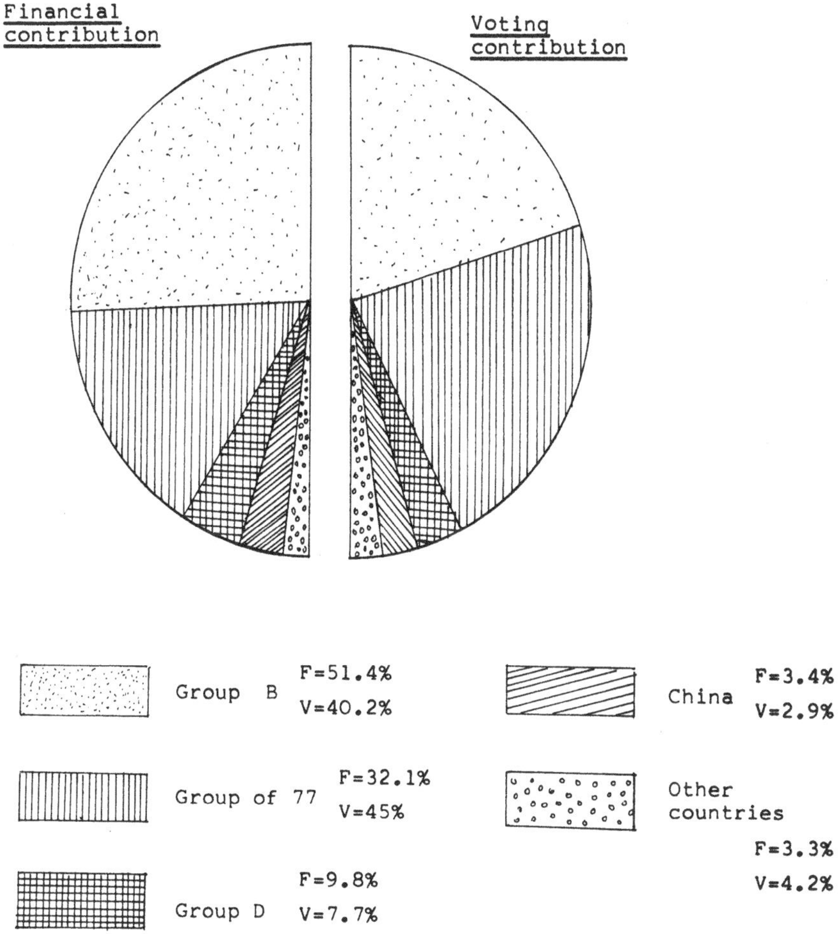

The western industrial countries account for 40.2 per cent of the votes, while the developing countries are accorded 45 per cent;then come the socialist countries of Eastern Europe with 7.7 per cent, followed by China with 2.9 per cent, and other countries with 4.2 per cent. These figures show clearly that the developing countries, as a group, are well placed. Does this give the Group of 77 effective control? It does not automatically give them a predominant position. This emerges from Figure 22, where the countries' financial contributions are presented. The Group of 77 accounts for 32.1 per cent. On the other hand, Group B has fewer votes (40.2 per cent) but the financial contributions of the countries are far greater since they represent 51.4 per cent of the financing obligations. This would seem to suggest the important point that, for the first time, there is no automatic correlation between voting rights and financial structure, i.e. the majority of votes for those who make the biggest financial contributions. However, this is not the only point. It is also of great importance that no single group has the majority of votes. A voting majority of two-thirds of the participating members is required when important decisions of financial consequence are involved, and a three-quarters majority is needed for decisions affecting the constitution.

It goes without saying that developing countries have the majority of votes but, nevertheless, power is reduced by the rules concerning the two-thirds or three-quarters majorities. This enables Group B, the western industrialized countries, to exercise their veto in the event of certain decisions.

2. Financial structure

The complex task of building the financial structure of the Common Fund was achieved during the long and difficult years of negotiation, and the hard resistance, notably of the Group B countries, was overcome by making concessions on the question of its capital structure. It is not our purpose to give a detailed interpretation of developments but simply to take them into consideration and concentrate on the most important problem of the Common Fund, that is trying to answer the following question: why was it decided not to finance buffer stocks by the direct contribution of members of individual agreements?

a) The pool and its financial significance

To be more specific, we must begin by outlining the principle of the "pooling" concept. In particular, this concept should provide evidence of a good deal of collaboration between producing and consuming countries. Group D, the socialist countries of Eastern Europe, agreed with Group B, the western industrial countries, that the Common Fund is meant to be a "pool" of ICA resources.

H. O'Neill reports that "the individual commodity organizations would themselves raise the money necessary to finance their own activities under their individual commodity agreements, and deposit their funds into a common pool (the Common Fund) and borrow it is necessary" (40). This could lead to potential savings because conditions make it unlikely that the prices of all primary products will fluctuate at the same time. The concentration of financial resources on the multiple-commodity buffer stock, through the pooling system, would enable them to be directed to meet specific commodity requirements. This procedure would, in turn, make it feasible to reduce the total financial resources needed. Here it should be noted that this concept is accompanied by a unique financial body for the ICAs, which functions simultaneously as

---

(40) O'NEILL, Helen, A Common Interest in Common Fund, UNCTAD publication, New York, 1977, p. 22.

creditor and debitor of the ICAs (41).

This suggests, to a certain extent, why the Common Fund was chosen as the means of financing the buffer stocks established for the selected primary commodities. At this point, a word should be said about the importance of the Common Fund as a catalyst, since it was planned that negotiations and agreements concerning the buffer stocks would be facilitated by the existence of the Fund's financial resources. For this reason, a Common Fund should be established either when there is a series of ICAs to be concluded or, according to a time table, before ICA negotiations. The relevance of such an approach is that it avoids "a vicious circle: no common fund because there are no commodity agreements and no commodity agreements because there is no common fund" (41). Therefore, the sooner the Agreement on the Common Fund is ratified, the better the prospects for the successful conclusion of additional individual commodity agreements are (42).

b) Financial contributions

The financial contributions to the Common Fund of each group of countries are shown in Table 30. As has been seen, the biggest contribution is made by Group B, the western industrial countries. This purely descriptive remark may be useful in distinguishing between the general financial structure of the Common Fund, the underlying relations and the superordinate system in which they are connected.

---

(41) CUTTAT, Jacques, "Le fond commun pour les produits de base", in: L'organisation de l'économie internationale au seuil des années 1980, by CUTTAT, Jacques, DUNKEL, Arthur, GAUDARD, Gaston, HEIMO, Marcel, SCHLEIMINGER, Günther, SOMMARUGA, Cornelio, Editions Universitaires, Fribourg, Suisse, 1981, p. 30.

(42) UNCTAD IV and Beyond: A Common Fund; Questions and Answers, TAD/INF/PUB/77.4, October 1977, No. 2, p. 3.

With regard to its financial structure, the Common Fund has three sources of capital:

- the direct contributions from governments, and members of the Common Fund (43),
- cash deposits and guarantee capital, and the guarantees of Individual Commodity Organizations - (ICOs) (44), and
- borrowings from the international capital markets (45).

The directly-contributed capital amounts to $ 470 million. Of this, 400 million are allocated to the first account. The remaining $ 70 million are allocated to the second account and, added to the $ 280 million of voluntary contributions, give a total of $ 350 million.

The minimal direct financial contributions of the governments of each member state are $ 1 million. Each member state contributes an amount which is assessed in relation to its paying capacity and is also free to pay in a voluntary contribution to the second account.

Governments can pay their capital subscription in three instalments:

- First instalment: 30% of total $ 470 million in cash,
- Second instalment: one year later, 20% in cash and 10% in the form of promissory notes to be cashed as and when decided by the Executive Board,
- Third instalment: payable after two years, 40% in promissory notes.

The rôle of the Individual Commodity Organizations is seen in the fact that they provide most of the resources needed for the operation of the Common Fund's first account.

---

(43) Agreement Establishing the Common Fund for Commodities TD/IPC/CF/CONF/24, 29th July 1980, art. 9, p. 8.

(44) Ibid., art. 14, p. 2.

(45) Loc. cit., art. 16, par. 5, p. 15

Every ICO has to deposit in the first account the cash amount in the successive instalments for use by the Fund when needed for stocking operations.

It is very difficult to be precise about the effective financial capacity of the Common Fund as it stands in a feedback relation with the commodity agreements concluded.

2. The two accounts or "windows"

The negotiations concerning the Common Fund's structure, envisaged in the form of two accounts, more often called "windows", were already under way in 1976 although they gave rise to constant disagreement between the Group of 77 and Group B. For two years there was an atmosphere of blackmail in negotiations. The Group of 77 insisted on the second account, which was hard for the Group B countries to accept. In the earliest estimates their hesitation was partly justified by the fact that the determination of the second account might bring about unwanted effects - encroachment upon the the operations of the biggest world financial institutions such as the World Bank (46).

The conflicting interests of the Group of 77 and Group B, were at last respected in a solution that was satisfactory for both sides: the pooling concept was accepted in place of the second "window" proposal.

Although a great deal has been said about the two "windows" of the Common Fund, a glance should be taken at both of them in order to see if these approaches contain enough details to be applied in the present market situation.

---

(46) CUTTAT, Jacques, "Le fond commun pour les produits de base", op.cit., p. 33.

a) The first "window"

The purpose of the first account or "window" was to meet the requirements of the ICAs financing the international buffer stock of the ICOs.

The initial capacity of the first account is $ 400 million. It would be constituted by subscriptions from

- member governments, in the form of shares of Directly Contributed Capital (DCC) as in the three instalments (46),
- ICO cash deposits, in the form of one-third of its Maximum Financial Requirements (47),
- proceeds of borrowings (e.g. potential cash contributions from the international capital markets).

The operating principle of the first "window" is based on the need to protect the interests of importing developing countries under the IPC. The financial facilities granted by the first account could be accorded only to ICOs which intend to conclude an international agreement under the auspices of the IPC. The basic requirements of the IPC had to be fulfilled: in other words, both producing and consuming countries had to participate and the agreement had to cover the major part of world trade in the commodity concerned (48). The first account would, therefore, provide sufficient financial resources for the buffer stock regulation of commodity agreements which provided for commodity control through this sort of mechanism to reduce excessive price fluctuations in the world market.

---

(46) In the previous section,the envisaged capacity of each DDC instalment has already been presented in more detail.

(47) The precise explanation of the MFR is given in Article 17, C, par. 8 of the Agreement Establishing the Common Fund for Commodities, UNCTAD, TD/IPC/CF/CONF/24, 29th July 1980: "the MFR of an Associated ICO shall include the acquisition cost of stocks, determined by multiplying the authorized size of its stocks, as specified in the Association Agreement by the appropriate purchase price, as determined by that Associated ICO. In addition, an associated ICO may include in its MFR specified carrying costs, exclusive of interest charges on loans, in an amount not exceeding 20 per cent of the acquisition cost".

(48) Le fond commun pour les produits de base, UNCTAD/CD/237/rev-1, p. 5, para.15.

Indeed, the same facilities in the international capital market, in the form of most favoured loans, are also granted by the first "window" to internationally-co - ordinated national stocks. Although the ICOs are obliged to "keep the Fund informed of conditions and development in the commodity markets with which the Associated ICO is concerned" (49), the Fund would fully respect the autonomy of the ICOs: it would abstain from all direct intervention in the ICAs concluded under the IPC.

b) The second "window"

The purpose of, and need for, the second account became evident after careful investigation of international commodity problems. At the very start of the negotiations to set up the Common Fund as an international financial institution, it was clear that a single account would not satisfy the expectations of all countries.

The initial amount of the second "window" was $ 350 million. Although impressive, this is not enough to assist the expected measures.

The resources of the second account are twofold: there are $ 70 million of voluntary direct government contributions (50), while the remaining $ 280 million are cash commitments and potential cash contributions.

The operations of the second "window" are to sponsor improvement of the structural conditions in markets, research and development, improvements in productivity and marketing, and assistance in diversification (51). Beyond this, one of the main principles of the second account is to increase competitiveness (52) and the prospects of particular primary commodities for which measures other than stocking are more appropriate (bananas, vegetable oils, etc.).

---

(49) Op.cit., in note (20), art, 16, para. 9(e), p. 19.

(50) Loc. cit., art. 10, para. 3, p. 9.

(51) Ibid.,art, 18, para. 3(a), p. 21.

(52) Ibid., art. 18, para. 3(a), p. 21.

What kind of general advantages can be expected from the second "window"? More profound analysis of this framework reveals that the most effective contribution of the second "window" lies in its rôle of improving the structure of world commodity trade by providing assistance to the poorest developing countries for their economic progress and development.

To attain this goal, the second "window" is intended to take "the form of loans and grants to an ICB (international commodity body) or an agency,therefore, having regard to the economic situation of the ICB or the Member or Members concerned and the nature and requirements of the proposed operation. Such loans may be covered by governmental or other suitable guarantees from the ICB or the Member or Members designated by such ICB" (53). In particular, this might shed new light on the research and development needed for food products and related commodities. In consequence, the Food and Agricultural Organization (FAO), could serve as the intergovernmental commodity body for attaining the proposed goal. The importance of the second account is evident, but the main priority is still the first account, which was the original reason for setting up the Common Fund.

To conclude this section, one last question should be asked: was the creation of the Common Fund really an ideal solution from the economic point of view? Numerous analyses have shown that, although presented as the essential part of the IPC, it is not, in fact, indispensable for the application of the IPC.

Nevertheless, the principle advantage of the creation of the Common Fund remains its authority and obligation to lend financial resources to associated ICOs and, therefore, provide sufficient encouragement for more realistc international commodity agreements to be concluded.

---

(53) Ibid., art. 18, para. 3(c), p. 22.

B - CAN THE FINANCING SYSTEM OF THE COMMON FUND BE IMPROVED?

The objective of this section is to see whether the financing system of the Common Fund can be improved by looking into the possibility of one, two or three accounts.

It is evident that the operation of the financing system of the Common Fund involves not only economic but also political aims which are difficult to reconcile so as to ensure a stable relationship between the LDCs and DCs.

There are clearly a number of constraints,consideration of which could be interesting for various reasons. Furthermore, if the issues mentioned above could be clarified and explained in depth, this might suggest some judicious conclusions.

1. Constraints

One serious risk is that the Common Fund has so much political significance that this is overtaking the economic issue. The Common Fund was not meant to provide the final solution to international economic and political problems.

It was set up to try out the methods envisaged and make a solution feasible.

The first problem to be overcome, i.e. its ratification, showed that all expectations concerning the Common Fund had to be treated with great caution. In consequence, the assumptions behind the creation of the Common Fund have to be considered soberly.

It should be recalled, at this point, that the Common Fund is regarded as an excellent compromise to commodity problems, but this does not mean that it will solve all questions arising from the commodity trade; it should not, therefore, be considered perfect in design or in the way it functions.

There remains the major problem of overcoming certain limitations and trying to balance the conflicting tendencies of the participating members.

a) The Common Fund - more a political than an economic issue

It is becoming increasingly urgent to improve the situation and prospects of LDCs that export primary commodities because of the recent instability of commodity prices, which have reached their lowest level for the last twenty years (54).

The widespread fall in commodity prices reflects the low and diminishing levels of economic activity and income which, in the early 1980s, no longer balanced the levels of output of primary commodities. The magnitude of the price decrease has been so great that other factors, apart from imbalances between real demand and supply at current price levels, have clearly been at work.

The first implication to be drawn from this is that political and economic considerations have come to predominate. In this respect, it should be realised that the magnitude of the constraints, the real crux of the problem, lies in the fact that they are more political than economic in nature and that they have a big impact on the Common Fund and the way it functions.

A great deal of analysis has produced clear evidence on this score. The most troublesome difficulties are related to the fact that the success of the compromise between the LDCs and DCs has been rather limited. The series of measures intended by the Common Fund were too ambitious for it to function as planned. The significance of this can be seen by observing the impact of the disappointment of the LDC's at the fact that, up to now, ICAs have been concluded for only 7 commodities (sugar, rubber,cocoa, coffee, tin, jute and olive oil) out of 18 as covered by the IPC. One result was that the Common Fund was not ratified by the dead-line, 31st March 1982(55).

---

(54) The fall in commodity prices recorded at the end of 1981 and beginning of 1982 was the bigest for the last twenty years, according to the Journal de Genève, 10th February, 1982.

(55) By the 1st July 1983 the situation had hardly changed. The number of signatory countries was 108 and those which ratified it 54.The new dead-line for the fulfilment of the requirements for the Common Fund Agreement to come into force is 30th September, 1983. Therefore, the Common Fund still remains within the theoretical limits.

Common sense suggests, therefore, that the relationship between the LDCs and DCs could be described as resembling a closed loop. Nevertheless, these difficulties and contradictions do not reduce the essential value of the buffer stock hypothesis in the framework of North/South relations as seen through the IPC's Common Fund. However, the question remains as to whether the Common Fund, with its present internal characteristics, will be able to regulate the economic and political constraints, or whether it can be used only to even out the fluctuations affecting producing and consuming countries.

Owing to its universality and the number of distinctions and suggestions made, the buffer stock solution, as developed under the auspices of the Common Fund, without doubt, represents an important concept concerning the substance of the relationship between the LDCs and DCs. However, this does not mean that it qualifies as the famous 3 G's panacea (general-genial-generator) for solving the LDCs'problems. Urgent action is needed to deal with the extreme gravity of the situation now facing the LDCs. The efforts to ratify the Common Fund are of the utmost importance to North/South issues. Ratification will improve future LDC - DC relations whereas non-ratification "would be a serious constraint given the existing linkages whereby the fortunes of the developing countries are related to those of developed ones" (56). The importance of this can be better understood if one imagines this eventuality as fact (57).

---

(56) Comments made by the Secretary-General of UNCTAD, Gamani COREA, on trade and development issues; Trade and Development Report 1981, UNCTAD, November 1981, p. 5.

(57) This idea was expressed by the President of the Ivory Coast, Mr. Houphouêt-Boigny:"Actuellement, non seulement les prix de nos produits agricoles proposés par l'Occident ne suivent pas l'inflation mondiale, mais ils baissent.On ne garantit même pas les prix pour la campagne actuelle. Les prix de nos exportations vitales sont livrés au caprice des boursiers. L'Europe joue sur la vie de nos paysans, sans se rendre compte qu'elle joue en même temps son propre destin... Spéculer sur nos matières premières, c'est déstabiliser notre économie. Votre ennemi en Afrique, à vous Occidentaux, ce sont vos propres Bourses de commerce plus que les Russes".Interview given to Paris-Match, October 1980.

Therefore, among the complex tasks concerning the creation and existence of the Common Fund, the most important is to co-ordinate the international policy strategies and thus facilitate the efforts of member countries to find their way to growth and development.

Meanwhile, there is the practical question of whether the Common Fund should, as a more political tool, meet all the economic needs of the LDCs, for whom it represents "a substantial power of intervention in international commodity markets?"(58).

b) Could the Common Fund face the risk of an excessively large stock accumulation?

The implications of this question are immediately apparent, and might be considered a powerful constraint on the improvement of the financing system of the Common Fund.

The fact is that every approach to buffer stock policy elaborated up to now offers its own particular solution to the problem. Theoretically, it may seem easy to recognize and establish certain conditions essential for adequate estimations, but in practice it is often difficult. Besides, do we need to worry about large stock accumulations when it is known from past experience that they have never actually occurred? There are deep-rooted problems here, as the Common Fund is meant to have adequate resources at its disposal to meet the needs of the 18 commodities proposed by the IPC.

The above remark suggests that far more attention should be given to the danger that a disproportionate supply of certain commodities might occur simultaneously.

Such an imbalance could lead to excessive accumulation, which might, in turn, call in question the major mechanism, since the resources of the Common Fund might not be sufficient to deal with such a situation.

Accordingly, attention should be given to the possible risk of overabundant supply, possibly accompanied by a floor price that is set too high. This would definitely cause

(58) AVRAMOVIC, Dragoslav, "Common Fund: Why and of What Kind?", Journal of World Trade Law, vol.12,1978, p. 275.

trouble. In such a situation the Common Fund might not be able to afford a sufficient intervention.

The fact must, therefore, be accepted that nothing can be stated with certainty as an element of risk always has to be reckoned with. The important point is that the effects of the risk should be estimated precisely enough to obtain optimal results in commodity stabilization through the Common Fund facility.

This example serves to call attention to the fact that the constraints imposed by a potential risk are likely to start significant policy changes. They therefore deserve serious consideration. The most important thing is to reduce the existing difficulties to a minimum, since they are hard to eliminate, so as to arrive at the best practical solution for the Common Fund in the contemporary situation.

2. Could new conditions improve the present functioning of the current two-account system?

Given the present situation and prospects of the Common Fund, it is difficult to be confident about future developments since they are hard to predict.

It is true that, as things stand, some remedial action is required, and there exist various alternatives which might be regarded as complementary tools to the generally-accepted institution of a Common Fund.

The following presentation discusses two possible structural forms, seen as major alternatives. However, there are many possible combinations and other models could be taken into consideration or developed by intuition. Our discussion is focused on two issues:

- creation of a third account: could it produce the amelioration needed?
- could the very first proposal of a single account be the solution?

If the solution could be found, it would reinforce a variety of measures to strengthen the LDCs' position, bring about improvements in general economic development and facilitate relations with DCs with regard to further actions.

a) Is there any advantage in creating a third account?

In fact, the proposal to provide assistance through a third account is not completely original. A form of it can be seen in the World Bank's "supplementary" financing proposal. The World Bank's suggestion was put forward to cope with the problems arising from the export incomes of the LDCs when a short-term solution in the form of balance-of-payments support proved inadequate. The point of this proposal regarding the method of calculating export shortfalls was

- no compulsory reference to the levels of past earnings,and
- "reasonable expectations" to be calculated for the next five years (59).

Essentially, the World Bank proposal offers a new concept in compensatory financing. This scheme envisaged that the LDCs concerned should be provided with enough financial support to cover export shortfalls below the forecast trend. Such action would be beneficial for the country concerned as it would ensure substantial resources for its economic growth and development.

The scheme was based entirely on loans. These loans were to be repaid out of the income realized from exports which exceeded the forecast trend and would be valid for the five-year period, after which they would be treated as long-term loans. In this case the interest rate would differ from that for a five-year period. The rate of interest would be based on the particular LDC's balance-of-payments situation and its reserves. Those were, in brief, the financing proposals advanced by the World Bank in 1974.

---

(59) The period of five years was chosen because it corresponds to most development plans and programmes. The calculations were to be based on the projected exports of the LDC concerned. How accurate would such calculations be and how would "reasonable expectations" for the future be defined for the countries which are highly dependent on the income from exports? This point is by no means clear.

The history of compensatory financing continued to develop and, in 1975, the EEC's STABEX facility entered the economic arena to provide a "new model" for the relations between the LDCs and DCs. This scheme and its features were described in Chapter I, Section A, of this Part.

Let us now come back to the question asked in the heading of this section and see whether the ex post compensatory stabilization system of export receipts could be relevant where the Common Fund is concerned. If so, in what way, and how?

The measures envisaged and covered by the first and second accounts might not be enough. For instance, a number of countries might remain the victims of export instability and depressed trends. These would be countries with a clear and significant dependence on exports, for which stocking agreements are not feasible, and with serious and worrying fluctuations in their prices or export earnings. Would these countries have significant influence on the trade and payments of importing countries? The answer is that the probability of such an influence is low. A suitable measure is therefore required to meet the manifest needs of exporting countries. Could it take the form of a third account from which assistance and aid could be provided in the form of compensation effect through a combination of the IMF and STABEX financing schemes? From our point of view, such a proposal might serve as the basis for a third account.

Within the integrated programme dealing with commodity problems, it might be enough to devise additional compensatory measures that might be required in certain circumstances, such as those of the countries mentioned above. Therefore, to attain a sufficient level of assistance to exporting countries, the following facilities have to be given appropriate consideration:

- sufficiently flexible conditions regarding the balance-of-payments criterion for assistance,

- more flexibility regarding the limits set on the funds available, as determined by the IMF quotas for covering the shortfalls of exporting countries,
- the import purchasing power of the country's exports,
- adequate statistical information concerning the shortfalls in exports over a relatively short period, and
- the repayment period, usually five years, but with possibility of extension.

Let us look at another side of this question in order to clarify the real purpose of a third account.

The third account could not be expected to have the same importance and weight as the first account. It should be of a residual character and its measures for compensatory financing should be regarded as residual measures, to be applied when the other measures, i.e. those provided by the first account, prove insufficient or inappropriate for the fixed objective: stabilization of the real export income of the LDCs.

The third account should be designed to provide loans to LDCs subject to export instability due to shortfalls in export earnings from the commodities concerned. These loans should be related to the country's balance-of-payments and its reserves, and the rate of interest payable on this financial assistance should be rather low. The repayment of the loans should be effected in part from earnings in excess of a certain agreed level which would be considered as standard. This standard level should be used as the basis for calculation of the country's shortfalls in export income. Besides such loans, the proposed third account scheme might also provide grants, to be given in many cases to the poorest countries of the Third World. Among other things, provision might be made for converting unpaid loans into grants. For these countries, therefore, the compensatory financing assistance would be on a grant basis.

As has already been seen, price stabilization does not always ensure the stabilization of export earnings. In consequence, the aim of the compensatory financing measures of the third account would be to ease the economic situation of individual countries where difficulties might arise even if world market prices were successfully stabilized. This might happen if the export supply dropped because of an insufficient or reduced output of the commodity concerned.

This discussion brings us to the important problem of whether the Common Fund should be regarded as:

- purely a financing mechanism (clearly determined by the functions of the first account) or, in addition,
- a financing mechanism providing loans and grants (possibly through the functioning of the third account).

Even if the content of the UNCTAD proposal remains unchanged, the technical experts claim that the Common Fund for the primary commodities is more than a purely financial arrangements. It is true that the first account, in financing the ICO's buffer stock operations, would be a straightforward financing mechanism, but the second account is envisaged as providing loans, at concessionary rates or in the form of grants, for commodity-related measures other than stocking. It should not be forgotten that the financing mechanism of the Common Fund already has a dual character.

In general, therefore, it can be said that the nature of these two accounts does not exclude the possibility of including a compensatory financing scheme on the already-existing pattern in the form of a third account, which would simply add a further dimension to the Common Fund.

It is worth saying that such an approach would be beneficial to the poorest Third World countries for whose economic development and growth a third account would provide new possibilities.

The next step is to explore the kind of questions that would need to be answered if and when it comes to setting up the third account. Here are some relevant questions:

- What attitude would the third account be expected to take?
- To function satisfactorily, what should be its size?
- What potential benefits can be expected?
- Whom should the third account benefit?
- Would the third account have a positive impact on the economic growth and development of the LDCs?
- If the financial resources required for the establishment of the third account were not, for various different reasons, adequate, could it still be regarded as a feasible proposition?

All these questions are concerned with the guidelines for testing the feasibility of setting up and operating the third account. Instead of examining each of these questions separately, we have decided to answer them in tabular form (Table 44). Our proposed combination of the IMF and a world regionalized STABEX compensatory financing scheme in the form of a third account of the Common Fund, might provide an answer to the economic situation of the Third World and there are two major arguments in favour of the preference for a combination of these two schemes:

- Firstly, although neither of these schemes if fully satisfactory in design and operation, they have both gradually improved with experience and the result is that their advantages are not to be disregarded. However, they should be seen as complementary rather than alternatives because the IMF facility compensates LDCs for only about 50 per cent of the fall in export earnings, and the need to cover the remaining 50 per cent might be met through the STABEX facility, which experience has shown to be relevant in this connection.

Table 44.

Proposal of a combination of IMF and a world regionalized STABEX Compensatory Financing Scheme as a Third Account of the Common Fund

Characteristics	The Third Account	As now under
Source of finance	Fund financed by the DCs by fixing the maximum with-drawal of the members' quota	CFF/IMF
magnitude of operations	$ 3.25 billion, sort of transfer temporary tiding -over loan. If calculations are made on the basis of the shortfalls in the period 1960-1976 of $ 29.1 billion for 74 non-oil countries, then $ 1.8 billion is needed per year. Therefore the proposed sum of $ 3.25 would be sufficient.	CFF/IMF
capacity of considerations	commodity-by-commodity, but to cover all commodities: foods, agricultural raw materials, minerals and metals.	STABEX
applicable to	all exports	IMF
position of the scheme towards participating countries	discriminatory: available only to LDCs	sort of STABEX
method of calculating shortfalls	to find the commodity-specific shortfalls: a) four-year period of reference to the past earnings and levels as a necessary ground, and then b) five-year moving averages. For centre taken, the current year and forecasts are only for the two further years.	IMF+STABEX
availability of loans and grants	loans: yield more liberal interest (based on the position of balance-of-payments and reserves of LDC concerned). grants: given in many cases where the poorest of the Third World countries are concerned.	IMF+STABEX

- *Secondly*, because the conclusion was reached (60), in our comparison of the STABEX and IMF compensatory schemes, that they possess several points of contact on which an appropriate combination of the two could be safely based. A marriage of the complementary elements of the two schemes might produce a more orderly regulation of the export earnings problem of the Third World LDCs by providing sufficient ex post stabilization.

It should be added that " a Third World left to its fate,beset with ever-growing payments diffilucties and ever-increasing indebtedness would also be disastrous for the DCs. The industrialized North can have no interest in the (continued) poverty of the southern hemisphere" (61). A solution such as the scheme proposed above is therefore required to meet the need of the least developed countries to finance balance-of-payments deficits which are of a temporary nature.

Although this suggestion sounds like a rather handy remedy, especially for the short-term problems of the poorest LDCs of the Third World, it goes without saying that it has certain shortcomings which seem to be inherent in any sort of plan or scheme. Perfection in this domain is highly improbable.

While advancing this scheme as a possible means of ameliorating the financing system of the Common Fund, we can take another small step forward by envisaging the construction of the third account as its separate but " complementary facility and lender of last resort" (62).

---

(60) See Chapter I, section B, of this Part.

(61) Neue Zürcher Zeitung, 5th April 1977.

(62) *Complementary Financing: Issues and Proposals for Further Action*, UNCTAD V, Manila 1979, TD/229/Supp.1, 7th March 1979, p. 24, para. 60.

As stated in Table 44, the capital requirements for this complementary financing facility would depend on a set of elements which could follow those formulated by UNCTAD:

- "country coverage,
- commodity coverage,
- definition of shortfall,
- extent of shortfall to be covered,
- terms of payment,
- rate of interest to be charged to the borrowers, and
- rate of interest payable to lenders on amounts borrowed to finance such a complementary facility" (63).

The aim of such an approach is not only to show its underlying purpose but to bring out the structure which makes the achievement of such functions possible. Here it is impossible to be categoric and speak with confidence about future developments since there are many factors which have to be regarded with extreme caution. Should the expected conditions enable the DCs and LDCs finally to arrive at the best global solution so far, it still remains to be tested through the concessions made in diplomatic negotiations, where the DCs will have to face their responsibilities.

b) Could the Common Fund financial system have been improved by the use of a single account?

In contrast to the proposal for a three-account system for the Common Fund, let us see if only one account would, in practice, be sufficient to meet present economic requirements.

---

(63) Ibid., p. 24, para. 62.

As a matter of fact, the one-account system was the original idea advanced in the very first efforts to set up the Common Fund financial facilities. Its main function would have been to finance international buffer stocks chiefly in order to even out fluctuations in commodity prices.

The solution was seen to lie in a Common Fund for stock financing as in international agreements since the scope of stocking procedures had been limited by financial constraints either arising from the scheme itself or due to the influence of other factors unrelated to the commodity agreements.

The fact is that the creation of the Common Fund showed that the time had come for a common conceptual framework with a positive approach to international economic problems. We are now well-placed to detect the relevance of such a change. Past experience has shown that it is almost impossible for individual ICAs to incorporate the principle that both exporting and importing countries should make compulsory financial contributions. With the creation of the Common Fund that principle was accepted, for the first time, as a function of international trade in commodities.

This participation of producers and consumers is one point; the other is the fact that they can borrow, for this purpose, from the Common Fund. Borrowing from the Common Fund require a smaller total outlay than would be the case if the ICOs had to meet their requirements through the direct contributions of their members or from the capital markets (64). These were the proposals accepted in the Nairobi 1976 Resolution 93(IV) as the core of the Common Fund, which was seen as the principal instrument of the Integrated Programme. The content of the UNCTAD proposal remained, on the whole, unchanged. The function of the first account formulated in the agreement establishing the Common Fund for commodities, is to act as a source of credit to ICOs for financing their buffer stock. The criteria employed

(64) This is the pooling principle, which was examined in Section A of this Chapter.

and the facilities accorded to the ICOs have been outlined in the previous section. However, besides the technical provisions of the UNCTAD Common Fund, there remains the question of whether the Common Fund's first account engenders enough economic unity from the LDCs' point of view or whether it creates more discord owing to the political differences between North and South?

From the economic point of view,the LDCs have, through the first account system, achieved the advantage that both sides are compelled to join together in dealing with commodity problems by negotiating international commodity agreements.

By accepting the method of pure buffer stocks and its system of financing as a means of regulating and reducing the price fluctuations of primary commodities entering the international market, the LDCs have obtained access to more orderly marketing arrangements.

As established, the Common Fund's first account has to provide for the financing of stocks which are internationally or nationally held but internationally co-ordinated. This calls for a new form of financial regulation that has never existed in the past. Although it sounds rather sophisticated in structure,it is not expected to solve all the problems and questions raised by the IPC. These are numerous and go far beyond the problems of commodity agreements and the determination of whether the measures to be used are

- to reduce the price fluctuations in the primary commodities, or
- to increase prices.

The nature and the scope of the questions raised by the IPC are more complex. They concern international co-operation in development, trade, aid and investment programmes, and are of as much interest to the LDCs as to the DCs. The problem, as has already been said, is too difficult to be solved by a Common Fund with the first account as its mode of operation, which, as the instrument of the Programme, provides financial assistance only for stocking schemes. It is true that it would have a certain impact on overall development, but it cannot be regarded as the only possible solution to this problem.

From this follows an important deduction: one account, based on the system of pure buffer stocks, is not sufficient to meet all the needs of the LDCs, especially in the Third World category, for international economic aid and development, and therefore cannot be seen as the only way of assisting development. This is why it has to be combined with some other appropriate measure or measures which can cope with the questions raised by the IPC regarding international co-operation and development. Consequently, the first account illustrates what might be considered as an alternative solution, but one that cannot stand alone or be regarded as final.

The creation of the Common Fund turned out to be a thorny problem. Although it was the first example of collaboration between the producing and consuming countries, its non-ratification by the date planned, 31st March, 1982, once again drew attention to the long history of their conflicting interests:

- price support: financing the interests of the LDCs as exporters, and
- price stabilization: favouring the interests of the DCs as importers.

Balancing these interests means finding the best way of improving the terms of trade, which would then lead to a general improvement in trade. To achieve this, the Common Fund has to be in a situation to promote the optimal solution with its financial assistance, and therefore meet the needs and expectations of both sides.

Achievement of the closest possible co-operation between producing and consuming countries would reduce that well-known obstacle which is so hard to overcome: who wins and who loses in such an enterprise? Here we find ourselves on dangerous ground. Many theoretical and practical findings clearly suggest that everything in this area is relative. In what direction does the solution lie? It is easy to see that none of our three possibilities (one account, two accounts or three accounts) stands out from the others. They have their advantages and disadvantages. However this need not be regarded as a great handicap as it also means that any of these approaches might prove reasonable and stable. Moreover, different methods can be combined, and such combinations may turn out very effective. Therefore, it might be concluded that the best solution would be purely a question of strategy.

* * *

This chapter has examined proposals for the improvement of the IPC's multiple-commodity buffer stock system and the amelioration of its financial approach within the framework of the Common Fund.

This investigation has provided a fair amount of information which might be worth developing further with the purpose of overcoming difficulties regarding its implementation. The success of the Common Fund will largely depend on the skill and competence of the world's economic experts in successfully dealing with the political strategies and economic tactics which are of great importance to the LDC - DC challenge and a visible and essential aspect of the North-South problem.

C O N C L U S I O N S

I

In the context of these concluding remarks, several points can be raised which might stand out as being of particular importance.

It goes without saying that the international commodity markets were always characterized by permanent price movements. These will undoubtedly play a part in the future evolution of the former. They are particularly important in the present situation where they represent one of the most important questions that the LDCs and DCs are faced with. The significance of such a statement might be measured by the fact that contemporary investigations are characterized by extreme complexity due to the world economic and political situation.

The aim of this work is to present the buffer stock method of control in theory and practice. It has been seen that, even when theoretical solutions exist, it is clear that there are a number of functional problems as regards putting them into practice. This should not be regarded as either a discouraging or pessimistic situation for further approaches.

The nature, structure and functioning of the buffer stock control scheme have been explored in different settings which have illustrated, once more, the controversy existing between theoretical problems and practical choice. The trend of their gradual development has also been traced.

The purpose of the approach developed in this work was not to offer a definite optimal solution for existing problems, but to analyse the buffer stock control mechanism and its real possibilities. Therefore, it might be considered as a contribution in this domain, since it brings to light a new aspect - typology - which might be of use in future investigations. In this regard, it must be remembered that the purpose of this technique was threefold:

- to formulate the typology hypothesis,
- to develop a deductive approach, and
- to bring about its application.

Here our aim was not to achieve perfection in putting forward the theoretical points, but was, primarily, to develop the empirical approach to the typology. We hope that the efforts made in this inquiry might be of service to future research.

It may be noted that the buffer stock mechanism does not represent the only possibility of control in commodity markets. Nevertheless, the above analysis suggests that more attention deserves to be given to its concepts and less to its enumerated assumptions. It follows from this that it should in future, become, once again, a matter of interest to find possible improvements and see how they progress in dealing with the same basic problems of primary commodity markets.

II

The outcome of this analysis suggests that,for the successful application and utilization of the buffer stock method of control, it is not only important to know the basic elementary technique, but also to be able to use it in an appropriate way in accordance with changing political circumstances. The way in which the political dimension should be regulated depends on the ability and willingness, as well as on the present and future conditions, of the participating nations. All this is very hard to predict. Given such a formulation, it is immediately apparent that the treatment of primary commodities is of strategic and economic importance. This leads to the conclusion that political balance would be preferred before the attempt to attain primary commodity market stability can be made, especialy in to-day's situation where it is a fact that the world economy is facing an arduous crisis.

It is evident that the steady collapse of commodity prices which began in the last months of 1980 and continues up to the present, preceded by the period of price improvement represents not only a frustration in itself, and for the further processing of primary commodities,but also a negative impact on the commodity export earnings of a large number of developing countries. The magnitude of the price decrease has been so great that it is evident that this effect was not due only to the imbalance between real demand and supply at current price levels.

It is quite understandable, therefore, that the evolution of world trade is affected by the substantial deterioration of the terms of trade and, consequently, by the increasingly dramatic situation for developing countries and their efforts to pursue their development objectives. This requires, more than ever, radical decisions in the approach to the problem of commodities,which is closely related to that of world general economic stability.

The minor improvements made during the last forty years in the field of commodity regulation have clearly led to the possibility of the Common Fund. This does not, of course, represent a complete success in the North/South Dialogue, but nevertheless could be accepted as a turning point in the history of international trade in primary commodities. Therefore, its ratification has been seen as a pressing need in order to lessen the existing tensions between LDCs and DCs.

It is important to remember that, if the ratification of the Common Fund can be brought about, its impact on world economic and political stabilization will be of importance, and satisfaction will be procured for all participants in the Dialogue. For the moment,it is a difficult task to achieve. The Common Fund question is still open.

III

The general problem remains one which might be called the problem of co-operative phenomena or, more commonly, the North/South Dialogue. Participating UNCTAD VI members were expected to find sufficient time to elaborate a substantial compromise. To achieve this, a different atmosphere is needed in debates between LDCs and DCs. It has to be noted that neither the LDCs nor DCs should be regarded as a monolithic block. The fact is that, in the North/South Dialogue, the Third World countries contribute their solidarity to the Group of 77 and non-aligned countries in the context of international activity. Therefore, they should be considered an important factor in the efforts made to achieve co-operation among LDCs, and their joint strategies to penetrate the markets of DCs (USA, Europe of Ten, Japan, etc.).

As the world economy is faced with the most difficult crisis since the 1930s, both sides of the Dialogue should bear in mind the fact that almost any agreement would be better than none. It is no longer a problem of deciding who is going to dominate the situation, but of finding urgently-needed, acceptable solutions, however insignificant they may appear, which can bring about the answer to the structural maladjustments in all areas of the international economic system.

Therefore, attention must be paid to the following:

- whether the real plans and prospects are effectively real,
- in what measure an inaccurate realisation of the plans would affect the future development, and
- whether the possibilities have been developed in the best way.

Furthermore, each side of the Dialogue has to be bold enough to face the fact that all plans and wishes do not necessarily need to be realized. That is the first step, however small, towards proving that reasonable negotiations might become possible. In addition, following this line, a number of problems would be avoided in advance and this would contribute to crystallizing what might be achieved in reality.

After the UNCTAD VI Conference, the situation of the general economic disagreement betweent the South and the North had not changed. The expected solutions were not arrived at and the negotiations of the UNCTAD VI can be considered a failure. The general situation concerning primary products was not resolved nor did the participants find a common denominator and, therefore, it can be regarded as having reached an impasse. The solution must be found, but when?

Again, nevertheless, the reference which invites attention is that one of the virtues of the UNCTAD IPC lies in its formulation of ICAs, which have remained basically faithful to the commodity-by-commodity approach, but differ from the traditional ones in the sense that they are managed as a unified "package" ready to meet the demands of both exporting and importing countries. Therefore, it is clear that it embodies some old disadvantages which could be overcome by the amelioration of the techniques necessary to attain its major objective, which is the regulation of prices.

IV

In order to complete the conception of international buffer stocks as a measure of price regulation, and their role in commodity trade, it should be mentioned again that their importance with regard to other instruments of control represented in the commodity agreements also lies in the satisfactory results (tin) obtained in the combination with the export quota system. With respect to past experiences, their positive tendency and feasibility are evident. However, it should also be added that there have been considerable difficulties in setting up the appropriate price range for their realization. Against this background,it should be repeatedly pointed out that the positive features of the buffer stock scheme could be evaluated from its operations, which do not have any impact on production and consumption levels. That is to say, production and consumption do not change as a result of the activities of the buffer stock. Moreover, the operation of the buffer stock control scheme does not fix the price. Due to the problems caused by the instability of commodity markets, producers and consumers are encouraged to reach agreement concerning the buffer stock control scheme as it acts as a plug between the supply and demand and therefore absorbs the negative points by stabilizing the international price within a specific price range.

Up to now it has been seen that the buffer stock scheme has had convincing,but moderate,success as an instrument of commodity price control. The future,therefore, has to be faced with a great deal of caution. The number of questions concerning buffer stocks might be endless. Among them, there are several that stand out. Could we arbitrate the future of the buffer stocks? What would the value of such arbitration be? To answer these questions a number of reasonable and realisable programmes are needed.

Given the above observations, as a general concluding note, it can be said that outlining an effective buffer stock programme requires,firstly,that the impediments which lie in the specific characteristics of the market of each commodity be overcome, and secondly that the structural instability of the challenging situation which confronts the LDCs and DCs participating in the programme be reduced.

Finally, in dealing with the economic problems of world commodity markets, there is no point in looking for a definite solution. These problems continue to necessitate a permanent time-consuming study of the changing political and economic conditions.

BIBLIOGRAPHY

I. BOOKS

ADAMS, G., and KLEIN, S., (ed.), Stabilizing World Commodity Markets, Lexington Books, D.C.Heath, Massacusetts, 1978, 335 p.

ALTING-GENSAN, (ed.), The Lomé Convention and a New International Economic Order, A.W.Sijthoff-Leyden, 1977.

BARANYAI, L., History of Commodity Agreements, IBRD, July 1959, 44 p.

BEHRMAN, Jere R., International Commodity Ageements - an evaluation of the UNCTAD Integrated Commodity Programme; Overseas Development Council, October 1977, 94 p.

BEIGIE, Carl, HAGER, Wolfgang SEKIGUCHI, Sueo, Seeking a New Accomodation in World Commodity Markets, New York, 1976.

BROWN, C.P., Primary Commodity Control, Oxford University Press, Kuala Lumpur, London, New York, Melbourne, 1975.

COPPOCK, Joseph D., International Economic Instability: the Experience after World War II, MacGraw-Hill Book Company. New York, Toronto, London, 1962.

CUTTAT, Jacques, DUNKEL, Arthur, GAUDARD, Gaston, HEIMO, Marcel, SCHLEIMINGER, Günter, SOMMARUGA, Cornelio, L'organisation de l'économie internationale au seuil des années 1980, Editions Universitaires, Fribourg, 1981. 104 p.

ECBO, Paul L., OPEC and the Experience of Previous International Commodity Cartels, Massachusetts Institute of Technology, Energy Laboratory, Paper No. 75.008 WP, August 1975, 38 p.

EVANS, David, International Commodity Policy: UNCTAD and NIEO in Search of a Rational, Institute of Development Studies at the University of Sussex (UK) May 1978, 44 p.

FOX, William, Tin: The Working of a Commodity Agreement, Mining Journal Books Ltd., London 1974.

GILBERT, C. L., Buffer Stocks, Exchange Rate Movements and Inflation, Commodities Research Unit, London and New York 1974.

GLISMANN, H. H., RODEMER, H., Bufferstocks als Mittel zur Stabilisierung konjukturbedingter Preisschwankungen auf den Welttrohstoffmärkten, Arbeitspapier Nr. 56, Institut für Weltwirtschaft, Kiel 1977.

HALWOOD, Paul, Stabilization of International Commodity Markets, JAI Press Inc., Greenwich, Connecticut, 1979.

HAYES, J. P., Terms of Trade Policy for Primary Commodities, Commonwealth Economic Paper,No. 4, Commonwealth Secretariat 1975.

HEXNER, Ervin, International Cartels, Chapel Hill, The University of North Carolina Press, 1945, 555 p.

JOHNSON, Harry G., Economic Policies Towards Less Developed Countries, London, George Allen & Unwin, 1967.

ISACHSEN, Arne Jon, A Note on Price Stabilization Schemes and the Terms of Trade, Oslo, 1976, 13 p.

KEBSCHULL, Dietrich, KUNNE, Wilfred, MENCK, Karl Wolfgang, Das integrierte Rohstoffprogramm, Verlag Weltarchiv GmbH, Hamburg 1977, 401 p.

KINDLEBERGER, C.P., International Economics, Richard D. Irwin Inc. Homewood Illinois 1968, 526 p.

KNNOR, K.E., Tin Under Control, Food Research Institute, Stanford University 1945.

LAIDLAW, Ken and LAISHLEY, Roy, Fund for the Future, UNCTAD's Common Fund for Commodities, UNCTAD Information Unit, 1980.

LAW, Alton D., International Commodity Agreements, Lexington Books, D.C.Heath and Company, Lexington Massachusetts, Toronto, London, 1975, 128 p.

LEWINSOHN, Richard, Trusts et cartels dans l'économie mondiale, Lib. de Médicis, 1958, 386 p.

MacAVOY, Paul W., Economic Perspective on the Politics of International Commodity Agreements, The Institute of Government Research, University of Arizona, 1977.

Mac BEAN, Alasdair I., Export Instability and Economic Development, George Allen & Unwin Ltd., London 1966, 364 p.

Mac BEAN, Alasdair and BALASUBRAMANYAN, V.N., A Positive Approach to the International Economic Order, Part II: North-Trade Issues, British-North American Committee, May 1980, 100 p.

Mc NICOL, David L., Commodity Agreements and Price Stabilization, Lexington Books, D.C.Heath & Co., Lexington 1978, 142 p.

MASON, Edward, Controlling World Trade, New York, MacGraw Hill, 1946, 289 p.

McCULLOCH, Rachel, Commodity Power and the International Community, Harvard University, Department of Economics, 1976 October.

MOUTON, Claude and CHALMIN, Philippe, Commerce international et matières premières, Economica, Paris 1980.

O'NEILL, Helen, A Common Interest in a Common Fund, UNCTAD, United Nations, New York 1977, 48 p.

NUSBAUMER, Jacques, L'enjeu du dialogue Nord-Sud: partage des richesses ou guerre économique, Economica, Paris, 1981, 261 p.

PATTERSON, G., Discrimination in International Trade: the Policy Issues 1945-1965, Princeton N.J., 1966.

PRINZING, Albert, The Bearing of International Cartel and Control Schemes upon International Trade Organization, Berlin 1939.

RADETZKI, Marian, International Commodity Market Arrangements, C.Hurst & Co., London 1970.

RANGARAJAN, L.N., Commodity Conflict, Chroom Helm, London 1978, 390 p.

REYNOLDS, Paul D., International Commodity Agreements and the Common Fund: a legal and financial analysis, New York, Preager Special Studies 1978, 233 p.

ROWE, J. W. E., Markets and Men, Cambridge University Press 1936.

" " Primary Commodities in International Trade, Cambridge, University Press 1965, 234 p.

STOCKING, George, WATKINS, Myron, Cartels or Competition?, New York, The Twenty Century Fund 1948, 516 p.

WILKINSON, Harold François, Etudes des initiatives internationales en vue de la stabilization des marchés des produits de base, Genève, Droz 1959, 162 p.

YATES, P. L., Commodity Control: a Study of Primary Products, MacMillan & Co. 1943, 248 p.

II. ARTICLES IN PERIODICALS AND IN COLLECTED WORKS

ADAMS, Gerard F., "Commodity Stabilization Policy and Economic Models", in: Econometric Modeling of World Commodity Policy (ed.), by ADAMS, G.F., BEHRMAN, J.R., Lexington Books, D.C.Heath, 1978, pp. 1-8.

ALI, Liaqat, "Principles of Buffer Stock and Its Mechanism and Operation in the International Tin Agreement", Weltwirtschaftliches Archiv , Band 96, 1966, Heft 1.

" " "The Regulation of Trade in Tea", Journal of World Trade Law, vol. 4, 1970, pp. 565-585.

AVRAMOVIC, Dragoslav, "Common Fund: Why and of What Kind?" Journal of World Trade Law, vol. 12, 1978, pp. 375-408.

BANKS, F. E., "Economics and Politics of Primary Commodities", Journal of World Trade Law, vol. 6, 1976, pp. 567-575.

BARKMAN, Kerstin, "The International Tin Agreements", Journal of World Trade Law, vol. 9, 1975, pp. 495-524.

" " "Costs and Finance of the Buffer Stacks", Journal of World Trade Law, vol. 10, 1976, pp. 585-592.

BERGSTERN, Fred C., "The Threat from the Third World", Foreign Policy, 11, 1973.

BROOK, E. M, and GRILLI, E.R., "Commodity Price Stabilization and Developing World", Finance and Development, vol. 14, March 1977, No. 1.

BROOK, E. M., GRILLI, E. R., and WALEBROECK, J., "Commodity Price Stabilization and the Developing Countries", Banca Nacionale del Lavoro, Quarterly Review, No. 124, March 1978.

BURGER, Sharon R., "The Fifth International Tin Agreement", Law and Policy in International Business, vol.9, 1977, pp. 578-591.

CLINE, William R., "International Commodity Agreements and the Common Fund", in: Policy Alternatives for a New International Economic Order, Preager Publishers, 1979, pp. 11-27.

COLEBROOK, Jay, "The Costs of Storing Primary Commodities", Journal of World Trade Law, vol. 11, 1977, pp. 369-377.

COOPER, Richard and LAWRENCE, R. Z., "The 1972-1974 Commodity Price Boom", Brooking Papers on Economic Activity, 3, 1975, pp. 671-715.

CUTTAT, Jacques, "Le fond commun pour les produits de base" in: L'organisation de l'économie internationale au seuil des années 1980,par CUTTAT, J, DUNKEL, A., GAUDARD, G., HEIMO, M., SCHLEIMINGER, G., SOMMARUGA, C., Edition Universitaires, Fribourg, 1981.

CUDDY, J.D.A., "Indexation in International Commodity Arrangements", Journal of World Trade Law, vol. 12, 1978, pp. 501-513.

DAVIS, Joseph S., "Experience under Intergovernmental Commodity Agreements, 1902-1945", Journal of Political Economy, 54, 1946, 193-220.

DUYNE, Carl Van, "Commodity Cartels and the Theory of Derived Demand", KYKLOS, vol. 28, 1975, pp. 597-612.

EDWARDS, John, "The International Tin Agreement", Journal of World Trade Law, vol. 3, 1969, pp. 237-250.

FINGER, Michael and DeROSA, Dean, "Commodity Price Stabilization and Ratchet Effect", The World Economy, London, vol. 1, No. 2, January 1978.

FORD, Gerald R., "International Coffee Agreement Transmitted to the Senate", Message from President Ford, The Department of State Bulletin, vol. LXXIV, No. 1924, May 10, 1976.

FRIED, Edward, R., "International Trade in Raw Materials: Myths and Realities", Science, February 1976, pp. 641-646.

GALTUNG, Johan, "The Lomé Convention and Neo Capitalism", The African Review, vol. 6, 1976.

GARIEPY, Richard N., "International Commodity Agreements", International and Comparative Law Quarterly, vol. 25, 1976, pp. 677-684.

GLISMAN, H. H., and RODEMER, H., "Wohlfahrtseffekte von Bufferstocks zur Glättung von Preisschwankungen auf den Welt rohstoffmärkten", Weltwirtschaftliches Archiv, Band 115, 1979, pp. 467-484.

GOODWIN, Geoffrey, "The UNCTAD Common Fund - Challenge and Response", The World Today, 33, 1977, 11, pp. 425-432.

GOREUX, Louis, "The Use of Compensatory Financing", Finance and Development, 14, No. 3, 1977.

" " "The Use of the Buffer Stocks", Finance and Development, December 1978, vol. 15, no. 4.

GRUBEL, H., "Foreign Exchange Earnings and Price Stabilization Schemes", The American Economic Review, vol. LIV, (June 1964), No. 4, Part I, pp. 378-485.

HARBERGER, Arnold, C., "Some Evidence on the International Price Mechanism", The Journal of Political Economy, vol. LXV, (December 1957) No. 6, pp. 506-521.

INGERSENT, K. A., "Sugar Prices and Stocks", Journal of Agricultural Economics, vol. 26, 1975, pp. 227-238.

JOHNSON, Harry G., "Commodities: Less Developed Countries' Demands and Developed Countries' Response", in: The New International Economic Order: The North-South Debate,(ed.), by BHAGWATI, Jagdish N., Cambridge, Massachusetts Institute of Technology Press, 1977.

JOSLING, Tim and HARRIS, Simon, "The Revolution in World Commodity Markets", The Round Table, Issue No. 254, April 1974.

JUNZ, Helen B., MacAVOY, Paul, "A Hard Look at Prospects for Commodity Agreements" in: Stabilizing World Commodity Markets,(ed.), by ADAMS, G., and KLEIN, S., Lexington Books, D.C.Heath and Co., 1978, pp. 271-287.

KATZ, Julius, "International Commodity Policy: Coffee, Cocoa, Sugar, Copper, Tin and Bauxite", U.S.Department of State Bulletin, 74, May 1976, pp. 607-614.

KEYNES, J. M., "The International Control of Raw Materials", Journal of International Economics, reprinted, vol. 4, No. 3, August 1974.

KEYNES, J. M., "The Policy of Government Storage of Foodstuffs and Raw Materials", Economic Journal, September 1938.

KIRKPATRIK, C. H., and NIXON, F. I., "The New International Economic Order: Trade Policy for Primary Commodities", British Journal of International Studies, 3, 1977, pp. 233-253.

KLEIN, Kenneth, "International Commodity Agreements", Georgia Journal of International Comparative Law, vol. 6, 1976, pp. 275-309.

KNNOR, K. E., "International Buffer Stocks", KYKLOS, 1958-2, pp. 224-230.

KOFI, T. A., "The International Cocoa Agreements", Journal of World Trade Law, vol. 11, 1977, pp. 37-51.

KRAVIS, Irving B., "International Commodity Agreements to Promote Aid and Efficiency: the Case of Coffee", Canadian Journal of Economics, I, No. 2, May 1968.

KRISHNA, Ahooja-Patel, "UNCTAD - I Committee on Commodities", Lournal of World Trade Law, vol. 3, 1969.

LABYS, Walter C. and PERRIN, Yves, "Multivariate Analysis of Price Aspects of Commodity Stabilization", Weltwirtschaftliches Archiv, 1976.

LAW, Alton D., "Raw Material Agreements as World Market Instruments in Agriculture", Weltwirtschaftliches Archiv, Band 108, 1972, Heft 2.

LOUMIET, Carlos, "Towards an International Commodity Agreement on Petroleum", Journal of International Law and Policy, 1975.

MacAVOY, Paul, and ORR, D., "Price Strategies to Promote Cartel Stability", Economica, vol. 32 (May 1965), pp. 186-197.

MAIZELS, Alfred, "A New International Strategy for Primary Commodities", in: A World Divided, (ed.), by G.K. HELLEINER, Cambridge University Press, 1976, pp. 31-51.

" " "Primary Commodity Markets and Their Regulation", in: Reshaping the New Economic Order, (ed.), by GIERSCH, Herbert, Institut für Weltwirtschaft an der Universität Kiel, Tübingen, 1977.

McKINNON, Roland I., "Futures Markets, Buffer Stocks and Income Stability for Primary Producers", Journal of Political Economy, 1967, pp. 844-861.

MEADE, J. E., "International Commodity Agreements", Lloyds Bank Review, July 1964, No. 73, pp. 28-45.

METZGER, Stanley D., "Cartels, Combines, Commodity Agreements and International Law", Texas International Law Journal, 11, 1976, pp. 527- 539.

MICHALOPOULOS, Constantin, PEREZ, Lorenzo L., "Commodity Trade Policy Initiatives and Issues", in: Stabilizing World Commodity Markets, (ed.), by ADAMS, G., KLEIN, S., Lexington Books, D.C.Heath and Co., Lexington 1978.

MIKDASHI, Z., "Collusion Could Work", Foreign Policy, 14(Spring 1974), pp. 59-65.

" " "Influencing the Environment for Primary Commodities", Journal of World Trade Law, vol. 8, 1974, pp. 144-175.

MIKESELL, R.F., "International Commodity Stabilization Schemes and the Export Problems of Developing Countries", AER Papers and Proceedings, vol.LIII, 1963,

NURKSE, Rangar, "Trade Fluctuations and Buffer Policies of Low-Income Countries", in: The Quest for a Stabilization Policy in Primary Producing Countries - A Symposium; KYKLOS, vol.XI, 1958.

PAPSON, Thomas C., "The International Cocoa Agreements", Law and Policy in International Business, 9, 1977, pp. 553-569.

PELCOVITS, Michael D., "The Equivalence of Quotas and Buffer Stocks as Alternative Stabilization Policies", Journal of International Economics, 9, 1979, pp. 303-307.

PERSAUD, Bishodat, "Export Earnings Stabilization in ACP/EEC Convention", in: The Political Economy of EEC Relations with African, Caribbean and Pacific States, (ed.), LONG, Frank, Queen Elizabeth House, Oxford 1980.

PORTER, R.S., "Buffer Stocks and Economic Stability", Oxford Economic Papers, vol. 2, January 1950, pp. 95-118.

RADETZKI, Marian, "Is it useful to establish International Commodity Agreements?", Skandinaviska Banken Quarterly Review, 4, 1968, pp, 124-129.

RADETZKI, Marian, "International Commodity Agreements and National Benefit", International Development Review, 16, No, 1, 1974, pp. 15-21.

" " "The Potential for Monopolistic Commodity Pricing by Developing Countries", in: A World Divided, (ed.), by HELEINER, G.K., Cambridge University Press, 1976, pp. 53-76.

RIEFLER, W. W., "A Proposal for an International Buffer Stock Agency", Journal of Political Economy, vol. 54, December 1946, pp. 538-546.

RASHISH, M., "A New Cocoa Agreement?", Law and Policy in International Business, 11 September 1975.

ROGERS, Christophen, "International Commodity Agreements". Lloyds Bank Review, April 1973, No. 108.

SMITH, Gordon W., "Modeling Commodity Policy:Issues and Objectives", in: Econometric Modeling of World Commodity Policy (ed.), by ADAMS, Gerard and BEHRMAN, Jere, Lexington Books, D.C.Heath and Co., Massachusetts, 1978, pp. 99-116.

SMITH, G.W., SCHINK, G.R., "The International Tin Agreement: A Reassessment", Economic Journal, 86, pp.715-728.

SMITH, Ian, "Structure and Policy Changes in World Sugar", Journal of World Trade, vol. 11, 1977, pp. 228-247.

" " "Sugar Markets in Disarray", Journal of World Trade Law, vol. 9, 1975, No. 1.

STAKHOVITCH, Alexander, "A European View of Commodity Problems: Stabilization of Receipts", in: Stabilizing World Commodity Markets, (ed.), by ADAMS, G., KLEIN, S., Lexington Books, D.C.Heath & Co., Massachusetts, 1978, pp.235-241.

STERN, Robert, "World Market Instability in Primary Commodities", Banca Nazionale del Lavoro, Quarterly Review, Rome 1976, No. 117, pp. 175-195.

SWERLING, Boris, "Buffer Stocks and International Commodity Problems", The Economic Journal, vol. LXIII, September 1953, No. 251.

" " "Problems of International Commodity Stabilization", American Economic Review, vol. LIII, 1963, pp. 65-75.

TSON, S. S., BLACK, J. D., "International Commodity Arrangements", The Quarterly Journal of Economics",vol.LVIII, August 1944, pp. 521-552.

VIGNAL, Renaud, "Fond commun et stabilization des prix des matières premières" (ed.), MOUTON, Claude, et CHALMIN, Philippe, Commerce internationale et matières premières, Economica, Paris 1980.

WARMINGTON, W. A., "Stabilization in Primary Products Markets: an Analysis of Conflicting Needs and Their Resolution", Journal of World Trade Law, vol. 8, 1974, No. 3.

WASSERMANN, Ursula, "Multi-Commodity Approach to International Agreements", Journal of World Trade Law, vol. 9, 1975, pp. 463-590.

" ""Key Issues in Development", Journal of World Trade Law, vol. 10, 1976, pp. 17-22.

" ""The 1975 International Cocoa Agreement", Journal of World Trade Law, vol. 10, 1976, pp. 300-302.

" ""International Tin Agreement", Journal of World Trade Law, vol. 10, 1976, pp. 95-96.

" ""The Common Fund", Journal of World Trade Law, vol. 11, 1977, pp. 377-379.

" ""International Sugar Agreement", Journal of World Trade Law, vol. 12, 1978, No. 1.

WATERS, Alan Rufus, "The Economic Reason for International Commodity Agreements", KYKLOS, 27, 1974, pp. 777-791.

ZAIGLITIS, Oscar, "International Price Control through Buffer Stocks", American Journal of Farm Economics, vol. 28, May 1946, No. 2, pp. 413-443.

"ACP/EEC Convention of Lomé" The Courier, No. 31, March 1975.

JOURNAL DE GENEVE, Economic Part, various issues, 1971-1983.

NEUE ZUERCHER ZEITUNG, Economic Part, various issues, March and April 1980.

WALL STREET JOURNAL, April 21, 1976.

III. OFFICIAL DOCUMENTS

F A O

FAO Commodity Yearbook, Rome 1960-, various issues.

FAO: The State of Food and Agriculture, Rome 1973.

Agricultural Commodities - Projections from 1975-1985, FAO Rome 1967, volume 1.

Intergovernmental Group on Jute, Kenaf and Allied Fibres, Statistical Situation, FAO Rome 1960- various issues.

Draft Economic Articles of an Export Quota Type Agreement for Tea, FAO Rome, C. C. P. : Tah/1A/69-5.

G A T T

International Trade 1980/1981, GATT, Geneva 1981, 187 p.

Trends in International Trade, Reported by a Panel of Experts, Geneva 1958, 129 p.

I B R D

The Problem of Stabilization of Prices of Primary Products, IBRD/IMF, 1969.

Commodity Trade and Price Trends, IBRD, Washington D.C., 1975.

United Nations Department of Economic Affairs

Commodity Trade and Economic Development, submitted by a Committee Appointed by Secretary General, New York 1953, (Sales No. 54.II.B.1).

International Compensation for Fluctuations in Commodity Trade, Report by a Committee of Experts appointed by the Secretary General, New York, 1961.

Measures for International Economic Stability, New York 1951, (Sales No. 1951.II.A.1).

United Nations Coffee Conference

Summary of Proceedings of the UN Coffee Conference 1962, New York. E/CONF.42/8.

International Coffee Agreement 1962, United Nations Treaty Series, 1963, No. 5505, 169 p.

U N C T A D

Stabilization of International Commodity Markets, (Measures for stabilization of primary commodity markets at equitable and renumerative prices including commodity agreements), 19 March 1964, E/CONF/46/8.

Monthly Commodity Price Bulletin, Geneva, January 1975, UNCTAD/CD/CPB/65.

Commodity Year Book, 1980.

Handbook of International Trade and Development Statistics, 1980.

Survey of Commodity Demand and Supply Elasticities, UNCTAD Research Memorandum, No. 48, 19 March 1974.

An Over-All Integrated Programme for Commodities, 8 August 1974, TD/B/498.

An Integrated Programme for Commodities:

TD/B/C.1/166	9 December 1974
TD/B/C.1/166/Supp.1	12 December 1974
TD/B/C.1/166/Supp.1/Add.1	13 December 1974
TD/B/C.1/166/Supp.2	12 December 1974
TD/B/C.1/166/Supp.3	13 December 1974
TD/B/C.1/166/Supp.4	13 December 1974
TD/B/C.1/166/Supp.5	18 December 1974

A Common Fund for Financing of Commodity Stocks: Amounts, Terms and Prospective Sources of Finance

TD/B/C.1/184	24 June 1975
TD/B/C.1/184/Add.1	27 June 1975

(Report by the Secretary General of UNCTAD)

Recent Developments in International Commodity Arrangements relevant to the Elaboration of an Integrated Programme for Commodities

TD/B/C.1/185	6 June 1975
TD/B/C.1/185/Add.1	7 June 1975

International Commodity Stocks: Capital Requirements and Financing Possibilities

TD/B/C.1/186	20 June 1975
TD/B/C.1/187	3 June 1975
TD/B/C.1/198	29 September 1975

Resolution adopted by the Conference 93(IV)
TD/RES/93(IV) 10 June 1976

Consideration of Issues relating to the Establishment and Operation of a Common Fund, Report by the Secretary General of UNCTAD

TD/B/IPC/CF/2 November 1976
TD/B/IPC/CF/L.2 29 November 1976

UNCTAD IV and Beyond: A Common Fund
TAD/INF/PUB/77 4 October 1977

Articles of Agreement of Common Fund Adopted
TAD/INF/1185 30 June 1980

Le fund commun pour les produits de base
UNCTAD/CF/237/Rev.-1 1980

Agreement Establishing the Common Fund for Commodities,
TD/IPC/CF/24 29 July 1980

The World Commodity Situation and Outlook, Report by the UNCTAD Secretariat,
TD/B/C.1/207/Add.1 26 August 1980

Negotiations and Consultations on Individual Commodities,
TD/B/666 28 July 1977

Fifth International Tin Agreement,
TD/TIN.1/10 24 June 1975

The Sixth International Tin Agreement,
TD/TIN.6/14 6 July 1981

International Cocoa Agreement,
TD/COCOA.4/8 10 November 1975

International Cocoa Agreement, 1980
TD/COCOA.6/EX/R.1 17 November 1981

International Sugar Agreement, 1977
TD/SUGAR.9/10 17 October 1977

International Wheat Agreement,
TD/WHEATH.6/EX/R.2 21 March 1978

UNCTAD V - Review of Implementation and Follow-Up Action, including the On-Going Preparatory Work and Negotiations, Manila 1979
TD/228 May 1979

Complementary Financing: Issues and Proposals for Further Action, UNCTAD V, Manila 1979
TD/299/Supp.1 7 March 1979

International Cocoa Organization

Quarterly Bulletin of Cocoa Organization,
vol. VII, No.2, March 1981.

International Tin Council

Statistical Bulletin,
vol. XXIV, No. 6, June 1980.

Bangladesh Jute Industries Corporation

Quarterly Summary of Jute Goods,
Statistics, 1976 - .

Printed by
CPI books GmbH, Leck